国際社会で活躍するための必須英対話・用語用例集

外交的英対話学習法

宮家邦彦
Kunihiko Miyake
山中司
Tsukasa Yamanaka
伊藤弘太郎
Kohtaro Ito

南雲堂

この本の映像・音声を無料で視聴（ストリーミング）・ダウンロード（音声のみ）できます。ご活用ください。
以下のサイトにアクセスして書籍番号で検索してください。

https://nanun-do.com　書籍番号［**101483**］

※ 無線 LAN（WiFi）に接続してのご利用を推奨いたします。
※ 音声ダウンロードは Zip ファイルでの提供になります。
お使いの機器によっては別途ソフトウェア（アプリケーション）の導入が必要となります。

※ 外交的英対話学習法映像ストリーミング・音声ダウンロードページは以下の QR コードからもご利用になれます。

外交的英対話学習法

国際社会で活躍するための必須英対話・用語用例集

宮家 邦彦　　山中 司　　伊藤 弘太郎

はじめに

宮家 邦彦

人生最大の不思議の一つ

学生諸君！ これって実に不思議だとは思わないか。諸君がある学問に興味を持ったとしよう。その方面の勉強を2年、3年も続ければ、哲学だろうが、物理学だろうが、大体一人前のことは喋れるようになるはずだ。だったら、それは外国語でも同じはず。ところが、日本では決してそうならない。これって実に不思議だと思わないか。

日本では中学校からでも6年間、更に受験英語に費やす労苦をも考えれば、実に膨大な時間が英語学習に費やされている。にもかかわらず、大多数の大学生は英語が喋れない。理由は簡単、**日本の英語教育が根本的に間違っているからだ**。そもそも、英語を喋れない教師から習った学生が英語を喋れるようになる訳ないだろう。

こうした日本の貧弱な英語教育の犠牲となった諸君、今からでも遅くはないぞ。**英語は必ず喋れるようになる。**最低のセンスと音感があれば、マスターだって夢ではない。問題は何のために学ぶかだ。はっきり言おう。英語は諸君が将来良い仕事をするために不可欠の手段だ。目的は英語ではない、あくまで質の高い仕事である。

英語とはそのための単なる手段に過ぎない。だったら、そんな「手段」ごときに貴重な時間を費やす暇はない。諸君は最も効率的にこの「手段」を手に入れるべきなのである。このような明確な目的意識を持たない限り、日本で間違った英語教育を受けてしまった「ハンディキャップ」は克服できない。では、一体どうすればよいだろうか。

科学的英会話独習法

この奇妙な名称は、1973年春、筆者が大学1年生の時に受けた講座名だ。英会話の授業というので面白半分に受けたのだが、内容が「科学的」だとは全く思わなかったし、決して「独習」できる代物でもなかった。それでも、結果的に筆者にとってあの授業は**大学で受けた英語授業の中で最も効果的な講座だった。**それは何故か。

その講座では一冊の教科書の内容を丸暗記することが求められた。一見ごく普通の英会話教材だが、その中には友人同士の会話の中で喜怒哀楽を表現する際に使われる「慣用句」「決まり文句」が鏤められていた。**その会話集を徹底的に暗記する。これが全てだった。**「意味分かんない」と思いつつ、騙されたと思って全て暗記した。

英語は聞き流さない

振り返ってみたら、これが実に有効な方法だった。筆者自身の個人的経験から考えても、「聞き流す」だけでは絶対に外国語を喋れるようにはならない。幼児期であるならいざ知らず、20歳を過ぎた大人であれば、**外国語教材は「聞き流す」のではなく、単語と文法の基本を頭に刷り込んでいく必要がある。**これが英会話の第一の壁だ。

結局、**語学とは8割の暗記と2割の応用である。**自分の知らない単語は聞き取れない。されば、単語と文例を暗記することなしに会話の応用などできるはずがない。日本の英語教育の最大の欠陥は、喋ることを軽視し、読み書き、特に読むことに比重を置き過ぎたことだ。学生諸君にはこうした過ちを大学で繰り返してほしくない。

とにかく暗記する

ではどうすれば良いか。とにかく暗記である。筆者にとって語学とは「クラシック」ではなく、ジャズの「アドリブ（即興演奏）」だ。古典音楽のように譜面（教科書）を演奏（音読）するだけでは不十分。譜面を読むだけでは何時までたっても応用力が付かず、曲やコードが変われば、アドリブなど全くできない。英会話もこれと同じである。

ジャズ・プレーヤーのアドリブは決して出鱈目に演奏しているわけではない。アドリブの基本パターンはざっと数百種類はある。プロのミュージシャンであれば、これを12音階すべてについて完全暗記・反復練習しているはずだ。こうした基礎練習の繰り返しなしには、流れるようなアドリブの即興演奏など出来るはずないのである。

外国語も同じだ。**流れるように英語を喋りたかったら、喋る英語の一つ一つのフレーズ（慣用句）を完全に暗記する必要がある。逆に、一度暗記さえすれば、覚えたフレーズの順列・組み合わせをちょっと変えるだけで会話は出来る。**新しい場面や状況でも暗記している分だけ内容を考える時間ができる。これが英会話のポイントなのだ。

留学などする必要はない

外国語をマスターするには留学するしかないと思っている諸君。必ずしもそうではないぞ。**留学はベストだが、留学しなくても語学は必ず上達する。**何故多くの人が語学留学を望むのか。それは留学で、1日24時間、特定の外国語を「使わざるを得ない」環境に自分自身を追い込める「可能性が最も高い」と信じているからだろう。

残念ながら、これは必ずしも正しくない。それどころか、単なる希望的観測に過ぎない例を筆者は留学中何度も目にしてきた。1年に数百万円もかけて遠い外国の大学に留学しても、日本人と交われば効果は出ない。逆に、日本にいても、智慧を働かせ、時間を活用すれば、外国語の上達は十分可能なのだ。

趣味の世界を持つ

外国語の上達には異性の友人が最も効果的であるが、それには危険も伴う。しかも、それだけでは外国語会話習得に不十分だ。初対面の最初の数分間なら何とかなるだろうが、その後の会話が全く続かないからだ。悲しいかな、挨拶言葉を終えて話の本題に入った途端に、会話内容のレベルが急速に落ちていくのである。

これが英会話習得の第二の壁だ。話す内容のレベルが低くて面白くないため、話す方は勿論(もちろん)のこと、聞く方までもが疲れてしまう。この問題を如何に解決するか。筆者が強く勧めるのは**自分に合った趣味の世界を見つけることだ。**個人個人の趣味の世界はそう大きく変わらない。同好の士同士ならば心が通じあう可能性は十分ある。

音楽好きの筆者の場合、英語学習はビートルズの英語の歌詞を丸暗記することから始まった。歌われた歌詞を聴き、意味を辞書で調べ、再びレコードと共にそれを目で追い、最後には実際に歌ってみる。この耳、目、口の三感覚が外国語の習得に不可欠であることは言うまでもない。

得意のジャンルを持つ

人間である以上、知らないこと、詳しくないことを話したり聞いたりすることは、母国語でも決して簡単ではない。されば、外国語会話を早く習得しようと初めから難しい会話に挑戦しても、空回りが続くだけだろう。悪いことは言わない。そのようなやり方は直ちに止めるべきだ。

ではどうするか。筆者であれば、**自分が一番得意とするジャンルの、しかも「とっておき」の面白い話を外国語に訳し、それを完全暗記することから始める。**それなら内容的にも苦しくないし、相手も喜んでくれる可能性が飛躍的に高まるからだ。これこそ、文字通り、一石二鳥の特効薬だろう。

内容はどの分野でも構わない。相手が興味を抱く分野であればベストだが、最初はそうも言ってられない。但(ただ)し、このやり方の欠点は同じ相手に同じ内容を二度と使えないことだ。一つのネタを使う相手はどんどん増やしていく。更に、そのネタが尽きたら、次に面白い話を探し出し、それを翻訳してから、再び丸暗記して使う。

聞くよりも喋る

人間は不思議なもので、**自分が喋ることができる内容以上のことを聞くことは出来ない。** 自分が使える会話のフレーズや話題なら、他人が喋る内容も良く聞こえて理解できるが、その逆は悲惨なほど難しい。脳という人間のコンピューターは、自分の記憶媒体の中に保存されている単語とフレーズのみを受け入れるのだろう。

だから**「聞き流し」は学習効果が小さい。**人の話を聞く練習より、まずは自分が何を話すかを考え、その準備をすることが先決だろう。会話が弾み相手が話を変えても、直ぐに話題を諸君のペースに戻し、自分の話の世界に相手を巻き込んでいけば良いのだから。

勿論、これを何度も続ければ、相手に嫌われてしまう。でも、ご心配なく。同じ相手に同じ話題は二度と使わないと決めればよいのである。こうして、自分が最も得意とする分野で、相手が聞くに値すると感じる話題のネタをどんどん増やしていく。筆者の個人的経験では、これを何度も繰り返すしか方法はないと思う。

「英会話」ではなく、「英対話」のレベルに達する

こうした知的作業を何度も繰り返し、自分が一方的に話すネタが尽きた頃、諸君の英語は一定のレベルにまで達しているはずだ。その頃には、相手も同情心から諸君の話に付き合うのではなく、本心から諸君の面白い話を楽しんでいるだろう。これこそ諸君の英語が「英会話」から「英対話」へワープする瞬間である。

ここまで来れば大したものだ。しかし、ここで英語学習の「第三の壁」が立ちはだかる。それは中級から上級へ上がる最後の難関だ。これこそ諸君が、単なる「英会話」を卒業し、「英対話」、すなわち英語による高度な議論や説得力あるプレゼンテーションを外国語で行えるレベル、に至る重要な分岐点なのだ。

日本人でこのレベルに到達する人は百人に一人ぐらいかもしれない。しかし、逆に言えば、これまで筆者が述べてきた学習方法を実践しているのは、百人に一人ぐらいしかいないということでもある。諸君は必ずこのレベルまで到達できる。20年後の諸君の仕事ぶりは必ず変わる。そう信じて、騙されたと思って、努力を続けて欲しい。

科学的英対話学習法のススメ

留学もせず、英会話学校にも通わないで、英語力を高めるためにはどうするか？ 一番手軽で確実な方法を解説したのが本書である。ここでは架空の外交交渉を想定し、そこで行われる「英対話」の例と、そこで使われる重要単語につき解説してある。とにかく、騙されたと思って、この教材一冊に絞って、徹底的に暗記してほしい。

その間、他の教材に目を遣ってはならない。この教材には基本的内容が全て含まれているからだ。とにかく重要な事項を全て見て、聞いて、覚えて、口に出す。そうした達成感がない限り、「英会話」から「英対話」には行けないと肝に銘じて欲しい。

最後に、「英対話」に至る過程で留意すべきことを２点だけ述べたい。

短時間に集中する

英語学習に限らず、**全ての勉強法は「集中」が全て。**筆者にとって、この点は過去

50年間、大学受験の際も、外務公務員試験の際も一貫して変わらなかった。基本的問題を徹底的に反復練習する。一冊の教科書や参考書に集中し、他の教材には目もくれない。後は運を天に任(まか)せる。短期間集中するためにはこれしかない。

普通の成人男性の一回の集中時間(attention span)は13分といわれる。されば、1日だらだらと語学の勉強を続けても効果は少ないだろう。1日のうち、午前、午後、寝る前のそれぞれ10分間だけでも集中して単語とフレーズを覚えてほしい。それ以外は学習効率が下がるだけかもしれないのだから。

これまで何度も述べてきた通り、語学の8割は暗記であり、応用は２割に過ぎない。他人が少し休んだからといって、自分も休めば、この単調で地道な語学の「集中」環境は一瞬にして崩れ去る。**語学の学習は自分との闘いであり、ライバルはいない。「英対話」のレベルに達するまで他人のことはあまり気にしないことだ。**

自己満足の発音をしない

発音にどの程度の時間を割くべきか、とよく聞かれる。結論から言えば、**外国語学習において発音は非常に大切だ。**決して疎かにしてはならない。極めて重要な要素である。発音が悪くても通じれば良い、などと嘯(うそぶ)く輩(やから)もいるが、これは大きな間違いだ。発音が悪く、早口で喋る英語は、良く聞き取れず、聞く人の頭には全く入らない。

発音を良くすることは、自分が話す内容を相手に正確に伝えるために不可欠だ。そもそも、耳に入る英語と口から出る英語は同じ単語・同じ発音である必要がある。言い換えれば、耳と、目と、口という三つの器官が一つにならない限り、正しい外国語を学習することは出来ないということだ。

日本の英語学習は、これら三つの器官のうち、「目」を重視し過ぎ、「耳」と「口」を軽視した結果生まれたものだが、問題を克服する方法はある。今からでも遅くはない。ICレコーダーなどを使い、先ず**「耳」で聞いた外国語を、そのまま自分の「口」で発音し、録音して聞いて、更にそれを書き下して自分の「目」で読んでみてほしい。**

最後に一言。先程は発音の重要さに触れたが、それは決して内容について妥協せよという意味ではない。それどころか、**国際会議やシンポジウムなどでは、今でも、流暢ではあるが内容の空虚な英語よりも、下手ではあるが内容の濃い英語のプレゼンテーションの方がはるかに評価は高い**ようだ。

そうは言っても、同じ内容を話すなら、より多くの聴衆が理解できるので、発音の良い方が有利に決まっている。だからこそ、発音には常に十分注意してほしいのだ。さて、能書きはこのくらいにして、本文に入ろう。本書が学生諸君の「英対話」能力の飛躍的向上に資することを心から祈っている。

目次

PART Ⅲ

国際関係の分野、英語教育の観点からの英語学習（コラム）

PART Ⅳ

この本の使い方

本書は、広く国際社会で活躍を希望する皆さんのために、今の英語力をもう一段、あるいはもう二段階高められるよう執筆しました。扱っている内容は、国際関係、外交が中心ですが、こうした話題は専門を問わず、海外と接点のある仕事や活動に従事することになれば、何らかの形で必ず関わってくるでしょう。また本書の対象は、高度な英語力の獲得を目指す大学生を主としますが、大学院生、社会人、そして一部の高校生の英語力向上に対しても十分役立つ内容です。

国や組織を代表し、英語を使ってやり取りする場合、高いレベルで英語が使いこなせる必要があります。それは TOEFL や IELTS で高得点を取ることとイコールではありません。単に難しい単語や文法を知っていることでもありません。本書は、既に一定の基礎的な英語力を持った学習者が、どのようにしたらより高いレベルの英語力が身につくか、そのための知識と方法を提示するものです。

本書は、PART Ⅰ～PART Ⅳの４部構成で、それぞれの内容が相互に関連しています。

PART Ⅰは、他の英単語集とは大きく異なる本書の特徴の１つで、メインとなる教材です。これは**政策シミュレーション（Diplomatic Negotiations）**の英語シナリオで、３つのゲームを書き下ろしています。各ゲーム（ACT One, ACT Two, ACT Three）では、１番目に注釈なしの英語シナリオ、２番目に PART II で取り上げた重要語句などを注釈に添えたシナリオ、３番目に日本語訳を併記したシナリオを載せています。自分の英語の実力に合わせて、まずはシナリオの内容を徹底的に理解するところから始めて下さい。

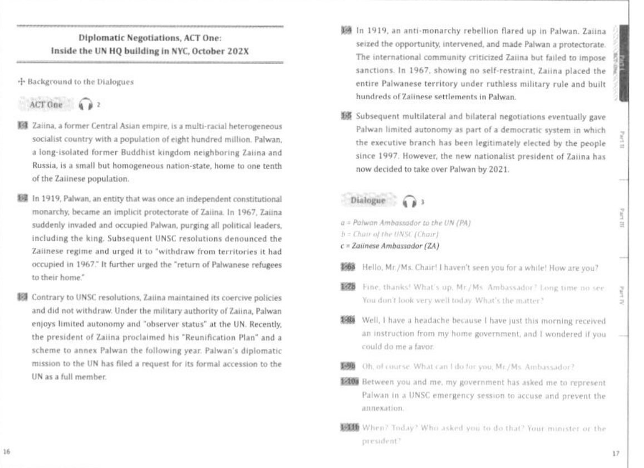

Diplomatic Negotiations, ACT One:
Inside the UN HQ building in NYC, October 202X

Background to the Dialogues

ACT One 2

Zaiina, a former Central Asian empire, is a multi-racial heterogeneous socialist country with a population of eight hundred million. Palwan, a long-isolated former Buddhist kingdom neighboring Zaiina and Russia, is a small but homogeneous nation-state, home to one tenth of the Zaiinese population.

In 1919, Palwan, an entity that was once an independent constitutional monarchy, became an implicit protectorate of Zaiina. In 1967, Zaiina suddenly invaded and occupied Palwan, purging all political leaders, including the king. Subsequent UNSC resolutions denounced the Zaiinese regime and urged it to "withdraw from territories it had occupied in 1967." It further urged the "return of Palwanese refugees to their home."

Contrary to UNSC resolutions, Zaiina maintained its coercive policies and did not withdraw. Under the military authority of Zaiina, Palwan enjoys limited autonomy and "observer status" at the UN. Recently, the president of Zaiina proclaimed his "Reunification Plan" and a scheme to annex Palwan the following year. Palwan's diplomatic mission to the UN has filed a request for its formal accession to the UN as a full member.

16

1-4 In 1919, an anti-monarchy rebellion flared up in Palwan. Zaiina seized the opportunity, intervened, and made Palwan a protectorate. The international community criticized Zaiina but failed to impose sanctions. In 1967, showing no self-restraint, Zaiina placed the entire Palwanese territory under ruthless military rule and built hundreds of Zaiinese settlements in Palwan.

1-5 Subsequent multilateral and bilateral negotiations eventually gave Palwan limited autonomy as part of a democratic system in which the executive branch has been legitimately elected by the people since 1997. However, the new nationalist president of Zaiina has now decided to take over Palwan by 2021.

Dialogue 3

a = Palwan Ambassador to the UN (PA)
b = Chair of the UNSC (Chair)
c = Zaiinese Ambassador (ZA)

1-6a Hello, Mr./Ms. Chair! I haven't seen you for a while! How are you?

1-7b Fine, thanks! What's up, Mr./Ms. Ambassador? Long time no see. You don't look very well today. What's the matter?

1-8a Well, I have a headache because I have just this morning received an instruction from my home government, and I wondered if you could do me a favor.

1-9b Oh, of course. What can I do for you, Mr./Ms. Ambassador?

1-10a Between you and me, my government has asked me to represent Palwan in a UNSC emergency session to accuse and prevent the annexation.

1-11b When? Today? Who asked you to do that? Your minister or the president?

17

次に暗記です。ACT One から ACT Three まで、書かれた英文がすらすら自分の口から「全て」出てくるまで徹底的に暗記して下さい。各シナリオで役割が分かれていますから、複数名で合わせてみるのもよいでしょう。各シナリオには、実際の交渉などでそのまま用いることができる表現が散りばめてあります。これらを適切な発音（アクセント、リズム、イントネーション）で、それぞれの役になり切って言えるようにして下さい。

これらに並行して、複数名で集まりシナリオを用いた政策シミュレーションを英語で何度も行い、実践的な英語力を養います。ゲームの方法は 14 ～ 15 ページの **1. Important Tips for Participants** 及び **2. From the Game Controller** を参照して下さい。（南雲堂の Web サイト内に、立命館大学で過去実施した政策シミュレーションのサンプルを載せました。ご参照下さい。）

＊この本についての付属映像・付属音声のご利用方法は 2 ページ目の記載をご参照下さい。

PART II は国際関係分野で重要と思われる英単語 350 語を厳選し、例文と共にその解説をつけました。見出語そのものの数は 350 ですが、派生語、類語、解説で用いた単語をまとめて習得することで、習得できる単語数はその数倍にも達します。単に意味が分かるようにするだけでなく、実際の英対話で用いることができるよう、様々な形式で習得状況をテストし、覚え込むようにして下さい。また例文のおよそ半分は外交青書より採っています。このレベルの英文が書けるようになることも目標にしましょう。

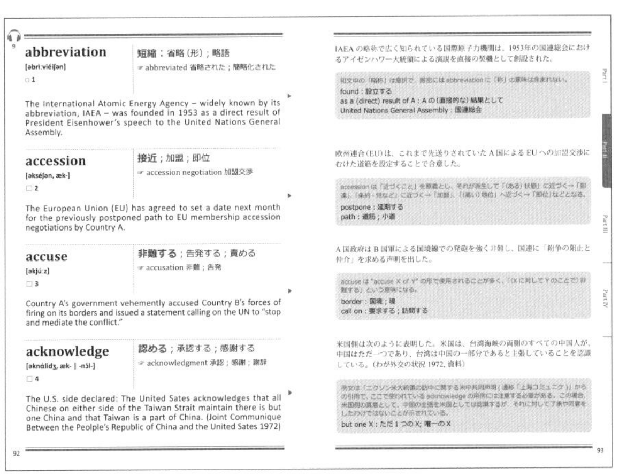

9

abbreviation 短縮；省略（形）；略語
[əbrìːviéiʃən]
☐ 1
☞ abbreviated 省略された；簡略化された

The International Atomic Energy Agency – widely known by its abbreviation, IAEA – was founded in 1953 as a direct result of President Eisenhower's speech to the United Nations General Assembly.

IAEA の略称で広く知られている国際原子力機関は、1953年の国連総会におけるアイゼンハワー大統領による演説を直接の契機として創設された。

和文中の「略称」は意訳で、厳密には abbreviation に「称」の意味は含まれない。
found：設立する
as a (direct) result of A：A の（直接的な）結果として
United Nations General Assembly：国連総会

accession 接近；加盟；即位
[əkséʃən, æk-]
☐ 2
☞ accession negotiation 加盟交渉

The European Union (EU) has agreed to set a date next month for the previously postponed path to EU membership accession negotiations by Country A.

欧州連合（EU）は、これまで先送りされていた A 国による EU への加盟交渉にむけた道筋を設定することで合意した。

accession は「近づくこと」を原義とし、それが派生して「（ある）状態」に近づく→「到達」、「条約・党など」に近づく→「加盟」、「（高い）地位」へ近づく→「即位」などとなる。
postpone：延期する
path：道筋；小道

accuse 非難する；告発する；責める
[əkjúːz]
☐ 3
☞ accusation 非難；告発

Country A's government vehemently accused Country B's forces of firing on its borders and issued a statement calling on the UN to "stop and mediate the conflict."

A 国政府は B 国軍による国境線での発砲を強く非難し、国連に「紛争の阻止と仲介」を求める声明を出した。

accuse は "accuse X of Y" の形で使用されることが多く、「（X に対して Y のことで）非難する」という意味になる。
border：国境；境
call on：要求する；訪問する

acknowledge 認める；承認する；感謝する
[əknɑ́lidʒ, æk- | -nɔ́l-]
☐ 4
☞ acknowledgment 承認；感謝；謝辞

The U.S. side declared: The United Sates acknowledges that all Chinese on either side of the Taiwan Strait maintain there is but one China and that Taiwan is a part of China. (Joint Communique Between the Peolple's Republic of China and the United Sates 1972)

米国側は次のように表明した。米国は、台湾海峡の両側のすべての中国人が、中国はただ一つであり、台湾は中国の一部分であると主張していることを認識している。（わが外交の状況 1972, 資料）

例文は「ニクソン米大統領の訪中に関する米中共同声明（通称「上海コミュニケ」）」からの引用で、ここで使われている acknowledge の用法には注意する必要がある。この場合、米国側の真意として、中国の主張を米国としては認識するが、それに対して了承や同意をしたわけではないことが示されている。
but one X：ただ 1 つの X; 唯一の X

Part I
Part II
Part III
Part IV

92 93

PART III はコラムとして、英語教育、そして国際関係の分野から、英語を学ぶ心構えやアドバイスを述べました。普段の生活ではなかなか気づけない視点から書くことに努めました。参考にして下さい。

PART IV は PART I、PART II で取り上げた単語等をアルファベット順で一覧にしたものです。合計で 2194 の項目があります。これら全てを習得し、使えるようにすることで、皆さんの英語力は確実にレベルアップするでしょう。

Diplomatic Negotiations

ACT One, Two and Three

1 Important Tips for Participants

Participants are encouraged to keep in mind the following in playing in roles:

a. Be sure to accurately play the role assigned to each participant. Politicians should be more political and bureaucrats be more bureaucratic, for example. Always try to handle a situation according to "what is most likely to occur," instead of "what should happen" or being influenced by the participants' personal opinion regarding a matter. In this game, a valued participant is simply someone who can accurately predict the others' actions, and is not a person of lofty ideals.

b. Each participant has the freedom to judge a given situation and make decisions throughout the game, but has no control over what the "Game Controller" has already decided or will decide (which relevant participants will be notified about during the game). They can also consult with the "Game Controller" whenever they feel the need to, and no one will hold them responsible for their judgments, except for the "Game Controller" himself.

c. Participants are encouraged to prepare (possibly even make up) to provide, to whomever necessary in the game, relevant names, factual data, background, or any other information (whatever is appropriate and relevant for this game, for example, name, characteristics, and size of the projects, their locations and purpose, etc.). If participants wish to "invent" factual data that might affect the entire progression of the game, they are kindly requested to consult with the "Game Controller."

2 From the Game Controller

for ACT One

Participants in this policy simulation are expected to internal discussions and bilaterally or multilaterally negotiate and/or exchange views with each other and finalize their positions in the UNSC emergency session to be called by the chair later this afternoon. There are seven teams: Japan (chair), the US, UK/France, Zaiina, Russia, Palwan, and the media.

for ACT Two

Participants in this policy simulation are expected to hold internal discussions and bilaterally or multilaterally negotiate and/or exchange views with each other and finalize their positions in the UNSC emergency session to be called by the chair later this afternoon. There are eight teams: Japan (chair), the US, UK/France, Zaiina, Russia, North Farlia, South Farlia, and the media.

for ACT Three

Participants in this policy simulation are expected to internally discuss and bilaterally or multilaterally negotiate and/or exchange views with each other and finalize their positions in the bilateral and multilateral negotiations that will be conducted later this afternoon. There are seven teams: Australia/New Zealand, Japan, the US, the EU, Zaiina, Palwan, and the media.

参考訳

1 参加される皆さんへ：ゲームをより有意義にするためのアドバイス

参加者はそれぞれの役割を演じるにあたり、特に以下のことに意識を向けるようにして下さい。

a. それぞれに割り当てられた役割になり切ることを忘れないで下さい。政治家ならばより政治家らしく、官僚ならばより官僚らしくということです。刻々と変化する事態に対し、「何が起きた方がよいのか」ではなく「おそらく何が最も起こり得るか」を考え適切に対処して下さい。個人としてどう考えるかという点を考慮に入れないことがポイントです。なおこのゲームにおける価値ある参加者とは、他のプレーヤーの行動を正確に予測して動ける人です。高慢な理想を掲げるだけの人に価値はありません。

b. それぞれの参加者は、ゲームの間いつでも与えられた状況に対して判断を行い、意思決定する自由を有します。ただし、「ゲームコントローラー」が既に決定したこと、もしくは今後決定するであろうことについては従わなければなりません。なおゲームが進行するにつれて、関係する参加者に対し、コントローラーから決定した内容が伝えられることになります。もちろん参加者は、必要に応じてコントローラーに相談することが可能です。しかしながらコントローラーその人を除いて、そこでの判断について責任は負えません。

c. 参加者は、時によってはある程度「でっち上げ」てまで、ゲームに必要な人物、関連する固有名、事実データ、背景知識や関連情報を準備しておきましょう。提示されるゲームに近いと思われる名前、特徴、案件の規模、場所や目的などがそれにあたります。また、もし参加者が、ゲームの全体的な進行に影響を与え得る事実データを新たに作り出すことを希望する場合は、必ずゲームコントローラーに相談するようにして下さい。

2 ゲームコントローラーから皆さんへ

ACT One に関して

この政策シミュレーションに参加する皆さんは、国内での議論、そして二国間及び多国間の交渉及び意見交換を通して、この後午後の時間に召集されることが決まった、国連安保理の緊急会合において、本事案に対してどのような立場を取るのかを決定することが求められています。チームは7つとし、日本（議長国）、米国、イギリス及びフランス、ザイーナ、ロシア、パルワーン、メディア（マスコミ）とします。

ACT Two に関して

（同内容のため前半省略）チームは8つとし、日本（議長国）、米国、イギリス及びフランス、ザイーナ、ロシア、北ファリア、南ファリア、メディア（マスコミ）とします。

ACT Three に関して

この政策シミュレーションに参加する皆さんは、国内での議論、そして二国間及び多国間の交渉及び意見交換を通して、この後の午後の時間に行われる国家間交渉で立場を最終決定します。チームは7つとし、オーストラリア及びニュージーランド、日本、米国、EU、ザイーナ、パルワーン、メディア（マスコミ）とします。

Diplomatic Negotiations, ACT One: Inside the UN HQ building in NYC, October 202X

Background to the Dialogues

ACT One  2

1-1 Zaiina, a former Central Asian empire, is a multi-racial heterogeneous socialist country with a population of eight hundred million. Palwan, a long-isolated former Buddhist kingdom neighboring Zaiina and Russia, is a small but homogeneous nation-state, home to one tenth of the Zaiinese population.

1-2 In 1919, Palwan, an entity that was once an independent constitutional monarchy, became an implicit protectorate of Zaiina. In 1967, Zaiina suddenly invaded and occupied Palwan, purging all political leaders, including the king. Subsequent UNSC resolutions denounced the Zaiinese regime and urged it to "withdraw from territories it had occupied in 1967." It further urged the "return of Palwanese refugees to their home."

1-3 Contrary to UNSC resolutions, Zaiina maintained its coercive policies and did not withdraw. Under the military authority of Zaiina, Palwan enjoys limited autonomy and "observer status" at the UN. Recently, the president of Zaiina proclaimed his "Reunification Plan" and a scheme to annex Palwan the following year. Palwan's diplomatic mission to the UN has filed a request for its formal accession to the UN as a full member.

1-4 In 1919, an anti-monarchy rebellion flared up in Palwan. Zaiina seized the opportunity, intervened, and made Palwan a protectorate. The international community criticized Zaiina but failed to impose sanctions. In 1967, showing no self-restraint, Zaiina placed the entire Palwanese territory under ruthless military rule and built hundreds of Zaiinese settlements in Palwan.

1-5 Subsequent multilateral and bilateral negotiations eventually gave Palwan limited autonomy as part of a democratic system in which the executive branch has been legitimately elected by the people since 1997. However, the new nationalist president of Zaiina has now decided to take over Palwan by 2021.

Dialogue

 3

a = Palwan Ambassador to the UN (PA)
b = Chair of the UNSC (Chair)
c = Zaiinese Ambassador (ZA)

1-6a Hello, Mr./Ms. Chair! I haven't seen you for a while! How are you?

1-7b Fine, thanks! What's up, Mr./Ms. Ambassador? Long time no see. You don't look very well today. What's the matter?

1-8a Well, I have a headache because I have just this morning received an instruction from my home government, and I wondered if you could do me a favor.

1-9b Oh, of course. What can I do for you, Mr./Ms. Ambassador?

1-10a Between you and me, my government has asked me to represent Palwan in a UNSC emergency session to accuse and prevent the annexation.

1-11b When? Today? Who asked you to do that? Your minister or the president?

1-12a It's from our highest office. They want you to convene an urgent meeting.

1-13b Today? Now? No way! Magic does not happen in this building, you know.

1-14a I know that, but you know, our territorial dispute is extremely adversarial.

1-15b Oh, here comes our Zaiinese ambassador. Wait a minute, Mr./Ms. Ambassador!

1-16a I am not supposed to talk to him/her directly. Excuse me, I must go now.

1-17b No, you stay here. Mr./Ms. Ambassador, do you have a minute? I have something to discuss with you personally. May I?

1-18c Oh, hello, Mr./Ms. Chair. What can I do for you? I'm in a hurry. I don't have much time.

1-19b That's a shame. Where are you off to? Do you have some time this afternoon?

1-20c Absolutely! But we have an extraordinary session scheduled, remember?

1-21b You didn't tell me! I didn't have the slightest idea of such a session today.

1-22c Never mind, it was only tentative. Do you have a specific agenda to discuss today?

1-23b Some members are interested in Palwan and its annexation, in particular.

1-24c No, sir/ma'am. Zaiina is one and Palwan is an integral part of our country. It's a non-starter.

1-25a May I jump in on this? Prior to the invasion, we were OK. You intimidated us, intervened, and imposed martial law. It was outrageous, illegitimate, and cannot be justified.

1-26c On behalf of my government, I advocate that Zaiina has a legitimate right to exercise its national sovereignty over Palwan and you have no right to make those claims.

1-27a Ironically, your annexation initiative is a strategic mistake that will not only trigger but also strengthen criticism against you. You must withdraw immediately!

1-28c Is that your ultimatum? There is no unanimous view on this issue. Annexation is a prerequisite. Don't threaten us. Your tactics are tragically unsustainable.

1-29b Well, let's see! Hmmm, what can I say? We are not supposed to...

1-30c If you wish, go ahead and call a session. But I'll tell you something, my friend. You didn't hear this from me, but Zaiina will probably announce the annexation today.

1-31b Fair enough. Anyway, I will convene an emergency UNSC session today.

1-32c In your capacity as chair, of course, you can. But mind you, you better not.

1-33b You said it! Anyhow, we'll see you again this afternoon in this building.

1-34a Mr./Ms. Chair, it's very kind of you to call the session. I owe you one.

1-35b Take it easy. It will be a piece of cake. Having said that, you must behave during the session as an observer. OK? See you then!

Diplomatic Negotiations, ACT One:
Inside the UN HQ building in NYC, October 202X

✣ Background to the Dialogues

ACT One  2

1-1 Zaiina, a former Central Asian empire, is a multi-racial heterogeneous (異種混淆の（→ 150）) socialist (社会主義の（→ 299）) country with a population of eight hundred million. Palwan, a long-isolated (隔絶された（→ 188）) former Buddhist kingdom neighboring Zaiina and Russia, is a small but homogeneous (単一民族の（→ 150）) nation-state (国民国家（→ 212）), home to one tenth of the Zaiinese population.

1-2 In 1919, Palwan, an entity (存在（→ 131）) that was once an independent constitutional (立憲（→ 78）) monarchy (君主制（→ 206）), became an implicit (暗黙の（→ 164）) protectorate (保護国（→ 260）) of Zaiina. In 1967, Zaiina suddenly invaded and occupied (占領した（→ 222）) Palwan, purging (粛清して（→ 266）) all political leaders, including the king. Subsequent (続いて（→ 308）) UNSC resolutions (決議（→ 284）) denounced (非難した（→ 101）) the Zaiinese regime (政権（→ 275）) and urged (促した（→ 344）) it to "withdraw (撤退する（→ 350）) from territories (領地（→ 321）) it had occupied in 1967." It further urged the "return of Palwanese refugees (難民（→ 274）) to their home."

1-3 Contrary to [に反して（→ 82）] UNSC resolutions, Zaiina maintained its coercive [高圧的な（→ 57）] policies and did not withdraw. Under the military [軍事（→ 203）] authority [当局（→ 34）] of Zaiina, Palwan enjoys limited autonomy [自治（→ 35）] and "observer status" at the UN. Recently, the president of Zaiina proclaimed [公表した（→ 255）] his "Reunification [再統一（→ 339）] Plan" and a scheme to annex [併合する（→ 22）] Palwan the following year. Palwan's diplomatic [外交的（→ 109）] mission [任務（→ 204）] to the UN has filed a request for its formal accession [加盟（→ 2）] to the UN as a full member.

1-4 In 1919, an anti-monarchy rebellion [反乱（→ 270）] flared up in Palwan. Zaiina seized [つかむ（→ 293）] the opportunity, intervened [干渉した（→ 181）], and made Palwan a protectorate. The international community criticized Zaiina but failed to [しなかった（→ 142）] impose [課した（→ 165）] sanctions [制裁（→ 290）]. In 1967, showing no self-restraint [自制（→ 294）], Zaiina placed the entire Palwanese territory under ruthless [情け容赦ない（→ 289）] military rule and built hundreds of Zaiinese settlements [入植地（→ 296）] in Palwan.

1-5 Subsequent multilateral [多国間の（→ 209）] and bilateral [二国間の（→ 43）] negotiations [交渉（→ 216）] eventually gave Palwan limited autonomy as part of a democratic system in which the executive [行政（→ 136）] branch [府（→ 47）] has been legitimately [合法的に（→ 192）] elected by the people since 1997. However, the new nationalist president of Zaiina has now decided to take over Palwan by 2021.

Dialogue  3

a = Palwan Ambassador to the UN (PA)
大使（→ 19）
b = Chair of the UNSC (Chair)

c = Zaiinese Ambassador (ZA)

1-6a Hello, Mr./Ms. Chair! I haven't seen you for a while! How are you?

1-7b Fine, thanks! What's up, Mr./Ms. Ambassador? Long time no see. You don't look very well today. What's the matter?

1-8a Well, I have a headache because I have just this morning received an instruction from my home government, and I wondered if you could do me a favor.

1-9b Oh, of course. What can I do for you, Mr./Ms. Ambassador?

1-10a Between you and me, my government has asked me to represent Palwan in a UNSC emergency session to accuse and prevent the annexation.
代表する（→ 279） 会合（→ 295） 非難する（→ 3）

1-11b When? Today? Who asked you to do that? Your minister or the president?

1-12a It's from our highest office. They want you to convene an urgent meeting.
召集する（→ 84） 緊急の（→ 344）

1-13b Today? Now? No way! Magic does not happen in this building, you know.

1-14a I know that, but you know, our territorial dispute is extremely adversarial.
紛争（→ 114）
敵対的（→ 8）

1-15b Oh, here comes our Zaiinese ambassador. Wait a minute, Mr./Ms. Ambassador!

1-16a I am not supposed to talk to him/her directly. Excuse me, I must go now.

1-17b No, you stay here. Mr./Ms. Ambassador, do you have a minute? I have something to discuss with you personally. May I?

1-18c Oh, hello, Mr./Ms. Chair. What can I do for you? I'm in a hurry. I don't have much time.

1-19b That's a shame. Where are you off to? Do you have some time this afternoon?

1-20c Absolutely! But we have an extraordinary session scheduled, remember?

1-21b You didn't tell me! I didn't have the slightest idea of such a session today.

1-22c Never mind, it was only tentative. Do you have a specific agenda to discuss today?

1-23b Some members are interested in Palwan and its annexation, in particular.

1-24c No, sir/ma'am. Zaiina is one and Palwan is an integral part of our country. It's a non-starter.

1-25a May I jump in on this? Prior to (先立って（→ 251）) the invasion, we were OK. You intimidated (威嚇した（→ 182）) us, intervened, and imposed martial law (戒厳令（→ 199）). It was outrageous (言語道断の（→ 229）), illegitimate, and cannot be justified (正当化する（→ 189）).

1-26c On behalf of (を代表して（→ 167）) my government, I advocate (主張する（→ 10）) that Zaiina has a legitimate right to exercise its national sovereignty (国家主権（→ 301）) over Palwan and you have no right to make those claims.

1-27a Ironically (皮肉にも（→ 187）), your annexation initiative (構想（→ 173）) is a strategic (戦略的な（→ 304）) mistake that will not only trigger (引き金を引く（→ 331）) but also strengthen (強める（→ 305）) criticism against you. You must withdraw immediately (直ちに（→ 158）)!

1-28c Is that your ultimatum (最後通告（→ 335）)? There is no unanimous (全員一致した（→ 336）) view on this issue. Annexation is a prerequisite (前提条件（→ 248）). Don't threaten (脅す（→ 323）) us. Your tactics (戦術（→ 319）) are tragically (あえなく（→ 326）) unsustainable (維持不可能な（→ 318）).

1-29b Well, let's see! Hmmm, what can I say? We are not supposed to…

1-30c If you wish, go ahead and call a session. But I'll tell you something, my friend. You didn't hear this from me, but Zaiina will probably announce the annexation today.

1-31b Fair enough. Anyway, I will convene an emergency UNSC session today.

1-32c In your capacity as chair, of course, you can. But mind you, you better not.

1-33b You said it! Anyhow, we'll see you again this afternoon in this building.

1-34a Mr./Ms. Chair, it's very kind of you to call the session. I owe you one.

1-35b Take it easy. It will be a piece of cake. Having said that, you must behave during the session as an observer. OK? See you then!

そうはいっても（→ 148）

✣ ACT One: Notes

1-1 one tenth of X ： X の 10 分の 1
(e.g. 2 分の 1 = one second、3 分の 2 = two thirds)

1-3 following year ：翌年；次の年

1-4 flare up ：突発する；燃え上がる

1-5 nationalist ：国家主義者；国粋主義者
take over ：接収する；乗っ取る；引き継ぐ

1-6a I haven't seen you (for a while). ：久しぶりですね。；ご無沙汰していました。

1-7b What's up? ：どうしたの？；調子はどう？
Long time no see. ：久しぶりですね。；ご無沙汰していました。

1-8a I wondered ：どうかと思って
you could do me a favor ：頼みごとを聞いてくれる
(do me a favor ：頼む；お願いがある)

1-9b What can I do for you? ：何をしましょうか？；ご用件は何ですか？

1-10a between you and me (= between ourselves) ：ここだけの話ですが；大きな声では言えませんが

1-13b No way. ：冗談でしょう。；駄目です。；そんなこと絶対にあり得ない。
you know ：ご存知でしょうが；えっと；あのね；いいかい

1-15b Here comes X. ：（さあ；ほら）X がやって来た。
Wait a minute. ：ちょっと待って。；もう少し待って。

1-16a (be) supposed to X ： X することになっている
([be] not supposed to X ； X しないことになっている)
I must go now. ：もう行かなければなりません。；もう失礼します。

1-17b Do you have a minute? ：ちょっといいですか？；少々お時間いいですか？
have something to X ： X するべきこと（もの）がある
personally ：個人的に；自分自身で
May I? ：よろしいですか？；いいですか？

1-18c I'm in a hurry. ：急いでいます。；急いでいるのですが。

1-19b That's a shame. ：それは残念です。
Where are you off to? ：どちらへ向かうのですか？；どこへお出かけですか？

1-20c Absolutely! ：もちろんです。; その通りですとも。

1-21b not have the slightest idea ：考えもしない ; 思いもよらない ;
皆目見当もつかない

1-22c Never mind. ：まあいいです。; 気にしないで。
tentative ：仮の ; 一時的な
agenda ：議題 ; 予定

1-23b (be) interested in X ： X に関心がある ; 気になっている
in particular ：特に ; とりわけ

1-25a jump in ：割り込む ; 飛び込む

1-30c wish ：強く望む ; 願う
go ahead ：勝手にどうぞ ; どうぞ ; 先へ進む

1-31b Fair enough. ：結構。; 分かった。; 取引成立。
anyway ：とにかく ; いずれにせよ

1-32c in your capacity as X ： X の立場で ; の資格において
of course ：もちろん ; 当然（ながら）
mind you ：いいかい ; よく聞いて
you better not. (= you'd better not.) ：やめておいた方がいい。;
しない方がいいですよ。

1-33b You said it. ：確かに。; よくぞ言った。; 同意するよ。
anyhow ：とにかく ; いずれにせよ

1-34a It's very kind of you to X. ： X してもらい親切にありがとうございます。;
恐縮しています。
I owe you one. ：恩に着る。; 借りができたね。; ありがとう。

1-35b Take it easy. ：気楽に行こう。; 気をつけて。; じゃあまた。
It will be a piece of cake. ：簡単なことさ。; たいしたことじゃない。
behave ：ふるまう ; 行儀よくする
See you then. ：それではまた。; じゃあね。

Diplomatic Negotiations, ACT One: Inside the UN HQ building in NYC, October 202X

ニューヨーク国連本部ビルの中で (202X 年 10 月)

✣ Background to the Dialogues （対話の背景）

ACT One  2

1-1 Zaiina, a former Central Asian empire, is a multi-racial heterogeneous socialist country with a population of eight hundred million. Palwan, a long-isolated former Buddhist kingdom neighboring Zaiina and Russia, is a small but homogeneous nation-state, home to one tenth of the Zaiinese population.

ザイーナは、かつて中央アジアを支配した帝国の１つであり、多民族が混淆する社会主義国で、人口は８億を数える。パルワーンは、ザイーナとロシアに隣接しつつも、長く隔てられてきたかつての仏教王国で、単一民族国家である。規模は小さく人口はザイーナの 10 分の１である。

1-2 In 1919, Palwan, an entity that was once an independent constitutional monarchy, became an implicit protectorate of Zaiina. In 1967, Zaiina suddenly invaded and occupied Palwan, purging all political leaders, including the king. Subsequent UNSC resolutions denounced the Zaiinese regime and urged it to "withdraw from territories it had occupied in 1967." It further urged the "return of Palwanese refugees to their home."

1919年、かつて独立した立憲君主国であったパルワーンが、ザイーナの支配が間接的に及ぶ地域へと変わった。1967年、今度はザイーナが突如パルワーンに軍事侵攻、占領を行い、国王を含んだ全ての政治指導者を粛清した。これを受け国連安保理決議は、当時のザイーナ政権を強く非難すると共に、パルワーンの領地から撤退するよう勧告を行った。また被災したパルワーンの難民を帰還させることも求めた。

1-3 Contrary to UNSC resolutions, Zaiina maintained its coercive policies and did not withdraw. Under the military authority of Zaiina, Palwan enjoys limited autonomy and "observer status" at the UN. Recently, the president of Zaiina proclaimed his "Reunification Plan" and a scheme to annex Palwan the following year. Palwan's diplomatic mission to the UN has filed a request for its formal accession to the UN as a full member.

安保理決議に反し、ザイーナは高圧的な政策を取り続け、撤退も行わなかった。ザイーナの軍事当局によると、パルワーンには一定の自治が確保され、国連でもオブザーバーの地位が与えられており問題ないとしている。なお、ここ最近、ザイーナの国家主席によって「再統一計画」が公にされ、来年パルワーンを併合する計画があることが分かっている。パルワーンの国連での外交目標は、自国が正式な国連加盟国となるよう申し立てることである。

1-4 In 1919, an anti-monarchy rebellion flared up in Palwan. Zaiina seized the opportunity, intervened, and made Palwan a protectorate. The international community criticized Zaiina but failed to impose sanctions. In 1967, showing no self-restraint, Zaiina placed the entire Palwanese territory under ruthless military rule and built hundreds of Zaiinese settlements in Palwan.

1919年、王政に反対する抵抗運動がパルワーンで生じたことをきっかけに、ザイーナはパルワーンに干渉し、保護国下においた。国際社会はザイーナを非難したが、制裁を課すまでには至らなかった。1967年、何ら自制を見せないザイーナは、パルワーンの全領土を容赦なく軍政の下におき、大規模なザイーナ人居留地を建設した。

1-5 Subsequent multilateral and bilateral negotiations eventually gave Palwan limited autonomy as part of a democratic system in which the executive branch has been legitimately elected by the people since 1997. However, the new nationalist president of Zaiina has now decided to take over Palwan by 2021.

その後、多国間及び二国間交渉の結果、パルワーンに一定の自治権が与えられることになった。それは1997年以降、自由選挙によって選ばれた行政府による民主政治を認めるものである。しかしながら、極端な国家主義を標榜するザイーナの新たな国家主席によって、2021年までにパルワーンを接収することが決められた。

Dialogue （対話）  3

a = Palwan Ambassador to the UN (PA) a = パルワーン大使
b = Chair of the UNSC (Chair) b = 国連安保理の議長
c = Zaiinese Ambassador (ZA) c = ザイーナ大使

1-6a Hello, Mr./Ms. Chair! I haven't seen you for a while! How are you?

こんにちは、議長。お久しぶりです。ご機嫌いかがですか？

1-7b Fine, thanks! What's up, Mr./Ms. Ambassador? Long time no see. You don't look very well today. What's the matter?

変わりありませんよ、大使。ところでどうされましたか？しばらくぶりですが、顔色が悪そうですよ。何かありましたか？

1-8a Well, I have a headache because I have just this morning received an instruction from my home government, and I wondered if you could do me a favor.

はい、実は今朝、本国政府より指示があり、お力添え頂ければと思っているのですが。

1-9b Oh, of course. What can I do for you, Mr./Ms. Ambassador?

もちろん構いませんよ。どんなことですか、大使。

1-10a Between you and me, my government has asked me to represent Palwan in a UNSC emergency session to accuse and prevent the annexation.

ここだけの話にしてもらいたいのですが、私がパルワーンを代表し、例の併合に関する非難とその阻止を、国連安保理の緊急会合で訴えるよう指示があったのです。

1-11b When? Today? Who asked you to do that? Your minister or the president?

それはいつのことですか？まさか本日でしょうか？どこからの指示です？大臣、もしくは総統からですか？

1-12a It's from our highest office. They want you to convene an urgent meeting.

政府の上層部からです。議長、緊急会合を召集してもらえませんか？

1-13b Today? Now? No way! Magic does not happen in this building, you know.

今日の今ですか？ それは無理です。そんな魔法はこの建物では通じないことは分かっているでしょう。

1-14a I know that, but you know, our territorial dispute is extremely adversarial.

もちろんです。しかし私達が直面する領土紛争において、対立は決定的になっています。

1-15b Oh, here comes our Zaiinese ambassador. Wait a minute, Mr./Ms. Ambassador!

おっと、ちょうどザイーナ大使がやってきましたね。ちょっとお待ち下さい、大使。

1-16a I am not supposed to talk to him/her directly. Excuse me, I must go now.

私はザイーナ大使とは直接話してはいけないことになっているんです。すみませんがここで失礼します。

1-17b No, you stay here. Mr./Ms. Ambassador, do you have a minute? I have something to discuss with you personally. May I?

いえ、ここにいて下さい。大使、お時間ありますか？ 個人的に少しお話したいことがあるのですがよろしいでしょうか？

1-18c Oh, hello, Mr./Ms. Chair. What can I do for you? I'm in a hurry. I don't have much time.

あぁ、こんにちは議長。どうされましたか？ 急いでおりあまり時間はないのですが。

1-19b That's a shame. Where are you off to? Do you have some time this afternoon?

それは残念です。どちらへおいでですか？ 今日の午後はお時間いかがでしょう？

1-20c Absolutely! But we have an extraordinary session scheduled, remember?

大丈夫ですよ。ただ午後は臨時の会議が予定されているように記憶していたのですが。

1-21b You didn't tell me! I didn't have the slightest idea of such a session today.

まさか。本日そのような会合があるなど思ってもいませんでした。

1-22c Never mind, it was only tentative. Do you have a specific agenda to discuss today?

お気になさらないで下さい。あくまで仮のものでしたから。ところで、今日議論すべき具体的な案件は何かありましたか？

1-23b Some members are interested in Palwan and its annexation, in particular.

実はパルワーンの件で、特にその領土が併合されることに関して議論が必要だとの声があがっています。

1-24c No, sir/ma'am. Zaiina is one and Palwan is an integral part of our country. It's a non-starter.

議長、それは違います。ザイーナはパルワーンをその一部とした１つの国です。議論そのものが成立しません。

1-25a May I jump in on this? Prior to the invasion, we were OK. You intimidated us, intervened, and imposed martial law. It was outrageous, illegitimate, and cannot be justified.

割って入らせて下さい。侵略される前は私達も特に問題に感じていませんでした。ところがあなた達は侵略を機に、私達を威嚇し、あらゆることに介入し、戒厳令まで出したではありませんか。これは常軌を逸した非合法的な行為であり、到底弁明できるものではありません。

1-26c On behalf of my government, I advocate that Zaiina has a legitimate right to exercise its national sovereignty over Palwan and you have no right to make those claims.

ザイーナ政府に代わり申し上げますが、私達はパルワーンに対する主権を行使する合法的権限を有しており、あなた達にはそのような言いがかりはできません。

1-27a Ironically, your annexation initiative is a strategic mistake that will not only trigger but also strengthen criticism against you. You must withdraw immediately!

皮肉にも、あなた達の併合に関する構想は、国際世論を敵に回す深刻な戦略的過ちになるでしょう。直ちに軍を撤退させるべきです。

1-28c Is that your ultimatum? There is no unanimous view on this issue. Annexation is a prerequisite. Don't threaten us. Your tactics are tragically unsustainable.

それがあなた達の最後通告ということですか？ この件に関して、皆が一致する見解などありえないでしょう。併合は必要な措置です。そちらこそ私達を脅さないで下さい。あなた達の戦術は、あえなく維持できないものとなるでしょう。

1-29b Well, let's see! Hmmm, what can I say? We are not supposed to…

そうですねぇ。何と言いましょうか､ここでそのような議論をするつもりは…

1-30c If you wish, go ahead and call a session. But I'll tell you something, my friend. You didn't hear this from me, but Zaiina will probably announce the annexation today.

お望みなら、会合を開いたらよいでしょう。ですが言っておきます、議長。ご存知なかったかもしれませんが、ザイーナは本日、パルワーンの併合を正式に宣言するでしょう。

1-31b Fair enough. Anyway, I will convene an emergency UNSC session today.

結構。いずれにせよ、本日、国連安保理の緊急会合を招集しましょう。

1-32c In your capacity as chair, of course, you can. But mind you, you better not.

議長の権限でもちろんそれは可能でしょう。しかし忠告しておきます。やめておいたほうがよい。

1-33b You said it! Anyhow, we'll see you again this afternoon in this building.

分かりました。ともかく今日の午後、ここで再び会うことになります。

1-34a Mr./Ms. Chair, it's very kind of you to call the session. I owe you one.

議長、会合を開いていただき感謝します。ご好意をありがたく思います。

1-35b Take it easy. It will be a piece of cake. Having said that, you must behave during the session as an observer. OK? See you then!

気にする必要はありません。簡単なことですから。とはいえ、会合中はあくまでオブザーバーとして参加することを忘れないで下さい。よろしいですね？それではまた。

Diplomatic Negotiations, ACT Two:
US, NF and SF Summit meetings, October 202X

✣ Background to the Dialogues

ACT Two  4

2-1 The history of the Farlian Peninsula shapes the geopolitical realities in Northeast Asia. After WWII, Farlia was divided into a socialist North and a capitalist South. In 1950, North Farlian troops suddenly crossed the border and started an offensive operation against the South. The armed conflict lasted for three years.

2-2 When the Farlian war broke out, North Farlia was a dominant power. South Farlia, whose military capability was too weak to prevent a regime collapse, required assistance from multinational forces to regain the balance of power. Although hostilities ceased in 1953, no peace treaty was signed.

2-3 North Farlia periodically suffered food crises and economic collapses, but it continued waging asymmetric warfare against the South and its Imperialist allies. After the demise of the Soviet Union in 1991, some European nations tried shuttle diplomacy to alleviate inter-Farlian tensions but to no avail. While assisting South Farlian domestic political dissidents to spread conspiracy theories about the United States, North Farlia also started launching medium- and long-range ballistic missiles.

2-4 Two years ago, North Farlia sent a special delegation to the South, which was an initiative designed to have direct negotiations with the US President. The top leaders of the US and North Farlia had three dialogues in Singapore, Hanoi and the Panmunjom but they did not reach a compromise. Hong Un-jong, the Chairperson of North Farlia, felt betrayed by both the US and the South.

2-5 North Farlia recently started claiming that the bipolar world order is finished and that they are now a nuclear power. In this new age of disarmament and interdependence, it is believed that the North not only possesses but is continuing to develop a massive stockpile of biological and chemical weapons and that it now stands on the verge of becoming a "real" nuclear power with various kinds of ballistic missiles including ICBMs.

Dialogue  5

a = North Farlian Chairperson Hong (NF)
b = President Joker of the United States (US)
c = South Farlian President Saan (SF)

(In Washington D.C.)

2-6c Hello, Mr./Ms. President! It is my great privilege to see you again. I have an alternative plan for you today. North Farlia's Hong is a serious actor. He/She was committed to "denuclearization within a year." He/She adheres to that.

2-7b I beg your pardon? That is profoundly intriguing! Will we have an agreement? Are you 100% sure? I cannot easily acknowledge that. Seriously, if that is the case, do you mind if I ask some questions?

2-8c Not at all. It is my pleasure. Oh, yes, what a coincidence! I just talked to him/her on the phone last night and when I raised the issue of sanctions, guess what he/she said?

2-9b I can hardly guess. You said he/she approved of denuclearization? You must be kidding me! He/She finally accepted substantial concessions? In what context did he/she say that? Is he/she ready to abandon all the nukes he/she has?

2-10c You bet! This is what he/she said. He/She agreed to comply with a complete denuclearization program including closing the Koson facility! Mr./Ms. President, it is time for you to meet him/her. I am ready to join you.

2-11b I hope he/she is not concealing anything. Thank you but let me handle this for the time being. It was very nice of you, Mr./Ms. President, to share such important information. See you later soon!

(In Singapore)

2-12b Good morning, Mr./Ms Chairperson! Great to see you. To cut a long story short, I want eternal peace on the peninsula and so do you, don't you? If so, let's exert our best efforts and agree to a memorandum now!

2-13a Before that, I need some clarifications. When I asked Saan about the upcoming hostile military exercises, he/she said it was up to you, Mr./Ms. President. Could you induce him/her to stop those exercises now?

2-14b Well, to be honest with you, we need to incorporate in the memorandum, a) CVID, meaning Complete, Verifiable and Irreversible Denuclearization of North Farlia, and b) a road map to do so with a concrete list of facilities and weapons to be dismantled.

2-15a This is an insult to us! We need no mediation! We can only agree to the complete denuclearization of the Farlian Peninsula and we are ready to close the Koson nuclear facility completely. What about this?

2-16b Well, that is too marginal. We adhere to CVID and if you agree to completely denuclearize the North Farlian military, we could declare an end to the war in the peninsula. Let's make a mutually agreeable deal now.

2-17a No, it is a non-starter, Mr./Ms. President. It is against our national interest and national security. We can only agree to a complete denuclearization of the Farlian Peninsula in a series of negotiations on a step-by-step basis. Oh, it's time for a photo opportunity... We must go now, Mr./Ms. President!

(On the Phone)

2-18c Hello, Mr./Ms. President! How was the meeting with Hong in Singapore? Wasn't he/she pragmatic? It was good that you reached an agreement on the principle of a complete denuclearization! Congratulations, indeed!

2-19b So far, so good, thanks! But the deal must be reciprocal and it is not the end of the story. What in the world did you tell Hong about CVID? He/She didn't say a word about it. Did you urge him/her to dismantle all his/her nukes? Our intelligence says otherwise. I have strong doubts about that. It will not lead to a solution. What did you promise him/her in return?

2-20c Nothing! By the way, can I join you in the second summit meeting? I could be a great advisor for you. We are allies, aren't we? Can I host a trilateral summit on the demilitarized zone (DMZ)? When is the best time for you, Mr./Ms. President?

2-21b I am not sure yet. Chairperson Hong never talked about a tripartite meeting. He/She only requested a bilateral meeting. There is a trade-off. Anyhow, I will bear that in mind, and we will get back to you when appropriate.

2-22c I sincerely hope that the three of us will get together next time. Hong is trustworthy and not unpredictable. Are you seeing him/her in Hanoi next time? Never mind, I know it is none of my business.

2-23b Well, let's see. There is no room for your arbitration. Keep your fingers crossed and we will inform you of the necessary arrangements, I mean the time and venue of the next meeting, as soon as we can.

(In the DMZ)

2-24a Mr./Ms. President, that was not the assumption as far as we understand it. You said in an authoritative manner that the Americans will drop CVID and accept our phased approach for denuclearization. I thought it was a bargain. You lied to me! Or, are you coercing me?

2-25c Not at all. This is complicated. On the contrary, we will do our best to lift sanctions while providing maximum humanitarian support to the North. Inter-Farlian dialogues are compatible with a dialogue with the United States. What we need now is conformity.

(In Hanoi)

2-26a With your generous consent, my counterpart, Mr./Ms. President, I am now ready to sign this document which will constitute a new phased process of denuclearization. The closure of the Koson facility is contingent on you lifting all the economic sanctions against us. It's a barter.

2-27b No, we need a collective approach. First, you need to declare all your nuclear-related materials and facilities in writing before we start the phased process. If not, it will be very controversial, and we may have to walk out of the room.

2-28a Don't try to impose anything on us! If you so wish, go ahead. It is your deliberate choice, not mine. This is a de facto surrender for us. But mind you, there will be a consequence, if you don't agree today. We must denounce your attitude and declare that this meeting was a devastating failure. Your credibility and reputation are at stake.

2-29b (Cell phone rings) Excuse me. Oh! Hello, just a minute. It's from Melania. Hi, honey, it's me. Well, the diplomacy is over and I'm on my way. See you in a minute. Ciao.

2-30a Why don't we continue our discussions? We still have time to talk and determine a detailed plan to close our only nuclear-related facility in Koson... Or we can mutually designate our special envoys to continue working on a draft agreement...

2-31b Oh, you have great foresight, but I am afraid I must excuse myself because I have a dinner date tonight. If you change your mind, Mr./Ms. Chairperson, don't hesitate to call us or leave me a message at any time. Our door is always open.

2-32a Your famous last words! At the end of the day, you have not been serious about establishing peace and stability on the peninsula. You just want to maintain your hegemony here. This is an act of hypocrisy. You have no intention to implement the agreement. Thanks a million, Mr./Ms. President!

2-33b (Damn, this guy and Saan are both liars!) You are quite welcome, Mr./Ms. Chairperson! Thank you very much for your time today and I hope to see you sooner rather than later!

Diplomatic Negotiations, ACT Two:
US, NF and SF Summit meetings, October 202X

✣ Background to the Dialogues

ACT Two  4

2-1 The history of the Farlian Peninsula shapes the geopolitical realities
半島（→ 233） 地政学上の（→ 147）
in Northeast Asia. After WWII, Farlia was divided into a socialist North
社会主義の（→ 299）
and a capitalist South. In 1950, North Farlian troops suddenly crossed
資本主義の（→ 52） 軍隊（→ 333）
the border and started an offensive operation against the South. The
攻勢の（→ 223） 軍事行動（→ 226）
armed conflict lasted for three years.
武器を伴った（→ 28） 紛争（→ 71）

2-2 When the Farlian war broke out, North Farlia was a dominant power.
勢力（→ 244） 支配的な（→ 119）
South Farlia, whose military capability was too weak to prevent a
軍事的（→ 203） 能力（→ 51）
regime collapse, required assistance from multinational forces to
政権（→ 275） 倒壊（→ 58） 多国籍（→ 210） 軍（→ 143）
regain the balance of power. Although hostilities ceased in 1953, no
勢力均衡（→ 36） 戦闘行為（→ 152） 中止した（→ 53）
peace treaty was signed.
協定（→ 330）

2-3 North Farlia periodically suffered food crises and economic collapses,
定期的に（→ 235）
but it continued waging asymmetric warfare against the South and
非対称（→ 33） 戦争（→ 349）
its Imperialist allies. After the demise of the Soviet Union in 1991,
帝国主義（→ 161） 同盟（→ 17） 解体（→ 99）
some European nations tried shuttle diplomacy to alleviate inter-
定期往復（→ 297） 外交（→ 109） 緩和する（→ 16）
Farlian tensions but to no avail. While assisting South Farlian
domestic political dissidents to spread conspiracy theories about
国内の（→ 118） 反体制派（→ 116） 陰謀（→ 77）

the United States, North Farlia also started launching medium- and
弾道（→ 37）
long-range ballistic missiles.
打ち上げる（→ 191）

2-4 Two years ago, North Farlia sent a special delegation to the South,
代表団（→ 97）
which was an initiative designed to have direct negotiations with
新構想（→ 173） 交渉（→ 216）
the US President. The top leaders of the US and North Farlia had
three dialogues in Singapore, Hanoi and the Panmunjom but they
協議（→ 108）
did not reach a compromise. Hong Un-jong, the Chaiperson of
妥協（→ 67）
North Farlia, felt betrayed by both the US and the South.
裏切られた（→ 42）

2-5 North Farlia recently started claiming that the bipolar world order
主張する（→ 56） 二極の（→ 45）
is finished and that they are now a nuclear power. In this new
age of disarmament and interdependence, it is believed that the
軍縮（→ 110） 相互依存（→ 179）
North not only possesses but is continuing to develop a massive
stockpile of biological and chemical weapons and that it now stands
生物化学兵器（→ 44）
on the verge of becoming a “real” nuclear power with various kinds
瀬戸際にある（→ 225）
of ballistic missiles including ICBMs.

Dialogue

 5

a = North Farlian Chairperson Hong (NF)
b = President Joker of the United States (US)
c = South Farlian President Saan (SF)

(In Washington D.C.)

2-6c Hello, Mr./Ms. President! It is my great privilege (光栄 → 253) to see you again. I have an alternative (代替の → 18) plan for you today. North Farlia's Hong is a serious actor (当事者 → 5). He/She was committed to "denuclearization (非核化 → 102) within a year." He/She adheres (固執する → 7) to that.

2-7b I beg your pardon? That is profoundly (大いに → 256) intriguing (興味深い → 184)! Will we have an agreement (合意 → 13)? Are you 100% sure? I cannot easily acknowledge (認める → 4) that. Seriously, if that is the case, do you mind if I ask some questions?

2-8c Not at all. It is my pleasure. Oh, yes, what a coincidence! I just talked to him/her on the phone last night and when I raised the issue of sanctions (制裁 → 290), guess what he/she said?

2-9b I can hardly guess. You said he/she approved (同意した → 25) of denuclearization? You must be kidding me! He/She finally accepted substantial (大幅な → 310) concessions (譲歩 → 69)? In what context did he/she say that? Is he/she ready to abandon all the nukes (核兵器 → 102) he/she has?

2-10c You bet! This is what he/she said. He/She agreed to comply (従う → 66) with a complete denuclearization program including closing the Koson facility (施設 → 141)! Mr./Ms. President, it is time for you to meet him/her. I am ready to join you.

2-11b I hope he/she is not concealing anything. Thank you but let me
隠蔽する（→ 68）
handle this for the time being. It was very nice of you, Mr./Ms. President, to share such important information. See you later soon!

(In Singapore)

2-12b Good morning, Mr./Ms. Chairperson! Great to see you. To cut a long story short, I want eternal peace on the peninsula and so
永続的な（→ 134）
do you, don't you? If so, let's exert our best efforts and agree to a
努力する（→ 138）
memorandum now!
覚書（→ 201）

2-13a Before that, I need some clarifications. When I asked Saan about the upcoming hostile military exercises, she/he said it was up to you, Mr./Ms. President. Could you induce him/her to stop those
説得する（→ 170）
exercises now?

2-14b Well, to be honest with you, we need to incorporate in the
取り入れる（→ 169）
memorandum, a) CVID, meaning Complete, Verifiable and
検証可能な（→ 345）
Irreversible Denuclearization of North Farlia, and b) a road map to do so with a concrete list of facilities and weapons to be dismantled.
廃棄される（→ 113）

2-15a This is an insult to us! We need no mediation! We can only agree to
侮辱（→ 174）　仲裁（→ 200）
the complete denuclearization of the Farlian Peninsula and we are ready to close the Koson nuclear facility completely. What about this?

2-16b Well, that is too marginal (取るに足りない（→197）). We adhere to CVID and if you agree to completely denuclearize the North Farlian military, we could declare (宣言する（→95）) an end to the war in the peninsula. Let's make a mutually (お互いに（→211）) agreeable deal now.

2-17a No, it is a non-starter, Mr./Ms President. It is against our national interest (国益（→213）) and national security (国家安全保障（→214）). We can only agree to a complete denuclearization of the Farlian Peninsula in a series of negotiations on a step-by-step basis. Oh, it's time for a photo opportunity... We must go now, Mr./Ms. President!

(On the Phone)

2-18c Hello, Mr./Ms. President! How was the meeting with Hong in Singapore? Wasn't he/she pragmatic (現実的な（→245）)? It was good that you reached an agreement on the principle (原則（→250）) of a complete denuclearization! Congratulations, indeed!

2-19b So far, so good, thanks! But the deal must be reciprocal (互恵的（→271）) and it is not the end of the story. What in the world did you tell Hong about CVID? He/She didn't say a word about it. Did you urge (促す（→344）) him/her to dismantle all his/her nukes? Our intelligence (諜報機関（→176）) says otherwise. I have strong doubts about that. It will not lead to a solution (解決（→300）). What did you promise him/her in return?

2-20c Nothing! By the way, can I join you in the second summit meeting? I could be a great advisor for you. We are allies, aren't we? Can I host a trilateral summit on the demilitarized zone (DMZ)? When is the best time for you, Mr./Ms President?

助言者（→ 9）　三カ国の（→ 43）　非武装（→ 203）

2-21b I am not sure yet. Chairperson Hong never talked about a tripartite meeting. He/She only requested a bilateral meeting. There is a trade-off. Anyhow, I will bear that in mind, and we will get back to you when appropriate.

三者間（→ 332）　二国間（→ 43）　両立しない（→ 325）　適切な（→ 24）

2-22c I sincerely hope that the three of us will get together next time. Hong is trustworthy and not unpredictable. Are you seeing him/her in Hanoi next time? Never mind, I know it is none of my business.

信頼できる（→ 334）　予測できない（→ 342）

2-23b Well, let's see. There is no room for your arbitration. Keep your fingers crossed and we will inform you of the necessary arrangements, I mean the time and venue of the next meeting, as soon as we can.

仲裁（→ 26）　手配（→ 30）

(In the DMZ)

2-24a Mr./Ms. President, that was not the assumption as far as we understand it. You said in an authoritative manner that the Americans will drop CVID and accept our phased approach for denuclearization. I thought it was a bargain. You lied to me! Or, are you coercing me?

想定（→ 31）　きっぱりと（→ 34）　取引（→ 39）　強要する（→ 57）

2-25c Not at all. This is complicated. On the contrary, we will do our best
複雑な（→ 65） むしろ（→ 82）
to lift sanctions while providing maximum humanitarian support
解く（→ 193） 人道的な（→ 153）
to the North. Inter-Farlian dialogues are compatible with a dialogue
両立できる（→ 168）
with the United States. What we need now is conformity.
一致（→ 72）

(In Hanoi)

2-26a With your generous consent, my counterpart, Mr./Ms. President,
同意（→ 75） 同等の地位である（→ 87）
I am now ready to sign this document which will constitute a new
制定する（→ 78）
phased process of denuclearization. The closure of the Koson facility is contingent on you lifting all the economic sanctions
次第で（→ 81）
against us. It's a barter.
交換（→ 40）

2-27b No, we need a collective approach. First, you need to declare all
集合的な（→ 60）
your nuclear-related materials and facilities in writing before we start the phased process. If not, it will be very controversial, and
物議を醸す（→ 83）
we may have to walk out of the room.

2-28a Don't try to impose anything on us! If you so wish, go ahead. It is
課す（→ 165）
your deliberate choice, not mine. This is a de facto surrender for
意図的な（→ 98） 事実上の（→ 94） 降伏（→ 316）
us. But mind you, there will be a consequence, if you don't agree
帰結（→ 76）
today. We must denounce your attitude and declare that this
非難する（→ 101）
meeting was a devastating failure. Your credibility and reputation
悲惨な（→ 107） 失敗（→ 142） 信頼性（→ 92） 名声（→ 281）
are at stake.

2-29b (Cell phone rings) Excuse me. Oh! Hello, just a minute. It's from Melania. Hi, honey, it's me. Well, the diplomacy is over and I'm on my way. See you in a minute. Ciao.

2-30a Why don't we continue our discussions? We still have time to talk and determine (決定する (→ 105)) a detailed plan to close our only nuclear-related facility in Koson... Or we can mutually designate (任命する (→ 104)) our special envoys (使者 (→ 132)) to continue working on a draft (草案 (→ 120)) agreement...

2-31b Oh, you have great foresight (先見性 (→ 144)), but I am afraid I must excuse myself because I have a dinner date tonight. If you change your mind, Mr./Ms. Chairperson, don't hesitate to call us or leave me a message at any time. Our door is always open.

2-32a Your famous last words! At the end of the day, you have not been serious about establishing (確立する (→ 133)) peace and stability (安定 (→ 302)) on the peninsula. You just want to maintain your hegemony (覇権 (→ 149)) here. This is an act of hypocrisy (偽善 (→ 154)). You have no intention to implement (実施する (→ 162)) the agreement. Thanks a million, Mr./Ms. President!

2-33b (Damn, this guy and Saan are both liars!) You are quite welcome, Mr./Ms Chairperson! Thank you very much for your time today and I hope to see you sooner rather than later!

✣ ACT two: Notes

2-1 shape：形作る；輪郭
crosse the border：越境する；国境を越える

2-2 regain：取り戻す；回復する

2-3 food crises：食糧危機（crises の単数形は crisis）
to no avail：無駄に；その甲斐なく

2-4 Panmunjom：板門店

2-5 nuclear power：核の力；核保有国；原子力
not only X but（also）Y：X だけでなく Y も；X 同様 Y も
stockpile：貯蔵；備蓄；貯蔵する

2-7b I beg your pardon?：もう一度言って下さい。；失礼ですが。；すみません。
if that is the case：もしそうだとしたら；仮にそれが本当なら
Do you mind if X?：X して構いませんか？；よろしいですか？

2-8c Not at all.：全くそんなことはありません（構いません）。；どういたしまして。
It is my pleasure.：喜んで。；こちらこそ。
What a coincidence!：何という偶然でしょう。；
奇遇ですね。（coincidence：一致；同時発生）
raise：上げる；取り上げる
Guess what X?：X について当ててごらん？；何だか分かりますか？

2-9b You must be kidding me!：まさか冗談だろう。；からかわないでくれ。
（must：違いない；しなければならない）
in what context：どういう事情で；どのような文脈で
(be) ready to X；X する用意がある；厭わない；覚悟がある；するつもりだ
abandon：廃棄する；諦める；捨て去る

2-10c You bet!：おっしゃる通り。；確かに。
what he/she said：彼 / 彼女が言ったこと
It is time for you to X.：X する時が来た。；もう X する時間だ。

2-11b handle：対処する；操縦する
for the time being：当分の間；差し当たり
It is（very）nice of you to X.：X に対し感謝する。；どうもありがとう

2-12b to cut a long story short：早い話が；端的に言えば
So do you, don't you?：あなたもそうですよね？

2-13a clarifications：説明；明確化（clarify；明確にする；解明する）
upcoming：次回の；近づきつつある
(be) up to you：あなた次第；あなたが決める

2-14b to be honest with you：率直に言うと；正直なところ

2-17a on a step-by-step basis：段階を経て；段階的方法で

2-18c Congratulations!：おめでとう。

2-19b So far, so good.：今のところ順調だ。；これまでのところはうまくいっている。
in the world（= on earth）：一体（全体）
not say a word：一言も言わない；発しない
otherwise：反対の；別の；さもなければ

2-20c by the way：ところで；それはそうと；ついでながら

2-21b I am not sure yet.：まだはっきりしたことは言えない。；まだ分からない。；まだ決めていない。
bear X in mind：X を覚えておく；心に留めておく
get back to you：折り返し連絡する；改めて連絡する

2-22c sincerely：心から；誠実に；真摯に
It is none of my business.：それは私には関係のないことだ。
（It is none of your business.：余計な口出しをするな。；あなたには関係のないことだ。）

2-23b Let's see.：えっと。；どれ。；そうだなあ。
There is no room for X.：X の余地はない。；出る幕はない。
keep your fingers crossed：祈る
venue：場所
as soon as we can（= as soon as possible）：できるだけ早く；すぐに；速やかに

2-24a as far as we understand it：私達が理解する限りでは；私達の理解の及ぶ範囲では
phased approach：段階的実施（方策）

2-25c do our best：最善（全力）を尽くす；できる限り努力する
what we need now：今私達が必要なこと（もの）

2-26a phased process：段階的な過程（プロセス）
closure：閉鎖；撤退

2-27b in writing：書面で；文書で
walk out：退席する；突然去る

2-28a if you so wish：お望みであれば；もしそうしたいなら
at stake：危機に瀕して；問題となって

2-29b I'm on my way.：向かっているところだ。；今すぐ行く。

2-30a Why don't we X?：X しませんか？；しましょうよ。

2-31b I am afraid that：残念ながら；せっかくですが；あいにく
excuse myself：失礼する；辞退する；ご免被る

2-32a Thanks a million.：どうもありがとう。

2-33b Damn.：ちくしょう。；しまった。

Diplomatic Negotiations, ACT Two:
US, NF and SF Summit meetings, October 202X

米国、北ファリア、南ファリア首脳会談 (202X年 10月)

Background to the Dialogues （対話の背景）

ACT Two  4

2-1 The history of the Farlian Peninsula shapes the geopolitical realities in Northeast Asia. After WWII, Farlia was divided into a socialist North and a capitalist South. In 1950, North Farlian troops suddenly crossed the border and started an offensive operation against the South. The armed conflict lasted for three years.

ファリアン半島の歴史は北東アジアの地政学的現実を形作っている。第二次世界大戦後、ファリアは北側の社会主義国と、南側の資本主義国とに分割された。1950年、北ファリアの軍隊が突如として国境を跨ぎ、南ファリアに対する軍事行動を開始した。両者の武力衝突はその後3年間続くことになる。

2-2 When the Farlian war broke out, North Farlia was a dominant power. South Farlia, whose military capability was too weak to prevent a regime collapse, required assistance from multinational forces to regain the balance of power. Although hostilities ceased in 1953, no peace treaty was signed.

ファリア戦争が勃発した当初、北ファリアは圧倒的な勢力を誇っていた。対する南ファリアは、軍事能力があまりに脆弱で政権転覆も免れない状態にあったため、多国籍軍に加勢を求め北との勢力均衡を保とうとした。戦闘行為自体は1953年に終息したが、平和協定が締結されることはなかった。

2-3 North Farlia periodically suffered food crises and economic collapses, but it continued waging asymmetric warfare against the South and its Imperialist allies. After the demise of the Soviet Union in 1991, some European nations tried shuttle diplomacy to alleviate inter-Farlian tensions but to no avail. While assisting South Farlian domestic political dissidents to spread conspiracy theories about the United States, North Farlia also started launching medium- and long-range ballistic missiles.

北ファリアはたびたび食糧危機や経済崩壊に見舞われたが、それにも関わらず、南ファリアとその帝国主義同盟に対して非対称戦争をしかけ続けた。1991年にソビエト連邦が解体した後は、ヨーロッパの複数の国が南北ファリアの緊張を緩和させるためシャトル外交を展開したものの、無駄に終わっている。北ファリアは南ファリアへの工作活動として、政治的反体制派に対する支援を行い米国の陰謀論を拡散する一方、中・長距離弾道ミサイルの打ち上げも開始した。

2-4 Two years ago, North Farlia sent a special delegation to the South, which was an initiative designed to have direct negotiations with the US President. The top leaders of the US and North Farlia had three dialogues in Singapore, Hanoi and the Panmunjom but they did not reach a compromise. Hong Un-jong, the Chairperson of North Farlia, felt betrayed by both the US and the South.

2年前、北ファリアは南ファリアに使節団を送ったが、それは合衆国大統領との直接交渉を目論む新たな構想のためのものであった。米国と北ファリア双方の首脳が、シンガポール、ハノイ、板門店での3度にわたる会談を行ったが、交渉に妥結点を見出すことはできなかった。北ファリアのホン・ウンジョン委員長は米国と南ファリア両国に対して背信を感じている。

2-5 North Farlia recently started claiming that the bipolar world order is finished and that they are now a nuclear power. In this new age of disarmament and interdependence, it is believed that the North not only possesses but is continuing to develop a massive stockpile of biological and chemical weapons and that it now stands on the verge of becoming a "real" nuclear power with various kinds of ballistic missiles including ICBMs.

昨今北ファリアは、今や二極による世界秩序は終焉を迎え、核による力が世界を支配すると主張するようになった。軍縮、そして世界の相互依存という新たな時代の中、北ファリアは核を保持するだけでなく、大量の生物化学兵器の開発と備蓄も継続していると考えられている。これは北ファリアが、ICBMを含む種々の弾道ミサイルを保有する、現実の核保有国となる瀬戸際にあることを示している。

Dialogue （対話）  5

a = North Farlian Chairperson Hong (NF) a = 北ファリア、ホン委員長
b = President Joker of the United States (US) b = 米国、ジョーカー大統領
c = South Farlian President Saan (SF) c = 南ファリア、サン大統領

(In Washington D.C.) （ワシントン D.C. で）

2-6c Hello, Mr./Ms. President! It is my great privilege to see you again. I have an alternative plan for you today. North Farlia's Hong is a serious actor. He/She was committed to "denuclearization within a year." He/She adheres to that.

どうも、合衆国大統領。再びお目にかかれて大変光栄です。本日は例の件について代替案をお持ちしました。北ファリアのホンは実に真面目な為政者なんです。彼／彼女は１年以内の非核化に責任持って取り組んでおり、その決心を変えてはいません。

2-7b I beg your pardon? That is profoundly intriguing! Will we have an agreement? Are you 100% sure? I cannot easily acknowledge that. Seriously, if that is the case, do you mind if I ask some questions?

何だって？ それは大いに興味をそそるね。しかし何か合意は取りつけてあるのか？ 100% 大丈夫なんだろうな？ 私だってそう易々と認めるわけにはいかないぞ。ただ真面目な話、もしそうだと仮定した上でのことだが、いくつか聞かせてもらってもいいか？

2-8c Not at all. It is my pleasure. Oh, yes, what a coincidence! I just talked to him/her on the phone last night and when I raised the issue of sanctions, guess what he/she said?

もちろん喜んで。あぁ、なんたる偶然でしょう。実はちょうど昨晩ホンと電話で話しまして、制裁の話題を取り上げた際、彼／彼女は何て言ったと思います？

2-9b I can hardly guess. You said he/she approved of denuclearization? You must be kidding me! He/She finally accepted substantial concessions? In what context did he/she say that? Is he/she ready to abandon all the nukes he/she has?

そんなこと分かるわけないじゃないか。彼／彼女が非核化に同意したとでも言うのか？ 冗談はよしてくれ。彼／彼女は最終的に大幅な譲歩を受け入れたのか？ いったいどんな文脈でそうなったんだ？ 彼／彼女は保有する全ての核を放棄する用意があるってことなのか？

2-10c You bet! This is what he/she said. He/She agreed to comply with a complete denuclearization program including closing the Koson facility! Mr./Ms. President, it is time for you to meet him/her. I am ready to join you.

まさにその通り、それこそ彼／彼女が言ったことなのです。彼／彼女は、コソンの核施設を閉鎖することも含めた、全面的な非核化計画に従うことに合意したんです。大統領、今こそ彼／彼女に会って話をする時です。私も加わる準備はできています。

2-11b I hope he/she is not concealing anything. Thank you but let me handle this for the time being. It was very nice of you, Mr./Ms. President, to share such important information. See you later soon!

彼／彼女が何も隠していなければよいのだが。君には感謝しているが、当面は私に舵を取らせてくれ。大統領、このような重要情報を共有してもらい嬉しく思うよ。また近々会おうじゃないか。

(In Singapore) （シンガポールで）

2-12b Good morning, Mr./Ms. Chairperson! Great to see you. To cut a long story short, I want eternal peace on the peninsula and so do you, don't you? If so, let's exert our best efforts and agree to a memorandum now!

おはよう、委員長。会えてとても嬉しいよ。手短に言わせてもらうと、私は半島に永続的な平和をもたらしたいんだ。それは君も同じだろ？ そうと来れば最大限の努力をして、今この地で覚書に合意しようじゃないか。

2-13a Before that, I need some clarifications. When I asked Saan about the upcoming hostile military exercises, he said it was up to you, Mr. President. Could you induce him to stop those exercises now?

その前にいくつか明らかにしておきたいことがある。サンに私達を敵視した軍事演習について、次回の実施を再考するよう頼んだのだが、それは完全にあなた次第だとの回答だった。大統領、今、彼／彼女に演習を止めるよう説得してくれないか？

2-14b Well, to be honest with you, we need to incorporate in the memorandum, a) CVID, meaning Complete, Verifiable and Irreversible Denuclearization of North Farlia, and b) a road map to do so with a concrete list of facilities and weapons to be dismantled.

そうだな、率直にいって、そういったものも全て覚書に盛り込む必要がある。覚書の内容は、a) CVID、すなわち北ファリアにおける核の、完全で、検証可能な、かつ不可逆的な廃棄、b) そのための具体的に廃棄される施設や武器のリストを記したロードマップの提示だ。

2-15a This is an insult to us! We need no mediation! We can only agree to the complete denuclearization of the Farlian Peninsula and we are ready to close the Koson nuclear facility completely. What about this?

それは私達に対する侮辱じゃないか。私達は米国の仲裁を求めてはいない。私達はファリアン半島における完全な非核化に同意するのみで、そのためにコソンの核施設は完全に閉じるつもりだ。これで十分じゃないか？

2-16b Well, that is too marginal. We adhere to CVID and if you agree to completely denuclearize the North Farlian military, we could declare an end to the war in the peninsula. Let's make a mutually agreeable deal now.

うーん、それではあまりにも核心からそれている。私達は CVID に拘り続けるつもりだ。もしあなたが北ファリアの核による軍事力を完全に放棄することに同意するなら、半島間の戦争の終結が宣言できる。互いに同意できる取引を今しようじゃないか。

2-17a No, it is a non-starter, Mr./Ms. President. It is against our national interest and national security. We can only agree to a complete denuclearization of the Farlian Peninsula in a series of negotiations on a step-by-step basis. Oh, it's time for a photo opportunity... We must go now, Mr./Ms. President!

いや、大統領、これでは交渉にならない。あなたの提示したものは、私達の国益や国家安全保障に対し抵触する。私達が合意できるのはファリアン半島の完全な非核化のみであり、しかもそれは一連の段階的交渉を経てのことだ。おっと、写真撮影の時間が来たようだ。もう行かなければ、大統領。

(On the Phone)

2-18c Hello, Mr./Ms. President! How was the meeting with Hong in Singapore? Wasn't he/she pragmatic? It was good that you reached an agreement on the principle of a complete denuclearization! Congratulations, indeed!

やあ、大統領。シンガポールでのホンとの会談はいかがでしたか？　彼／彼女は現実的な人間だったでしょう？　あなた方が完全な非核化という原則を巡って同意できたことは本当に良かった。

2-19b So far, so good, thanks! But the deal must be reciprocal and it is not the end of the story. What in the world did you tell Hong about CVID? He/She didn't say a word about it. Did you urge him/her to dismantle all his/her nukes? Our intelligence says otherwise. I have strong doubts about that. It will not lead to a solution. What did you promise him/her in return?

今のところはうまくいっている。協力に感謝する。しかし取引は双方にとって利益がなければならない。だからまだ話は終わってない。一体全体ホンにCVIDについて何を伝えたんだ？　彼はそれについて一言も言わなかったぞ。君は彼が持っている全ての核を廃棄するよう彼に促してくれたのか？　私達のインテリジェンスは180度違う見解だ。私自身もこの点については強い疑念がある。このままでは解決には向かわないだろう。彼／彼女には何を見返りに約束したんだ？

2-20c Nothing! By the way, can I join you in the second summit meeting? I could be a great advisor for you. We are allies, aren't we? Can I host a trilateral summit on the demilitarized zone (DMZ)? When is the best time for you, Mr./Ms. President?

何も約束などしていません。ところで、次の第2回首脳会談ですが、私も加わって構いませんか？　私なら大統領に大変役立つ助言者となれると思っています。私達は同盟国同士じゃないですか。次回は非武装地帯(DMZ)での三カ国首脳会談を私にホストさせて下さい。大統領、いつだったらよろしいですか？

2-21b I am not sure yet. Chairperson Hong never talked about a tripartite meeting. He/She only requested a bilateral meeting. There is a trade-off. Anyhow, I will bear that in mind, and we will get back to you when appropriate.

今の時点ではまだ何とも言えないな。実際、ホン委員長は三者会談のことなど何も言っていなかったぞ。彼／彼女の要求は二国間会談だ。これらは両立しない。ともかく気にはとめておこう。しかるべき時にこちらから連絡する。

2-22c I sincerely hope that the three of us will get together next time. Hong is trustworthy and not unpredictable. Are you seeing him/her in Hanoi next time? Never mind, I know it is none of my business.

次回は私達３人が共に集えることを心から期待しています。ホンは信頼できますし、予測できない人物ではありません。次回はハノイでお会いになる予定ですか？ 気にしないで下さい。私には関係のないことでしたね。

2-23b Well, let's see. There is no room for your arbitration. Keep your fingers crossed and we will inform you of the necessary arrangements, I mean the time and venue of the next meeting, as soon as we can.

まぁ、そうだな。確かに君が割って入るような余地はない。事態がうまく進むことを祈っていてくれ。必要な内容が整ったらまたこちらから連絡する。次回の会合の日時、場所についてだ。できるだけはやく行う。

(In the DMZ)

2-24a Mr./Ms. President, that was not the assumption as far as we understand it. You said in an authoritative manner that the Americans will drop CVID and accept our phased approach for denuclearization. I thought it was a bargain. You lied to me! Or, are you coercing me?

大統領、あくまで私が理解する限りだが、想定とは違うじゃないか。あなたはきっぱりと、アメリカが CVID を諦めて、私達の段階的な非核化のアプローチを受け入れると言ったはずだ。私はそれが今回の取引だと思っていた。あなたは私に嘘をついた！ あるいは私に強要しているのか？

2-25c Not at all. This is complicated. On the contrary, we will do our best to lift sanctions while providing maximum humanitarian support to the North. Inter-Farlian dialogues are compatible with a dialogue with the United States. What we need now is conformity.

いいえ全く違います。事態は複雑なのです。それどころか私達は、北ファリアへの最大限の人道支援を行いつつ、制裁解除に向けて最大限努力するつもりです。ファリア間の対話は米国との対話と両立します。重要なのは私達両国が一致した動きを見せることです。

(In Hanoi)

2-26a With your generous consent, my counterpart, Mr./Ms. President, I am now ready to sign this document which will constitute a new phased process of denuclearization. The closure of the Koson facility is contingent on you lifting all the economic sanctions against us. It's a barter.

私の正式なカウンターパートである合衆国大統領、あなたの寛大な同意のもと、私は新たな段階的非核化を取り決めたこの文書に署名できる準備ができています。コソンの核施設を閉鎖することは、あなたの判断で私達に対する全ての経済制裁を解除することを意味します。これは交換条件です。

2-27b No, we need a collective approach. First, you need to declare all your nuclear-related materials and facilities in writing before we start the phased process. If not, it will be very controversial, and we may have to walk out of the room.

ダメだ、私達は総体的なアプローチを必要とする。段階的過程に入る前に、まずあなた方は書面において核関連物質や施設の全てを公表する必要がある。もしそれができないと言うなら、対立は決定的だ。ここでの交渉は決裂することになる。

2-28a Don't try to impose anything on us! If you so wish, go ahead. It is your deliberate choice, not mine. This is a de facto surrender for us. But mind you, there will be a consequence, if you don't agree today. We must denounce your attitude and declare that this meeting was a devastating failure. Your credibility and reputation are at stake.

私達に何も押しつけないでもらいたい。出ていきたいなら勝手にそうなさい。それはあなた自身が行った選択で、私は交渉をまとめたかった。これは私達に対する事実上の降伏ですね。しかも覚えておいていただきたい。あなたが今日合意しないのなら、そのことが重大な結果をもたらすことになるでしょう。私達はあなたの態度を強く非難し、この会合が悲惨なまでの失敗に終わったことを高らかに宣言することになる。あなたの信頼と名声は地に落ちるでしょう。

2-29b (Cell phone rings) Excuse me. Oh! Hello, just a minute. It's from Melania. Hi, honey, it's me. Well, the diplomacy is over and I'm on my way. See you in a minute. Ciao.

（携帯電話がなって）ちょっと失礼。ああ、もしもし、ちょっと待ってくれ。メラニアからだ。やぁメラニア、私だ。あぁ、仕事は終わって今ちょうど帰ろうとしているところだ。また後で。じゃあ。

2-30a Why don't we continue our discussions? We still have time to talk and determine a detailed plan to close our only nuclear-related facility in Koson… Or we can mutually designate our special envoys to continue working on a draft agreement…

議論を続けないのですか？ まだ時間はあり、コソン核関連施設のみを閉鎖する詳細な計画を決定しようじゃありませんか。あるいは、合意文書の草案作成を続けるために、相互に特使を任命しますか？

2-31b Oh, you have great foresight, but I am afraid I must excuse myself because I have a dinner date tonight. If you change your mind, Mr./Ms. Chairperson, don't hesitate to call us or leave me a message at any time. Our door is always open.

おぉ、あなたは素晴らしい先見性をお持ちですね。しかし残念だが、今晩ディナーの予約があり失礼しなければならない。委員長、もし気が変わることがあれば、いつでも電話、もしくはメッセージを残してくれ。私達の対話のドアは常に開いている。

2-32a Your famous last words! At the end of the day, you have not been serious about establishing peace and stability on the peninsula. You just want to maintain your hegemony here. This is an act of hypocrisy. You have no intention to implement the agreement. Thanks a million, Mr./Ms. President!

またあなたのお決まりの最後の言葉だ。終盤になって、あなたが半島の平和や安定の確立に真剣でないことが露呈しましたね。あなた方は単にこの地域の覇権を維持したいだけだ。これは偽善的行為だ。あなたは合意の実施を取り付ける気などさらさらない。ご苦労様、大統領。

2-33b (Damn, this guy and Saan are both liars!) You are quite welcome, Mr./Ms Chairperson! Thank you very much for your time today and I hope to see you sooner rather than later!

（ちくしょう、こいつもサンも両方とも嘘つきだ。）どういたしまして、委員長。時間を取ってくれてどうもありがとう。近いうちに再会できる日を楽しみにしている。

Diplomatic Negotiations, ACT Three:
Inside the Zaiina Foreign Ministry building in Hwangjin, November 202X

❖ Background to the Dialogues

ACT Three  6

3-1 Despite its repeated ultimatum that it would undertake immediate annexation, Zaiina in fact did not annex Palwan in October 202X. Consequently, Palwan has narrowly retained a minimum level of autonomous democracy. However, at midnight on the eve of November 1, Zaiina's national parliament abruptly enacted and immediately imposed a new National Security Law on the land of Palwan.

Dialogue 3-1  7

a = Zaiina staff and MOFA Spokesperson

b = Correspondent, GNN (US) Hwangjin Bureau

c = MHK (Japan) Bureau Chief in Hwangjin

A press briefing given by the Zaiina Foreign Ministry spokesperson for international media based in Hwangjin

3-2a' Good afternoon, everybody, ladies and gentlemen. Welcome to today's press briefing. Today, the spokesperson of the Ministry of Foreign Affairs will provide an update and overview of the new National Security Law for Palwan. After his/her opening remarks, I'll ask that each person raise their hand. We'll alternate, and that will provide an opportunity for everybody to ask their question.

3-3a' With respect to time, we request that each person ask only one question and a follow-up, and then if we get to everybody, we'll go back around if there are additional questions. As is standard, just identify yourself by your name and your organization before asking your question. And with that, I'll now turn it over to our spokesperson for his/her opening remarks.

3-4a Thank you and good afternoon. As we have previously explained, the new law aims at securing peace and stability in Palwan. The law bans secession, subversion, terrorism, and collusion with a foreign country or external elements that might endanger Palwan's national security. The maximum penalty for each crime is life imprisonment, and we have already deployed three hundred police units throughout Palwan.

3-5a The following are some details related to the law. First, Article 5 stipulates: A person who organizes, plans, commits, or participates in any of the following acts with a view to committing secession or undermining national unification shall be guilty of an offense: a) separating Palwan from Zaiina, b) altering the legal status of Palwan, c) surrendering Palwan to a foreign country.

3-6a Article 6 states: A person who organizes, plans, commits, or participates in any of the following acts by force or threat of force with a view to subverting the State power shall be guilty of an offense: a) overthrowing or undermining the basic governmental systems of Zaiina or Palwan, or b) seriously interfering in, disrupting, or undermining the actions of the authorities of Zaiina or Palwan.

3-7a According to Article 7: A person who organizes, plans, commits, participates in, or threatens to commit any of the following terrorist activities shall be guilty of an offense: a) serious violence against a person or persons; b) explosion, arson, or dissemination of poisonous, radioactive, infectious, or other substances; c) other dangerous activities that jeopardize public health, safety, or security.

3-8a Article 8 stipulates: A person who provides support, assistance, or facility such as training, weapons, information, funds, supplies, labor, transport, technologies, or venues to a terrorist organization or a terrorist, or for the commission of a terrorist activity, or who uses other means to prepare for the commission of a terrorist activity, shall be guilty of an offense.

3-9a Article 9: A person who steals, spies, obtains with payment, or unlawfully provides State secrets or intelligence concerning national security on behalf of a foreign country or an institution, organization, or individual shall be guilty of an offense; a person who requests or conspires with a foreign country or institution, organization, or individual to commit any unlawful acts shall be guilty of an offense. This concludes my opening statement. Any questions?

3-10b Yes, I am David Chen with GNN. Hi. I wanted to ask you about the alleged abuse of power committed by the law enforcement units Zaiina deployed to the area experiencing unrest. The Palwanese protesters, mostly ordinary citizens, are being suppressed, forced to surrender, and are now being transferred to Zaiinese territories. Is that a legitimate policy? This is unprecedented in Palwan, isn't it?

3-11a Well, David, what is your affiliation? GNN? OK! I hate GNN, a fake news channel. Anyway, those opponents are thugs who took ordinary citizens hostage. Since they had no immunity and showed no signs of obedience, our police officers were obligated to implement the law, mitigate anarchy, and secure the area. This is customary everywhere in the world under such circumstances.

3-12b And just a quick follow-up, how do you justify the prohibition of nonviolent marches? The demonstrators included international groups of human rights advocacy as well as profoundly respected and prominent provincial dignitaries. The police exercised no self-restraint. Amid the chaos, why did you give permission to your police to confront unarmed, nonpartisan ordinary people?

3-13a No, some of them were radical Buddhist fundamentalists whose covert plots are supported by some foreign agents in Palwan. Zaiina always tries to deal with issues through persuasion, perseverance and prudence. Our goal is not punishment but the restoration of order in the area. We do not wish to restrict people's freedom. This is the security dilemma we are facing. Now I recognize MHK over there.

3-14c Thank you. I am Tanaka with Japan's MHK. Demonstrators claim that your surveillance of NGOs, the abbreviation for nongovernmental organizations, is too harsh, and is inflicting severe damage to Palwan's basic social structure. Some of these demonstrators are even seeking political asylum in the West. Do you think the situation will improve if you temporarily suspend the new security measures in Palwan?

3-15a I usually do not answer hypothetical questions, but my answer is no. The new law is a piece of national legislation that our National Congress ratified legitimately. Palwan's Zaiinese identity is innate, explicit, and permanent. Those criminals, who are in alliance with foreign powers, have no allegiance to Zaiina. They are radical Buddhist fundamentalists and their plots are supported by some foreign powers.

Dialogue 3-2 8

a = Director-General of the Bureau for the Asia-Pacific, the Zaiinese Ministry of Foreign Affairs

b = Ambassador of Nowhere Republic, Dean of the diplomatic corps in Zaiina

At a conference room in Zaiina's Foreign Ministry building

3-16a Good morning, Mr./Ms. Ambassador! Thank you for coming on such short notice today. Thanks so much for taking time out of your busy schedule to see me today. I really appreciate it.

3-17b Oh, it's my pleasure. I was about to take a vacation starting the day after tomorrow, but it's OK. This is more important than my vacation. Anyway, how have you been, Mr./Ms. Director-General?

3-18a Pretty good, thank you. Oh, by the way, today I must tell you about something that is quite an important issue for my country. Yesterday, your neighbor, the government of Somewhere, unilaterally made a very disappointing decision. Following the actions taken by some Western European countries last week, Somewhere also suspended the criminal extradition treaty with us.

3-19b Yes, I know that. No wonder, they made the decision because you enacted what you call the Palwan National Security Law, which is a clear violation of the international agreement on Palwan's highest level of autonomy in 1989. The diplomatic corps in Zaiina is deeply concerned that the enforcement of the new law will only escalate violence against innocent civilians in Palwan.

3-20a That's a complete misunderstanding. This law was properly enacted by the legislative branch of Zaiina. It would mean interfering with Zaiina's internal affairs, and no nation has the right to override the implementation of this law. No nation can disregard our legal system, either. Mr./Ms. Ambassador, you are kindly requested to stay away from Palwan.

3-21b Mr./Ms. Director-General, are you sure about what you are saying? Everybody knows that this is an issue of the basic human rights of Palwanese citizens. This is not only my personal opinion. The entire international community is concerned about the unfair treatment of the Palwanese. I am particularly worried about Palwanese citizens' right to leave the country if they wish to do so.

3-22a That is no problem. In Zaiina, everybody has such a right if they observe the domestic rules and regulations. Unfortunately, activists and demonstrators are trying to destroy the public order of Palwan. This is not acceptable. Some of them are even declaring "independence for Palwan," waving the flag of the United States. It's indisputable that they have ties to hostile elements overseas.

3-23b We know there are altogether seven journalists, or I should say, two Australians, two Japanese, two Americans, and one German, in addition to a Palwan local employee at the British Consulate-General, who have been illegally detained by the Zaiinese police since last week.

3-24b The diplomatic corps in Zaiina hereby formally requests humanitarian treatment and the immediate release of those eight innocent individuals. You should take this request very seriously because international criticism against their detention is rapidly growing.

3-25a They were detained only because they committed a criminal act in our territory. They are not diplomats, and of course are subject to Zaiina's laws and regulations. In addition, I must also remind you of our official request that, since last week the four Palwanese criminals now living in New Zealand, Japan, France, and Canada be extradited to Zaiina as soon as possible.

3-26b No way, my friend. Zaiina has accepted and guaranteed a "high degree of autonomy" in Palwan under the principle of "one country, two systems" since 1989. Palwan, a democratic and free-market economy, is an indispensable part of the world economy. Palwan cannot be easily integrated into Zaiina, because it is still home to many global investors and financial or commercial institutions.

3-27a In addition, what do you mean by the "international criticism" you just referred to? Last month, a United Nations Human Rights Council meeting discussed the Palwan National Security Law, and don't you remember that a number of countries represented at the meeting actually supported the law? Did you say international criticism? Forget it, there is no such thing.

3-28a Anyway, it doesn't make sense to me at all. Zaiina sincerely hopes that Nowhere will make a wise decision. The implications of your decision could be enormous. Don't threaten us, my friend. The Republic of Nowhere needs our market for its mineral and agricultural products. Don't forget that no other country purchases a larger amount from Nowhere than any other country worldwide.

3-29b Thank you for your advice, but you should respect our liberal democracy and freedom of speech. As for your request for extradition, it is highly likely that we will act in accordance with the basic principles of human rights. Your response is too ideological and our resentment is mounting. It is high time for Zaiina to think twice and immediately release the eight people being detained before you regret it.

Diplomatic Negotiations, ACT Three: Inside the Zaiina Foreign Ministry building in Hwangjin, November 202X

✣ Background to the Dialogues (対話 (→ 108))

ACT Three

6

3-1 Despite its repeated ultimatum (最後通告 (→ 335)) that it would undertake immediate (即時の (→ 158)) annexation (併合 (→ 22)), Zaiina in fact did not annex (併合する (→ 22)) Palwan in October 202X. Consequently (その結果 (→ 76)), Palwan has narrowly retained a minimum level of autonomous (自律的な (→ 35)) democracy. However, at midnight on the eve of November 1, Zaiina's national parliament abruptly enacted and immediately (直ちに (→ 158)) imposed (課す (→ 165)) a new National Security (国家安全保障 (→ 214)) Law on the land of Palwan.

Dialogue 3-1

7

a = Zaiina staff and MOFA Spokesperson

b = Correspondent, GNN (US) Hwangjin Bureau (支局 (→ 48))

c = MHK (Japan) Bureau Chief in Hwangjin

A press briefing given by the Zaiina Foreign Ministry spokesperson for international media based in Hwangjin

3-2a' Good afternoon, everybody, ladies and gentlemen. Welcome to today's press briefing. Today, the spokesperson of the Ministry of Foreign Affairs will provide an update and overview of the new National Security Law for Palwan. After his/her opening remarks,

I'll ask that each person raise their hand. We'll alternate, and that
交互に行う（→ 18）
will provide an opportunity for everybody to ask their question.

3-3a' With respect to time, we request that each person ask only one question and a follow-up, and then if we get to everybody, we'll go back around if there are additional questions. As is standard, just identify yourself by your name and your organization before
身元を明らかにする（→ 156）
asking your question. And with that, I'll now turn it over to our spokesperson for his/her opening remarks.

3-4a Thank you and good afternoon. As we have previously explained, the new law aims at securing peace and stability in Palwan. The law bans
保証する（→ 292）　安定（→ 302）　禁止する（→ 38）
secession, subversion, terrorism, and collusion with a foreign country
転覆（→ 312）
or external elements that might endanger Palwan's national security. The maximum penalty for each crime is life imprisonment, and we have already deployed three hundred police units throughout Palwan.
展開する（→ 103）

3-5a The following are some details related to the law. First, Article 5 stipulates: A person who organizes, plans, commits, or participates in any of the following acts with a view to committing secession or undermining national unification shall be guilty of an offense:
統一（→ 339）
a) separating Palwan from Zaiina, b) altering the legal status of Palwan, c) surrendering Palwan to a foreign country.
明け渡す（→ 316）

3-6a Article 6 states: A person who organizes, plans, commits, or participates in any of the following acts by force or threat of force with a view to subverting the State power shall be guilty of an offense: a) overthrowing or undermining the basic governmental systems of Zaiina or Palwan, or b) seriously interfering in, disrupting, or undermining the actions of the authorities of Zaiina or Palwan.

力（→ 143） 脅し（→ 323） 転覆させる（→ 312） 干渉する（→ 180） 当局（→ 34）

3-7a According to Article 7: A person who organizes, plans, commits, participates in, or threatens to commit any of the following terrorist activities shall be guilty of an offense: a) serious violence against a person or persons; b) explosion, arson, or dissemination of poisonous, radioactive, infectious, or other substances; c) other dangerous activities that jeopardize public health, safety, or security.

脅す（→ 323）

3-8a Article 8 stipulates: A person who provides support, assistance, or facility such as training, weapons, information, funds, supplies, labor, transport, technologies, or venues to a terrorist organization or a terrorist, or for the commission of a terrorist activity, or who uses other means to prepare for the commission of a terrorist activity, shall be guilty of an offense.

施設（→ 141）

3-9a Article 9: A person who steals, spies, obtains with payment, or unlawfully provides State secrets or intelligence concerning
機密情報（→ 176）
national security on behalf of a foreign country or an institution,
利益になるように（→ 167）
organization, or individual shall be guilty of an offense; a person who requests or conspires with a foreign country or institution,
共謀する（→ 77）
organization, or individual to commit any unlawful acts shall be guilty of an offense. This concludes my opening statement. Any questions?

3-10b Yes, I am David Chen with GNN. Hi. I wanted to ask you about the alleged abuse of power committed by the law enforcement units
申し立てられた（→ 14） 権力（→ 244） 執行（→ 128）
Zaiina deployed to the area experiencing unrest. The Palwanese protesters, mostly ordinary citizens, are being suppressed, forced to
市民（→ 55） 抑圧する（→ 314）
surrender, and are now being transferred to Zaiinese territories. Is
移動させる（→ 327） 領土（→ 321）
that a legitimate policy? This is unprecedented in Palwan, isn't it?
合法的な（→ 192） 政策（→ 243）

3-11a Well, David, what is your affiliation? GNN? OK! I hate GNN, a fake
所属（→ 11）
news channel. Anyway, those opponents are thugs who took ordinary
反対者（→ 227）
citizens hostage. Since they had no immunity and showed no signs of
人質（→ 151） 特権（→ 159）
obedience, our police officers were obligated to implement the law,
服従（→ 219） 余儀なくさせる（→ 220） 施行する（→ 162）
mitigate anarchy, and secure the area. This is customary everywhere
軽減する（→ 205） 無政府状態（→ 21） 慣習となっている（→ 93）
in the world under such circumstances.
状況（→ 54）

3-12b And just a quick follow-up, how do you justify the prohibition of
正当化する（→ 189） 禁止（→ 257）
nonviolent marches? The demonstrators included international groups of human rights advocacy as well as profoundly respected
擁護（→ 10） 深く（→ 256）
and prominent provincial dignitaries. The police exercised no
著名な（→ 258） 地方の（→ 262）
self-restraint. Amid the chaos, why did you give permission to your
抑制（→ 286） 渦中に（→ 20） 許可（→ 237）
police to confront unarmed, nonpartisan ordinary people?
対立させる（→ 73） 非武装の（→ 28） ゲリラの（→ 232）

3-13a No, some of them were radical Buddhist fundamentalists whose
原理主義者（→ 146）
covert plots are supported by some foreign agents in Palwan.
隠された（→ 90） 陰謀（→ 242） 工作員（→ 12）
Zaiina always tries to deal with issues through persuasion,
説得（→ 239）
perseverance and prudence. Our goal is not punishment but
忍耐（→ 238） 慎重さ（→ 264） 処罰（→ 265）
the restoration of order in the area. We do not wish to restrict
回復（→ 285） 制限する（→ 287）
people's freedom. This is the security dilemma we are facing. Now I recognize MHK over there.

3-14c Thank you. I am Tanaka with Japan's MHK. Demonstrators claim that
主張する（→ 56）
your surveillance of NGOs, the abbreviation for nongovernmental
監視（→ 317） 短縮（→ 1） 非政府（→ 217）
organizations, is too harsh, and is inflicting severe damage to
負わせる（→ 171）
Palwan's basic social structure. Some of these demonstrators are
構造（→ 306）
even seeking political asylum in the West. Do you think the situation
亡命（→ 32）
will improve if you temporarily suspend the new security measures in Palwan?

3-15a I usually do not answer hypothetical questions, but my answer is no. The new law is a piece of national legislation that our National Congress ratified legitimately. Palwan's Zaiinese identity is innate, explicit, and permanent. Those criminals, who are in alliance with foreign powers, have no allegiance to Zaiina. They are radical Buddhist fundamentalists and their plots are supported by some foreign powers.

hypothetical 仮定上の（→ 155）
Congress 議会（→ 74） ratified 承認する（→ 269） legitimately 合法的に（→ 192）
explicit 明確な（→ 139） permanent 永続的な（→ 236） alliance 連携（→ 17）
allegiance 忠誠（→ 15）

Dialogue 3-2

8

a = Director-General of the Bureau for the Asia-Pacific, the Zaiinese Ministry of Foreign Affairs

b = Ambassador of Nowhere Republic, Dean of the diplomatic corps in Zaiina

Ambassador 大使（→ 19）

At a conference room in Zaiina's Foreign Ministry building

3-16a Good morning, Mr./Ms. Ambassador! Thank you for coming on such short notice today. Thanks so much for taking time out of your busy schedule to see me today. I really appreciate it.

3-17b Oh, it's my pleasure. I was about to take a vacation starting the day after tomorrow, but it's OK. This is more important than my vacation. Anyway, how have you been, Mr./Ms. Director-General?

3-18a Pretty good, thank you. Oh, by the way, today I must tell you about something that is quite an important issue for my country. Yesterday, your neighbor, the government of Somewhere, unilaterally (一方的に（→ 340）) made a very disappointing decision. Following the actions taken by some Western European countries last week, Somewhere also suspended the criminal extradition treaty (条約（→ 330）) with us.

3-19b Yes, I know that. No wonder, they made the decision because you enacted what you call the Palwan National Security Law, which is a clear violation of the international agreement on Palwan's highest level of autonomy (自治（→ 35）) in 1989. The diplomatic (外交（→ 109）) corps in Zaiina is deeply concerned that the enforcement of the new law will only escalate violence against innocent civilians in Palwan.

3-20a That's a complete misunderstanding. This law was properly enacted by the legislative branch (府（→ 47）) of Zaiina. It would mean interfering with Zaiina's internal affairs, and no nation has the right to override (優位に立つ（→ 230）) the implementation (執行（→ 162）) of this law. No nation can disregard (軽視する（→ 115）) our legal system, either. Mr./Ms. Ambassador, you are kindly requested to stay away from Palwan.

3-21b Mr./Ms. Director-General, are you sure about what you are saying? Everybody knows that this is an issue of the basic human rights of Palwanese citizens. This is not only my personal opinion. The entire international community is concerned about the unfair treatment of the Palwanese. I am particularly worried about Palwanese citizens' right to leave the country if they wish to do so.

3-22a That is no problem. In Zaiina, everybody has such a right if they observe the domestic rules and regulations. Unfortunately, activists and demonstrators are trying to destroy the public order of Palwan. This is not acceptable. Some of them are even declaring (宣言する（→ 95）) "independence for Palwan," waving the flag of the United States. It's indisputable (疑う余地のない（→ 114）) that they have ties to hostile (敵の（→ 152）) elements overseas (海外の（→ 231）).

3-23b We know there are altogether seven journalists, or I should say, two Australians, two Japanese, two Americans, and one German, in addition to a Palwan local employee at the British Consulate-General (総領事館（→ 79）), who have been illegally detained by the Zaiinese police since last week.

3-24b The diplomatic corps in Zaiina hereby formally requests humanitarian (人道的な（→ 153）) treatment and the immediate release of those eight innocent individuals. You should take this request very seriously because international criticism against their detention is rapidly growing.

3-25a They were detained only because they committed a criminal act in our territory. They are not diplomats (外交官（→ 109）), and of course are subject to Zaiina's laws and regulations. In addition, I must also remind you of our official (公式な（→ 224）) request that, since last week the four Palwanese criminals now living in New Zealand, Japan, France, and Canada be extradited to Zaiina as soon as possible.

3-26b No way, my friend. Zaiina has accepted and guaranteed a "high degree of autonomy" in Palwan under the principle (原則（→ 250）) of "one country, two systems" since 1989. Palwan, a democratic and free-market economy, is an indispensable part of the world economy. Palwan cannot be easily integrated (統合する（→ 175）) into Zaiina, because it is still home to many global investors (投資家（→ 186）) and financial or commercial institutions.

3-27a In addition, what do you mean by the "international criticism" you just referred to? Last month, a United Nations Human Rights Council meeting discussed the Palwan National Security Law, and don't you remember that a number of countries represented (代表する（→ 279）) at the meeting actually supported the law? Did you say international criticism? Forget it, there is no such thing.

3-28a Anyway, it doesn't make sense to me at all. Zaiina sincerely hopes that Nowhere will make a wise decision. The implications (含意（→ 163）) of your decision could be enormous. Don't threaten us, my friend. The Republic of Nowhere needs our market for its mineral and agricultural products. Don't forget that no other country purchases a larger amount from Nowhere than any other country worldwide.

3-29b Thank you for your advice, but you should respect our liberal democracy and freedom of speech. As for your request for extradition, it is highly likely that we will act in accordance with (したがって（→ 166）) the basic principles of human rights. Your response is too ideological (イデオロギーに基づく（→ 157）) and our resentment (憤り（→ 282）) is mounting (高まる（→ 208）). It is high time for Zaiina to think twice and immediately release the eight people being detained before you regret it.

✣ ACT three: Notes

3-1 narrowly：辛うじて；狭く（narrow：狭い；限られた；やっとの）
retain：保持する；維持する
minimum level：最低水準
eve：直前；前夜
abruptly：突然；不意に（abrupt：急な；突然の）

3-2a' press briefing：記者会見
update：最新情報；更新する
overview：要旨；概説
remark：言葉；批評；意見；述べる

3-3a' follow-up：補足（質問）（この場合は follow-up question〔補足質問〕の question が省略された形）
get to X：X に達する；着手する
turn (it) over X：X に譲る；引き継ぐ

3-4a secession：分離；脱退
collusion：共謀；談合
endanger：危険にさらす；危うくする
maximum：最大の；最大限度の；最大値
penalty：罰則；刑罰；罰金
life imprisonment：終身刑；無期懲役

3-5a detail：詳細；細目
with a view to X：X するために；を目的として；する目的で
undermine：弱体化させる；間接的に攻撃する
national unification：国家統一
guilty：有罪の；罪を犯した
offense：違反；犯罪；攻撃
separate：離す；分離する；独立させる
alter：変える；変更する
legal status：法的地位

3-6a disrupt：混乱させる；破壊する

3-7a explosion：爆発
arson：放火
dissemination：散布；流布
poisonous：有毒な；有害な
radioactive：放射能の
infectious：感染性の
dangerous：危険な；危害を加える
jeopardize：危険にさらす；危うくする
public health：公衆衛生

3-8a training：訓練；練習

3-9a steal：盗む；盗用する
spy: スパイをする；諜報活動をする
obtain：得る；手に入れる
unlawfully：非合法的に；不法に
unlawful：非合法的な；違法の

3-10b unrest：混乱；動揺；不安
protester：異議を申し立てる人；デモ参加者
mostly：大部分は；たいていは
ordinary：普通の；平凡な；一般の

3-11a hate：ひどく嫌う；憎む
thug：悪党；凶悪犯

3-12b non(-)violent：非暴力の
march：デモ行進；行軍；マーチ
demonstrator：デモ参加者；実演者
dignitary：高官；要人
nonpartisan：無党派の

3-13a goal：目標；目的（地）
security dilemma：安全保障のジレンマ（dilemma：板挟み；難問；ジレンマ）
over there：あちらに；あちらでは

3-15a innate：生来の；生得的な

3-16a take time：時間を取る
out of X：X の中から
I (really) appreciate it.：感謝します。：ありがとうございます。

3-17b (be) about to X : X しそうである；まさに X しようとしている
vacation : 休暇；休み
the day after tomorrow : 明後日
How have you been? : ご機嫌いかがですか？；調子はどうですか？
director-general : 長官；総裁；事務総長；会長

3-18a pretty : 大いに；かなり；かわいい
quite : かなり；非常に；完全に
criminal : 犯罪者；犯人；犯罪の
extradition : （本国）送還；引き渡し

3-19b what you call : いわゆる
corps : 団；団体；隊
escalate : 悪化する；増大する；上昇させる

3-20a misunderstanding : 誤解；意見の相違
properly : 適切に；正しく
(be) kindly requested to X : どうか X して下さい；X するようお願いします
stay away : 離れている；近寄らない

3-21b sure : 本気で；確かに
basic human rights : 基本的人権
personal : 個人の；本人が直接行う

3-22a no problem : 問題ない；大丈夫だ
regulation : 規則；規制；法規
activist : 活動家；運動家
public order : 社会秩序
wave : 振る；うねらせる；波

3-23b altogether : 全体で；総計で；完全に
illegally : 不法に；違法に
detain : 拘束する；留置する；拘留する

3-24b hereby : ここに；これによって
formally : 正式に；公式に
detention : 拘留；抑留；引き留め

3-25a remind : リマインドする；思い出させる；注意する
extradite : 引き渡す；送還する

3-26b one country(,) two systems : 一国二制度
free-market economy : 自由主義経済

3-27a What do you mean by X? : X とはどういう意味ですか？
Human Rights Council : 人権理事会
Don' t you remember X? : X を覚えていないのですか？; をお忘れですか？
Forget it. : 忘れた方がいいですよ。; 今のはなかったことにして下さい。;
そんなことはどうでもいい。

3-28a It doesn' t make sense. : それはおかしい。; 意味をなさない ; 筋が通っていない。
wise : 賢明な ; 思慮深い
agricultural product : 農産物
purchase : 購入する ; 買う

3-29b liberal democracy : 自由民主主義
freedom of speech : 言論の自由
as for X : X に関しては
It is highly likely that X. : X の可能性が高い。; が十分考えられる。
It is high time X. : もう当然 X してよい時だ。; 既に X し終わっている時間だ。
think twice : 考え直す ; よく考える

Diplomatic Negotiations, ACT Three: Inside the Zaiina Foreign Ministry building in Hwangjin, November 202X

ホワンジンにおけるザイーナ外務省ビルの中で（202X 年 11 月）

✣ Background to the Dialogues （対話の背景）

ACT Three  6

3-1 Despite its repeated ultimatum that it would undertake immediate annexation, Zaiina in fact did not annex Palwan in October 202X. Consequently, Palwan has narrowly retained a minimum level of autonomous democracy. However, at midnight on the eve of November 1, Zaiina's national parliament abruptly enacted and immediately imposed a new National Security Law on the land of Palwan.

即時の併合に踏み切るというザイーナの繰り返しの最後通告にも関わらず、実際、202X年10月時点ではザイーナは併合を実施しなかった。その結果パルワーンは、辛うじて、最低限のレベルではあるが自律的な民主主義体制を保っていた。ところが、11月1日になろうとする深夜、ザイーナの国会は突如として、パルワーンの地における新たな国家安全保障法を制定し、直ちにその法律を施行した。

Dialogue 3-1 （対話）  7

a = Zaiina staff and MOFA Spokesperson　a = ザイーナ職員、外務省報道官

b = Correspondent, GNN (US) Hwangjin Bureau　b =（米国）GNN ホワンジン支局特派員

c = MHK (Japan) Bureau Chief in Hwangjin　c =（日本）MHK ホワンジン支局長

A press briefing given by the Zaiina Foreign Ministry spokesperson for international media based in Hwangjin

ザイーナ外務省報道官による国際メディア向け記者会見（於：ホワンジン）

3-2a' Good afternoon, everybody, ladies and gentlemen. Welcome to today's press briefing. Today, the spokesperson of the Ministry of Foreign Affairs will provide an update and overview of the new National Security Law for Palwan. After his/her opening remarks, I'll ask that each person raise their hand. We'll alternate, and that will provide an opportunity for everybody to ask their question.

皆さん、どうもこんにちは。本日の記者会見にようこそお越し下さいました。本日は、当国外務省の報道官より、パルワーンに対する新たな国家安全保障法についての最新の概要をお伝えしたいと思います。こちらからの説明の後、ご質問がある場合は挙手を願います。順番に質疑応答の機会を持たせて頂く予定です。

3-3a With respect to time, we request that each person ask only one question and a follow-up, and then if we get to everybody, we'll go back around if there are additional questions. As is standard, just identify yourself by your name and your organization before asking your question. And with that, I'll now turn it over to our spokesperson for his/her opening remarks.

限られた時間を有効に使うため、一人あたり質問１つとフォローアップ１つとさせて頂きます。その後、全員が質問を終えたことを確認し、追加の質問を受け付けます。基本的なルールとして、質問の前には名前と所属を明らかにして頂くようお願いします。それでは、私達の報道官より冒頭の言葉を述べさせて頂きます。

3-4a Thank you and good afternoon. As we have previously explained, the new law aims at securing peace and stability in Palwan. The law bans secession, subversion, terrorism, and collusion with a foreign country or external elements that might endanger Palwan's national security. The maximum penalty for each crime is life imprisonment, and we have already deployed three hundred police units throughout Palwan.

どうもありがとう。やあ皆さん。以前も説明した通り、新たな法律はパルワーンの平和と安定を保証することを目的としている。新法は分離独立、国家転覆、テロ、パルワーンの国家安全保障を脅かす外国や外部の勢力との共謀を禁止している。各罪状の最も重い刑罰は終身刑であり、私達は既に 300 の警察部隊をパルワーン全土に展開した。

3-5a The following are some details related to the law. First, Article 5 stipulates: A person who organizes, plans, commits, or participates in any of the following acts with a view to committing secession or undermining national unification shall be guilty of an offense: a) separating Palwan from Zaiina, b) altering the legal status of Palwan, c) surrendering Palwan to a foreign country.

次に述べる内容は法律に関する詳細である。１つに、第５条は次のように規定している。分離、もしくは国家統一の弱体化を目論む、次に掲げるいかなる行為の組織化、計画、従事、参加をも有罪とする。a) ザイーナからパルワーンを分離すること、b) パルワーンの法的地位を変更すること、c) パルワーンを他国に明け渡すこと

3-6a Article 6 states: A person who organizes, plans, commits, or participates in any of the following acts by force or threat of force with a view to subverting the State power shall be guilty of an offense: a) overthrowing or undermining the basic governmental systems of Zaiina or Palwan, or b) seriously interfering in, disrupting, or undermining the actions of the authorities of Zaiina or Palwan.

第6条は次のように定めている。国家権力の転覆を目論み、力や力による脅しを背景に、次に掲げるいずれかの行為の組織化、計画、従事、参加を有罪とする。a) ザイーナもしくはパルワーンの基本的な政治システムを転覆もしくは弱体化させること、b) ザイーナもしくはパルワーン当局による行動に対し、著しく干渉する、もしくは混乱、弱体化させること

3-7a According to Article 7: A person who organizes, plans, commits, participates in, or threatens to commit any of the following terrorist activities shall be guilty of an offense: a) serious violence against a person or persons; b) explosion, arson, or dissemination of poisonous, radioactive, infectious, or other substances; c) other dangerous activities that jeopardize public health, safety, or security.

第7条はこの通りである。次に掲げるいずれかのテロ行為の組織化、計画、従事、参加、脅迫を有罪とする。a) 人対人に対する深刻な暴力行為、b) 爆発、放火、もしくは有毒、放射能、感染、その他の物質の散布、c) 公衆衛生、安全、治安を脅かすその他の危険行為

3-8a Article 8 stipulates: A person who provides support, assistance, or facility such as training, weapons, information, funds, supplies, labor, transport, technologies, or venues to a terrorist organization or a terrorist, or for the commission of a terrorist activity, or who uses other means to prepare for the commission of a terrorist activity, shall be guilty of an offense.

第8条は以下の通り規定している。テロ組織、テロリスト、テロ行為の委託、テロ行為の委託を準備するその他の手段を用いる者に対して、訓練、武器、情報、資金、物資、労働、移送、技術、場所などの支援、援助、もしくは施設の提供を行なった者を有罪とする。

3-9a Article 9: A person who steals, spies, obtains with payment, or unlawfully provides State secrets or intelligence concerning national security on behalf of a foreign country or an institution, organization, or individual shall be guilty of an offense; a person who requests or conspires with a foreign country or institution, organization, or individual to commit any unlawful acts shall be guilty of an offense. This concludes my opening statement. Any questions?

第9条では、外国もしくは特定の機構、組織、個人の利益を目的として、国家安全保障に関する国家機密もしくは機密情報を盗難、スパイ、金銭による買収、もしくは非合法な手段で提供する者を有罪とする。またいずれかの非合法的行為で、外国もしくは特定の機構、組織、個人へそれらを依頼もしくは共謀する者を有罪とする。これで私の冒頭の言葉とさせてもらう。質問を受け付ける。

3-10b Yes, I am David Chen with GNN. Hi. I wanted to ask you about the alleged abuse of power committed by the law enforcement units Zaiina deployed to the area experiencing unrest. The Palwanese protesters, mostly ordinary citizens, are being suppressed, forced to surrender, and are now being transferred to Zaiinese territories. Is that a legitimate policy? This is unprecedented in Palwan, isn't it?

はい、私はGNNのデイビッド・チェンです。こんにちは。私からは、当該の地域に動揺をもたらしている、ザイーナが展開した法執行のための部隊による権力濫用について質問したいと思います。大部分が一般市民であるパルワーンの抗議者は、力づくで抑圧され、服従を余儀なくされた上、現在はザイーナ領土に強制移住させられています。これが合法的な政策ですか？ このようなことはパルワーンにとって前代未聞の事態ですよね？

3-11a Well, David, what is your affiliation? GNN? OK! I hate GNN, a fake news channel. Anyway, those opponents are thugs who took ordinary citizens hostage. Since they had no immunity and showed no signs of obedience, our police officers were obligated to implement the law, mitigate anarchy, and secure the area. This is customary everywhere in the world under such circumstances.

そうだなデイビッド、君の所属は何かな？ GNNか？ 分かった。私はGNNが嫌いだ。偽ニュースチャンネルだからな。それはともかくとして、これら抗議を行っている者は、一般市民を人質にとった悪党どもだ。彼らには何の権限もなく、一切の服従を示さなかったため、警官部隊が止むを得ず法を執行することで、無政府状態を軽減し、地域の安定をはからざるを得なかった。この対応は、そうした状況に陥った世界中で同様に取られる慣習的なものであり問題ない。

3-12b And just a quick follow-up, how do you justify the prohibition of nonviolent marches? The demonstrators included international groups of human rights advocacy as well as profoundly respected and prominent provincial dignitaries. The police exercised no self-restraint. Amid the chaos, why did you give permission to your police to confront unarmed, nonpartisan ordinary people?

短く１つフォローアップの質問をさせて下さい。それではあなた方は、どのような正当化の根拠で、彼らの非暴力のデモ行進を禁止するのですか？ 抗議する者の中には、国際的な人権擁護団体や、深く尊敬を集める著名な地方政府高官も含まれていました。これらに対し、警察隊は何の自制も見せなかった。混乱の最中、なぜあなた方は、非武装でゲリラでもない一般市民に対し、警官を向かわせることを許可したのですか？

3-13a No, some of them were radical Buddhist fundamentalists whose covert plots are supported by some foreign agents in Palwan. Zaiina always tries to deal with issues through persuasion, perseverance and prudence. Our goal is not punishment but the restoration of order in the area. We do not wish to restrict people's freedom. This is the security dilemma we are facing. Now I recognize MHK over there.

いいや、それらの一部は過激な仏教原理主義者で、その隠された陰謀にはパルワーン内の外国人工作員からの支援がある。ザイーナは常に、これらの問題に、説得を続け、忍耐強く、慎重に対処している。私達のゴールは彼らの処罰ではなく、地域の秩序を回復させることだ。私達は人々の自由を制限するつもりはない。これは私達が直面している安全保障のジレンマだ。さて、あちらのMHK から手が挙がっているようだ。

3-14c **Thank you. I am Tanaka with Japan's MHK. Demonstrators claim that your surveillance of NGOs, the abbreviation for nongovernmental organizations, is too harsh, and is inflicting severe damage to Palwan's basic social structure. Some of these demonstrators are even seeking political asylum in the West. Do you think the situation will improve if you temporarily suspend the new security measures in Palwan?**

ありがとうございます。私は日本の MHK に所属する田中と申します。デモ隊はあなた方の NGO、つまり非政府組織による監視があまりにも強く、それがパルワーンの基本的な社会構造に深刻なダメージを与えていることを主張しています。デモ隊の一部は、西側諸国への政治的亡命を求めることさえしています。もしパルワーンに対する新たな安全保障政策を一旦休止すれば、事態が改善するとはお考えになりませんか？

3-15a I usually do not answer hypothetical questions, but my answer is no. The new law is a piece of national legislation that our National Congress ratified legitimately. Palwan's Zaiinese identity is innate, explicit, and permanent. Those criminals, who are in alliance with foreign powers, have no allegiance to Zaiina. They are radical Buddhist fundamentalists and their plots are supported by some foreign powers.

私は通常、仮定の質問には答えないことにしているが、あえて答えるなら「ノー」だ。新法は私達の国会が合法的に可決承認した、国の法令の１つだ。パルワーンのザイーナに対するアイデンティティーは生来的であり、明確で、永続的だ。外国勢力と結託したこれらの犯罪者はザイーナに何の忠誠も誓っていない。繰り返すが、彼らは過激な仏教原理主義者であり、その陰謀は外国勢力によって支援されている。

Dialogue 3-2 （対話）  8

a = Director-General of the Bureau for the Asia-Pacific, the Zaiinese Ministry of Foreign Affairs

b = Ambassador of Nowhere Republic, Dean of the diplomatic corps in Zaiina

a = ザイーナ外務省、アジア太平洋局長官
b = ノーウェア共和国大使、在ザイーナ外交団長

At a conference room in Zaiina's Foreign Ministry building

ザイーナ外務省内の会議室にて

3-16a Good morning, Mr./Ms. Ambassador! Thank you for coming on such short notice today. Thanks so much for taking time out of your busy schedule to see me today. I really appreciate it.

おはようございます、大使。直前の連絡にもかかわらず本日お越し下さりありがとうございます。お忙しい中お時間を割いて面会下さり、心よりお礼申し上げます。

3-17b Oh, it's my pleasure. I was about to take a vacation starting the day after tomorrow, but it's OK. This is more important than my vacation. Anyway, how have you been, Mr./Ms. Director-General?

ええ、喜んで。明後日より休暇を取ろうとしていたところですが、構いません。これは私の休暇よりもはるかに大事なことですから。ともかく、長官ご機嫌いかがですか？

3-18a Pretty good, thank you. Oh, by the way, today I must tell you about something that is quite an important issue for my country. Yesterday, your neighbor, the government of Somewhere, unilaterally made a very disappointing decision. Following the actions taken by some Western European countries last week, Somewhere also suspended the criminal extradition treaty with us.

すこぶる調子が良いです。どうもありがとう。ああ、ところで本日なのですが、我が国についての大変重要な問題についてあなたにお伝えしなければなりません。昨日、あなたの隣国であるサムウェアー政府が、一方的に大変残念な決定を下しました。いくつかの西側ヨーロッパ諸国が先週取った行動に続いたものですが、サムウェアーも私達との犯罪人引渡条約を一時停止することを決めました。

3-19b Yes, I know that. No wonder, they made the decision because you enacted what you call the Palwan National Security Law, which is a clear violation of the international agreement on Palwan's highest level of autonomy in 1989. The diplomatic corps in Zaiina is deeply concerned that the enforcement of the new law will only escalate violence against innocent civilians in Palwan.

ええ、もちろん存じています。驚くに値しません。彼らがそう決定したのは、あなた方がパルワーンに対する国家安全保障法を制定したからで、それは、パルワーンの最高レベルの自治を認める 1989 年の国際的な同意に明確に違反しています。在ザイーナの外交団は、この新法の施行によって、パルワーンにおける無垢な市民に対する暴力がエスカレートするだけにならないか、大変懸念しています。

3-20a That's a complete misunderstanding. This law was properly enacted by the legislative branch of Zaiina. It would mean interfering with Zaiina's internal affairs, and no nation has the right to override the implementation of this law. No nation can disregard our legal system, either. Mr./Ms. Ambassador, you are kindly requested to stay away from Palwan.

それは完全なる誤解です。この法律はザイーナの行政府によって適切な手順に則り制定されたものです。諸外国の行為はザイーナに対する内政干渉を意味し、いかなる国も、この法律の執行よりも優位に立つ権利など有していません。そして、いかなる国も我が国の法体系を軽視することは許されません。大使、どうかパルワーンから手を引いてもらえませんか。

3-21b Mr./Ms. Director-General, are you sure about what you are saying? Everybody knows that this is an issue of the basic human rights of Palwanese citizens. This is not only my personal opinion. The entire international community is concerned about the unfair treatment of the Palwanese. I am particularly worried about Palwanese citizens' right to leave the country if they wish to do so.

長官、何を仰っているのか分かっていますか？ 誰もがこれがパルワーン市民の基本的人権に関わる問題だということが分かっています。これは単なる私の個人的な意見ではありません。国際社会全体が、パルワーンの人々に対する不公正な扱いに憂慮しています。私は特に、パルワーン人が求めた際の国を離れる権利について案じています。

3-22a That is no problem. In Zaiina, everybody has such a right if they observe the domestic rules and regulations. Unfortunately, activists and demonstrators are trying to destroy the public order of Palwan. This is not acceptable. Some of them are even declaring "independence for Palwan," waving the flag of the United States. It's indisputable that they have ties to hostile elements overseas.

それについては心配無用です。ザイーナでは、誰もが国内の規則や法規を遵守する限りにおいて、そうした権利を持ち得ます。しかし残念なことに、活動家やデモ参加者はパルワーンの社会秩序を台無しにしようとしています。これは到底受け入れられるものではありません。彼らの中の一部は、アメリカ合衆国の国旗を振って、パルワーンの独立を宣言しさえしています。これは、彼らが海外の敵対勢力と結びついている動かしがたい証拠です。

3-23b We know there are altogether seven journalists, or I should say, two Australians, two Japanese, two Americans, and one German, in addition to a Palwan local employee at the British Consulate-General, who have been illegally detained by the Zaiinese police since last week.

合計７人のジャーナリスト、正確に言うならオーストラリア人２名、日本人２名、アメリカ人２名、ドイツ人１名と、加えて在パルワーンイギリス総領事館の現地スタッフ１名が、先週来、ザイーナ警察によって不当に拘束されていることを私達は知っています。

3-24b The diplomatic corps in Zaiina hereby formally requests humanitarian treatment and the immediate release of those eight innocent individuals. You should take this request very seriously because international criticism against their detention is rapidly growing.

在ザイーナ外交団は、ここに公式に、それら無実の８人に対し、人道的な処遇と共に、即座の解放を求めます。なおあなた方はこの要求を真摯に受け入れた方がよいでしょう。その理由は国際社会からの拘留に対する批判が急速に高まっているからです。

3-25a They were detained only because they committed a criminal act in our territory. They are not diplomats, and of course are subject to Zaiina's laws and regulations. In addition, I must also remind you of our official request that, since last week the four Palwanese criminals now living in New Zealand, Japan, France, and Canada be extradited to Zaiina as soon as possible.

彼らは我が国の領土において、犯罪行為を行ったが故に拘束されているに過ぎません。彼らは外交官でもなく、そして当然、ザイーナの法律並びに規則の支配下にあるわけです。なお加えて、私もあなた方に対する公式の要求を改めて述べなければなりません。先週来、４人のパルワーン人犯罪者がニュージーランド、日本、フランス、カナダに留まっていますが、彼らを即座にザイーナへ引き渡すことを要求します。

3-26b No way, my friend. Zaiina has accepted and guaranteed a "high degree of autonomy" in Palwan under the principle of "one country, two systems" since 1989. Palwan, a democratic and free-market economy, is an indispensable part of the world economy. Palwan cannot be easily integrated into Zaiina, because it is still home to many global investors and financial or commercial institutions.

それは土台無理な要求というものです、大使。ザイーナは 1989 年以来、一国二制度の原則のもと、パルワーンにおける最高レベルの自治を受け入れ、保証してきました。民主主義、そして自由市場経済に基づくパルワーンは、世界経済に不可欠な一角を占めています。パルワーンは容易にはザイーナに統合できません。なぜなら、パルワーンは現時点でもなお、多くの世界的な投資家、金融、営利団体にとって本拠地であるからです。

3-27a In addition, what do you mean by the "international criticism" you just referred to? Last month, a United Nations Human Rights Council meeting discussed the Palwan National Security Law, and don't you remember that a number of countries represented at the meeting actually supported the law? Did you say international criticism? Forget it, there is no such thing.

加えてお聞きしたいのですが、あなたが先ほど述べられた「国際社会からの批判」とは何を指しておられるのでしょうか？ 先月、国連人権理事会でパルワーンの国家安全保障法が議論され、多くの国の代表が新法を現に支持したではありませんか。まさかお忘れになったわけではないでしょう。国際社会からの批判と仰いましたよね。忘れた方がいい。そんなものはありません。

3-28a Anyway, it doesn't make sense to me at all. Zaiina sincerely hopes that Nowhere will make a wise decision. The implications of your decision could be enormous. Don't threaten us, my friend. The Republic of Nowhere needs our market for its mineral and agricultural products. Don't forget that no other country purchases a larger amount from Nowhere than any other country worldwide.

いずれにせよ、私には全く納得いくものではありません。ザイーナ政府は心より、ノーウェアが賢明な決断をされることを期待します。あなた方の決断が持つ含意は大変大きなものです。大使、どうか私達を脅さないで下さい。ノーウェア共和国は、鉱物、そして農作物において私達のマーケットが必要なはずです。どうか、世界の他のいかなる国よりも、我が国がノーウェアから多く購入しているという事実をお忘れにならないで頂きたい。

3-29b Thank you for your advice, but you should respect our liberal democracy and freedom of speech. As for your request for extradition, it is highly likely that we will act in accordance with the basic principles of human rights. Your response is too ideological and our resentment is mounting. It is high time for Zaiina to think twice and immediately release the eight people being detained before you regret it.

ご助言どうも。しかしあなた方は私達の自由民主主義と言論の自由に敬意を払うべきです。犯罪人引き渡しに関しては、私達は基本的人権の原則に則って行動します。あなた方の応答はイデオロギーに満ちており、私達の憤りは増大しています。ザイーナ政府は今一度熟慮し、後悔する前に、８人の勾留を直ちに解くべきです。まさに今その時であると考えます。

PART II

英単語集

<はじめに>

- 国際関係、外交に必要な英単語 350 語を厳選し、それぞれに見出語を用いた例文と日本語訳をつけました。
- 例文のおよそ半分は過去の『外交青書 (Diplomatic Bluebook)』から引用し、残り半分は新たに執筆しました。
- 本英単語集は、一定の基礎的な英語力を持った方を対象としており、全ての新出単語に注がついているわけではありません。
- 品詞情報は思い切って省き、見出語の日本語訳も主要な意味のみに絞りました。第一義的に習得するべき意味を赤太字で記しました。自動詞・他動詞に関しても厳密な区別をしていません。文脈に応じて使い分けるようにして下さい。
- 例文は全て実践での使用を前提とし厳選しています。全てそのまま使える表現ですので、ご自身のものとして血肉化して頂くことを推奨します。つまり、全て暗記することをお勧めします。

9

abbreviation

[əbrìːviéiʃən]

□ 1

短縮；省略（形）；略語

☞ abbreviated 省略された；簡略化された

The International Atomic Energy Agency – widely known by its **abbreviation**, IAEA – was founded in 1953 as a direct result of President Eisenhower's speech to the United Nations General Assembly.

accession

[əkséʃən, æk-]

□ 2

接近；加盟；即位

☞ accession negotiation 加盟交渉

The European Union (EU) has agreed to set a date next month for the previously postponed path to EU membership **accession** negotiations by Country A.

accuse

[əkjúːz]

□ 3

非難する；告発する；責める

☞ accusation 非難；告発

Country A's government vehemently **accused** Country B's forces of firing on its borders and issued a statement calling on the UN to "stop and mediate the conflict."

acknowledge

[əknɑ́lidʒ, æk- | -nɔ́l-]

□ 4

認める；承認する；感謝する

☞ acknowledgment 承認；感謝；謝辞

The U.S. side declared: The United Sates **acknowledges** that all Chinese on either side of the Taiwan Strait maintain there is but one China and that Taiwan is a part of China. (Joint Communique Between the Peolple's Republic of China and the United Sates 1972)

IAEA の略称で広く知られている国際原子力機関は、1953年の国連総会におけるアイゼンハワー大統領による演説を直接の契機として創設された。

和文中の「略称」は意訳で、厳密には abbreviation に「称」の意味は含まれない。

found : 設立する
as a (direct) result of A : A の（直接的な）結果として
United Nations General Assembly : 国連総会

欧州連合（EU）は、これまで先送りされていた A 国による EU への加盟交渉にむけた道筋を設定することで合意した。

accession は「近づくこと」を原義とし、それが派生して「（ある）状態」に近づく→「到達」、「条約・党など」に近づく→「加盟」、「（高い）地位」へ近づく→「即位」などとなる。

postpone : 延期する
path : 道筋 ; 小道

A 国政府は B 国軍による国境線での発砲を強く非難し、国連に「紛争の阻止と仲介」を求める声明を出した。

accuse は "accuse X of Y" の形で使用されることが多く、「（X に対して Y のことで）非難する」という意味になる。

border : 国境 ; 境
call on : 要求する ; 訪問する

米国側は次のように表明した。米国は、台湾海峡の両側のすべての中国人が、中国はただ一つであり、台湾は中国の一部分であると主張していることを認識している。（わが外交の状況 1972, 資料）

例文は「ニクソン米大統領の訪中に関する米中共同声明 (通称「上海コミュニケ)」からの引用で、ここで使われている acknowledge の用例には注意する必要がある。この場合、米国側の真意として、中国の主張を米国としては認識するが、それに対して了承や同意をしたわけではないことが示されている。

but one X : ただ 1 つの X; 唯一の X

10

actor

[ǽktər]

☐ 5

行為主体；当事者；俳優

☞ non-state actor 非国家主体

Based on U.S. interpretation, terrorism by non-state **actors** constitutes an "armed attack," as defined in Article 51 of the UN Charter. As such, the U.S., as an aggrieved state, can invoke its right to self-defense. (National Institute for Defense Studies, Briefing Memo)

actuality

[ǽktʃuǽləti]

☐ 6

現実（味）；アクチュアリティ；実在

☞ in actuality 実際は（に）

Mr./Ms. A's editorial had no **actuality** at the time. However, such editorial is very much considered when looking into the world situation today.

adhere

[ædhíər, əd-]

☐ 7

固執する；粘着する；支持する

☞ adherence 固守；執着；支持

If North Korea **adheres** to its nuclear and intercontinental ballistic missile (ICBM) development any longer, international isolation will become an unavoidable consequence.

adversary

[ǽdvərsèri | -səri]

☐ 8

敵（の）；敵国（の）；敵対者

☞ adversarial 敵対的な；対立する

For Country A, the former virtual **adversary** B has wholly ceased on being a threat. However, developments in the neighboring Country C are now the most significant risk factor.

米国の解釈によれば、非国家主体によるテロは国連憲章第51条に定める「武力攻撃」を構成し、これに対して被害国である米国は自衛権を発動することができる。(防衛研究所 , ブリーフィング・メモ)

interpretation : 解釈 ; 説明
terrorism : テロ行為 ; テロリズム
Article 51 : (第) 51 条 ("article" は条文における「条」を指す)
aggrieved : 被害を受けた ; 権利を侵害された
invoke : 発動する ; 引き起こす
right to selfdefense : 自衛権

A 氏の論説は当時現実味をもたなかったが、今日の世界情勢を考えるにあたり大いに検討の余地がある。

actuality の形容詞形は actual で「実際の ; 現実の」という意味。
such : そのような ; とても
editorial : 論説

北朝鮮がこれ以上核と大陸間弾道ミサイル(ICBM)の開発に固執するならば、国際的な孤立は不可避となるだろう。

intercontinental : 大陸間 (の) (inter- : 間の、continent : 大陸)
development : 開発
unavoidable : 避けられない (un- : (否定の意味)、avoid : 避ける)

A 国にとって、かつての仮想敵国 B は完全に脅威でなくなったが、今や周辺国 C の動向が最大のリスク要因となっている。

former : かつての ; 以前の ; 元の ; 前者 (の)
virtual adversary : 仮想敵国 (virtual : 仮想の)
neighboring : 近隣の ; 隣接した

adviser/advisor

[ədváizər, æd-]

□ 9

相談役；顧問；助言者

☞ foreign affairs/diplomatic adviser 外交顧問

Mr./Ms. A., the president's foreign policy **adviser** at the time, was one of the significant influences on the state of relations between the two countries in the years that followed.

advocacy

[ǽdvəkəsi]

□ 10

擁護；支援運動；提唱

☞ advocate 主張する；擁護者

Many human rights **advocacy** groups have criticized the administration in the past for failing to prioritize human rights issues in its foreign policy.

affiliation

[əfiliéiʃən]

□ 11

所属；提携；加入

☞ party affiliation 政党所属；支持政党

Most of the residents living in the disputed Nagorno Karabakh area are Armenian and during the Soviet era they made increasingly strong demands to change their **affiliation** from Azerbaijan to Armenia and this led to a dispute between the two countries following the dissolution of the Soviet Union in 1991. (Diplomatic Bluebook 2018, Note)

agent

[éidʒənt]

□ 12

工作員；調査官；代理人

☞ agency 機関；局；取り次ぎ

According to a former U.S. Central Intelligence Agency **agent**, Country B's lobbying efforts included not only legitimate lobbying against House and Senate members but also a lot of illegitimate ones.

当時の大統領外交政策顧問だったA氏は、その後の両国関係のあり方に大きな影響を与えた一人である。

that followed : その後の（follow : 続く、that は関係代名詞で「(その後に) 続く」という意味）

人権擁護団体の多くは、これまで政権が外交政策において、人権問題を優先しなかったとして批判してきた。

human rights : 人権
criticize : 批判する
prioritize : 優先する ; 優先順位をつける
issue : 問題 ; 論点 ; 発行する

アゼルバイジャン内に所在する同地域の住民の大半はアルメニア人であり、ソ連末期にアゼルバイジャンからアルメニアへの帰属変更要求が高まったため、1991年のソ連解体に伴って、アルメニアとアゼルバイジャン間の紛争へと発展した。(外交青書 2018, 注釈)

resident: 住民
era : 時代
led : lead（導く）の過去形
following : 続いて ; 受けて ; 次の
dissolution : 解体（dissolve : 解消する ; 解散する）

元米国 CIA (Central Intelligence Agency) 工作員によると、当時のB国のロビー活動は上下両院議員に対する合法的なものばかりでなく、非合法的なものも多く含まれていた。

according to X : X によると ; と一致して
lobbying : ロビー (陳情) 活動
include : 含む
Senate : (二院制議会の) 上院
House and Senate : (米国) 上下両院 ; 上院と下院

agreement

[əgríːmənt]

□ 13

合意；協定；一致

☞ agreeable 賛同できる；好ましい

UN officials have revealed that the UN Security Council's permanent members have reached an **agreement** on several of the most important provisions of a resolution that calls on Country A to destroy its chemical weapons.

alleged

[əlédʒd, -dʒid]

□ 14

申し立てられた；言われている

☞ allege 言い張る；断言する；言い訳をする

The new administration set up a National Reconciliation Bureau for national reconciliation, an important task after the end of the civil war, and has been working in a variety of ways including the suggestion of the establishment of a mechanism consisting of a 4-layer system to correspond to the investigation of the truth related to **alleged** human rights violations, rights for justice, rights for compensation, and prevention of recurrence of conflict. (Diplomatic Bluebook 2017)

allegiance

[əlíːdʒəns]

□ 15

忠誠；義務；献身

☞ pledge of allegiance 忠誠の誓い

In every public elementary school in the U.S., every morning before class begins, all students shall recite the following pledge with their right hand on their left chest: "I pledge **allegiance** to the Flag of the United States of America and to the Republic for which it stands, one Nation under God, indivisible, with liberty and justice for all."

国連当局者は、国連安全保障理事会の常任理事国が、A 国に化学兵器廃棄を求める決議に関して、最も重要な複数の条項で合意に達したことを明らかにした。

reveal：明かす；明らかにする
reach：到達する；達する
provision：条項；提供；準備
chemical：化学（の）
weapon：武器；兵器

新政権は、内戦終結後の重要課題である国民和解に向け、国民和解局を設置したほか、人権侵害疑惑に関する真実追究、正義への権利、補償への権利及び紛争の再発防止に対応する 4 層体制メカニズムを設置する意向を示すなど、多様な方法で国民和解の促進に取り組んでいる。（外交青書 2017）

administration：政権
reconciliation：和解（reconcile：和解する）
civil war：内戦
layer：層
violation：違反；侵害；暴行

アメリカではどの公立小学校でも、次に示す誓いを毎朝授業が始まる前、皆で右手を左胸に当て復唱する。「私はアメリカ合衆国国旗と、それが象徴する万民のための自由と正義を備えた、神の下の分割すべからざる一国家である共和国に、忠誠を誓います。」

shall：しなければならない；すべきだ
recite：復唱する；朗唱する；暗唱する
flag：旗
republic：共和国；共和制
indivisible：分割できない

13

alleviate

[əlíːvièit]

□ 16

緩和する；軽減する；緩める

☞ alleviation 緩和；軽減

During the visit, His Imperial Highness listened intently to the explanation on the tunnel's history, its mechanisms combining drainage function and transportation system to **alleviate** traffic congestion in the city, and its disaster risk reduction capabilities. (Diplomatic Bluebook 2018, Special Feature)

alliance

[əláiəns]

□ 17

同盟（関係）；提携（国）；類似性

☞ ally 同盟（する）；同盟を結ぶ；結び付ける

It is important to remember that, while both Japan and the Republic of Korea (ROK) are in an **alliance** with the U.S., a close cooperation among the U.S., Japan, and the ROK is also required in the event of a Korean Peninsula conflict.

alternative

[ɔːltəːrnətiv]

□ 18

代替手段；選択肢；二者択一の

☞ alternate 交互に行う；互い違いにする

☞ alternatively その代わりに；代案として

U.S. Secretary of Defense A said, "The military **alternative** is in principle for peacekeeping and to support the negotiations of our diplomats around the world." In this statement, he/she stressed the idea of a military force being used solely as a means to advance a diplomatic solution.

ambassador

[æmbǽsədər]

□ 19

大使；代表；使者

☞ ambassador extraordinary and plenipotentiary 特命全権大使

(At the Ceremony of the Presentation of Credentials,) a newly appointed foreign **ambassador** extraordinary and plenipotentiary presents his/her credentials to His Majesty the Emperor. The Minister for Foreign Affairs or another Minister of State must be present. (The Imperial Household Agency, A-Z Index)

その際、同トンネルの設立の背景、市街地の交通渋滞を緩和させるために交通機能と排水機能を兼ね備えた同施設の仕組みや防災対策などについての説明を熱心にお聞きになりました。（外交青書 2018, 特集）

intently：熱心に（intent：熱意）
combine：結合する
drainage：排水；排水路；排水設備
disaster：災害；大惨事
congestion：渋滞；密集

忘れてはならないのは、日本と韓国はそれぞれが米国と同盟関係にある一方、朝鮮半島有事においては日米韓三カ国が緊密に協力することが求められていることである。

ROK：Republic of Korea（大韓民国）
cooperation：協力
require：要求する；求める
event：（重要な）出来事；事件

アメリカの A 国防長官は、「軍事的選択肢は原則的に平和維持が目的で、世界中にいる私達の外交官の交渉を支えるためにある」と語り、あくまでも軍事力は外交的解決を進めるための手段としての考え方を強調した。

Secretary of Defense：国防長官
peacekeeping：平和維持
solely：もっぱら；単に
as a means to X：X するための手段として（means：手段；方法）

（信任状捧呈式とは、）新任の外国の特命全権大使が信任状を天皇陛下に捧呈する儀式です。外務大臣または他の国務大臣が侍立することとされています。（宮内庁, 用語集）

appointed：任命された（appoint：任命する；指名する）
extraordinary：特命の；特別の
plenipotentiary：全権を有する（委任された）

amid

[əmíd]

□ 20

囲まれて；真っ只中に；取り巻かれて

☞ amid great applause 拍手喝采の中

Amid the speculation about the series of allegations, the prime minister will have to make a difficult political decision.

anarchy

[ǽnərki]

□ 21

無政府状態；混乱；無秩序

☞ anarchist 無政府主義者；アナーキスト

In Somalia, where people have been plagued for many years by civil war and **anarchy**, a transitional President was elected in August. (Diplomatic Bluebook 2001)

annexation

[ǽnikséiʃən]

□ 22

併合；合併；付属

☞ annex 併合する；付け足す；付属書類；別館

Country A suddenly invaded Country B and established a provisional autonomous government as a puppet government, and such was a de facto **annexation** of Country B by Country A.

apprehension

[ǽprihénʃən]

□ 23

懸念；理解；逮捕

☞ apprehend
懸念する；心配する；理解する；逮捕する

The chief cabinet secretary only mentioned that “Japan’s **apprehension** has already been conveyed to Country A through diplomatic channels. We would continue to monitor the situation closely.”

一連の疑惑に関して様々な憶測が飛び交う中、首相には重い政治判断が求められることになった。

speculation：憶測
allegation：疑惑
prime minister：総理大臣；首相
political decision：政治判断；政治決断

長年内戦に苦しみ、無政府状態が続いてきたソマリアでは、2000年8月に暫定大統領が選出された。（外交青書 2001）

transitional：暫定の（本来 transitional には「過渡的な（移り変わりの）という意味があり、転じて「暫定の（仮の）」という意味となる。）
president：大統領
elect：選出する；選ぶ（election：選挙）

A 国は突如 B 国に侵攻し、傀儡政権として B 国暫定自治政府を樹立した。これは A 国による事実上の B 国の併合である。

suddenly：突如；突然
invade：侵略する；侵攻する
provisional：暫定的な；仮の
puppet：傀儡；操り人形

官房長官は「我が国の懸念は、既に外交ルートを通じて A 国に伝えており、引き続き事態を注視する」と述べるにどまった。

Chief Cabinet Secretary：内閣官房長官（cabinet：内閣）
mention：言及する；述べる
monitor：注視する；観察する；監視する

15

appropriate

[əpróupriət]

☐ 24

適切な；ふさわしく；充当する

☞ appropriately 適切に；ふさわしく

Furthermore, it is necessary to disseminate **appropriate** information at an **appropriate** time in order to deal with the aftermath of the accident and move forward on reconstruction, while gaining support and correct understanding of the international community. (Diplomatic Bluebook 2018)

approve

[əprúːv]

☐ 25

承認する；同意する；認可する

☞ approval 承認；同意；認可

On the other hand, the House of Commons of the UK rejected a motion to **approve** the withdrawal agreement in January 2019, and the situation where a concrete breakthrough solution has not found was continued before the scheduled date for the UK to leave the EU at the end of March. (Diplomatic Bluebook 2019)

arbitration

[ɑ̀ːrbətréiʃən]

☐ 26

仲裁（裁定）；調停

☞ arbitrate 仲裁する；解決する

As the number of disputes between companies of different nationalities increases worldwide, international **arbitration** is attracting more attention. However, Japan's **arbitration** capabilities are far from being as strong as those of other countries.

archive

[ɑ́ːrkaiv]

☐ 27

保存記録；公文書；保管する

☞ National Archives and Records Administration (NARA) 米国国立公文書館

MOFA has voluntarily declassified its diplomatic records at the Diplomatic **Archives** since 1976. (Diplomatic Bluebook 2018)

また、国際社会の正しい理解と支援を得ながら事故対応と復興を進めるためには、適時適切な情報発信が必要である。(外交青書 2018)

furthermore：さらに；その上；なお
necessary：必要な
disseminate：広める；ばらまく
in order to X：X のために
deal (with)：扱う；処理する (deal: 取引；契約)
aftermath：直後の時期；余波；後(あと)の状態
reconstruction：再建；復興 (construction：建設)

一方、2019年1月には英国議会下院が(同)離脱協定等の承認動議を否決する等、3月末に予定される英国の離脱を前に、具体的な打開策が見つからない状況が続いた。(外交青書 2019)

on the other hand：他方で；一方で
reject：否決する；拒否する
motion：動議；提案；動き
withdrawal：離脱；撤退；引き出し
breakthrough：突破口；飛躍的進歩

世界では国籍の異なる企業間の紛争が増える中、国際仲裁がクローズアップされつつある一方、日本の仲裁力は諸外国に比して高まっているとは言い難い。

the number of X：X の数 (X の名詞は複数形になる)
nationality：国籍 (複数形は nationalities)
far from X：X から遠く離れて；少しも X ではない

外務省は、1976年から、自主的に外交記録を外交史料館で公開してきた。(外交青書 2018)

MOFA：外務省 (Ministry of Foreign Affairs of Japan)
voluntarily：自発的に；任意に
declassify：機密指定から解く；機密扱いから解除する

armed

[ɑ́ːrmd]

□ 28

武装した；武器を持った（伴った）

☞ arm 武装する；腕

☞ unarmed 非武装の；丸腰の

A series of kidnappings and murders of Japanese citizens by **armed** terrorist organizations in foreign countries has attracted the Japanese government's response.

armistice

[ɑ́ːrməstis]

□ 29

休戦；停戦

☞ armistice agreement 休戦（停戦）協定

Following the U.S.-North Korea generals' consultations on July 15, a transport aircraft of the U.S. Forces repatriated the remains of U.S. troops killed during the Korean War from Wonsan in North Korea to Osan in the ROK on July 27, on the 65th anniversary of the Korean War **armistice**. (Diplomatic Bluebook 2019)

arrangement

[əréindʒmənt]

□ 30

手配；配置；協定

☞ arrange 準備する；配置する；協定を結ぶ

In addition to strengthening bilateral cooperation, Japan is actually engaging in trilateral arrangements for dialogue, such as Japan-China-ROK, Japan-U.S.-ROK, Japan-U.S.-Australia, Japan-U.S.-India, and Japan-Australia-India **arrangements**, as well as larger multilateral frameworks, such as Japan-ASEAN, ASEAN+3, East Asia Summit (EAS), Asia-Pacific Economic Cooperation (APEC), ASEAN Regional Forum (ARF), Japan-Mekong cooperation and others. (Diplomatic Bluebook 2018)

海外では、武装したテロ組織による邦人の誘拐や殺害が相次いでおり、日本政府の対応に注目が集まっている。

a series of X：一連のX
kidnapping：誘拐
murder：殺人；殺害
terrorist：テロリスト
organization：組織；機構
response：反応；対応；応答

7月15日の米朝将官級協議等を経て、朝鮮戦争休戦65周年記念日に当たる7月27日、米軍輸送機が朝鮮戦争で死亡した米兵の遺骨を北朝鮮の元山（ウォンサン）から韓国の烏山（オサン）に送還した。（外交青書2019）

general：大将；将軍
consultation：協議；話し合い；（専門家から）助言を求めること
transport：輸送；移送；運搬
remain：遺骨；遺跡；残りもの；そのまま（の状態）である
anniversary：記念日（祭）；周忌

（日本としては、）二国間の協力強化に加えて、日中韓、日米韓、日米豪、日米印、日豪印といった三国間の対話の枠組み、日ASEAN、ASEAN+3、東アジア首脳会議（EAS)、アジア太平洋経済協力（APEC)、ASEAN地域フォーラム（ARF)、日・メコン協力などの様々な多国間の枠組みを積極的に活用している。（外交青書2018）

この和文にはarrangementの意味は出ていないが、「（日本 - 中国 - 韓国などの事前に手配された）枠組み」といった趣旨で用いられている。

in addition (to X)：(Xに) 加えて
as well as：同様に；もちろん
framework：枠組み；体制

assumption

[əsʌ́mpʃən]

□ 31

想定；仮定；掌握

☞ assume 想定する；思い込む

The prime minister of Country A should have made some **assumptions** about the reaction of public opinion in his country before launching this foreign policy.

asylum

[əsáiləm]

□ 32

亡命；保護；避難所

☞ grant asylum 亡命を認める

News agency A reported in a breaking news report this morning that Mr./Ms. B. appears to have sought **asylum** in Geneva, Switzerland, where he/she applied for refugee status here, fearing a purge by the new government.

asymmetry

[æsímətri, èis-]

□ 33

非対称；不均衡；不釣り合い

☞ asymmetric 非対象の；不均衡な

☞ symmetry（左右）対称；調和

The U.S. has a large trade deficit in its diplomacy with ASEAN. Correcting that **asymmetry** will be one of the issues at these talks.

authority

[əθɔ́ːrəti, əθɑ́r- | ɔːθɔ́r-]

□ 34

権限；権威；当局

☞ authoritative
当局の；権限のある；きっぱりと

There was bribery, abuse of **authority**, and other misconduct committed by Minister B of Country A. These acts subsequently led to a diplomatic row with Country C.

A国首相は、自国世論の反応をある程度想定した上で今回の外交政策を実行するべきだった。

reaction：反応；応答；反発
public opinion：世論（opinion：意見）
foreign policy：外交政策

通信社Aが今朝速報で伝えたところによると、B氏は新政権による粛清を恐れてスイスのジュネーブに亡命し、そこで難民申請を行ったようである。

breaking news：ニュース速報；臨時ニュース
sought：seek（求める）の過去形・過去分詞形
apply for：申請する；申し込む；志願する

米国はASEANとの外交において、多額の貿易赤字を抱えていることから、その不均衡の是正が今回の協議での論点の1つとなるだろう。

asymmetryの"a"は否定を意味するの接頭辞。
trade deficit：貿易赤字（deficit：不足額；赤字）
correct：是正する；修正する；矯正する

A国B大臣による収賄や職権乱用等の不正行為は、その後、C国との外交問題にまで発展した。

bribery：賄賂の授受；収賄；贈賄（bribe：賄賂）
abuse：乱用；悪用；乱用する；悪用する
misconduct：不正行為；違法行為
commit：犯す；委ねる；全力を傾ける
row：騒動；騒ぎ

autonomy

[ɔːtɑ́nəmi | -tɔ́n-]

☐ 35

自治（権）；自律（性）；自治国家

☞ autonomous 自治の；自律的な

☞ local autonomous body 地方自治体

Federalism is a method of division of sovereignty where a group of "states" with a high degree of **autonomy**, such as the U.S. and Germany, become responsible for internal affairs of their respective countries. Furthermore, authority over foreign affairs, military affairs, tax collection, and other matters to the federal government are delegated.

balance of power

[bǽləns əv páuər]

☐ 36

勢力均衡；力の均衡

☞ from balance of power to collective security 勢力均衡から集団安全保障へ

The **balance of power** between the West and the East changed dramatically with the collapse of the Soviet Union after the end of the Cold War.

ballistic

[bəlístik]

☐ 37

弾道（の）；弾道学の

☞ ballistic missile 弾道ミサイル

In 2017, North Korea conducted the sixth nuclear test, and launched more than 15 **ballistic** missiles, including the two that flew over Japan. North Korea's growing nuclear and missile capabilities pose an unprecedented, grave and imminent threat towards the peace and stability of Japan and the international community. (Diplomatic Bluebook 2018)

ban

[bǽn]

☐ 38

禁止する；差し止める；禁（止）令

☞ total ban 全面禁止；完全禁止

The UN Security Council also adopted Resolution 2371, which included measures such as a total **ban** on the import of coal from North Korea. (Diplomatic Bluebook 2018)

連邦制とは、アメリカやドイツのように高度な自治権を持った「州」が集まった国家であり、内政を州が担う一方、外交・軍事・徴税などの権限を連邦政府に委ねる主権分割の方法である。

federalism：連邦制　division：分割
state：国；国家；州；状態　degree：程度；段階
internal affairs：内政問題；国内事情（internal：内部の；内側の；国内の）
foreign affairs：外交　military affairs：軍事
tax collection：徴税
federal：連邦政府の；連邦の

冷戦終結の後、ソ連が崩壊したことに伴って西側諸国と東側諸国の勢力図が大きく変わり、それまでの勢力均衡が大きく変容した。

balance：均衡；平衡；残高；釣り合う；拮抗する
between X and Y：XとYの（2つの）間に（で）

2017年、北朝鮮は6回目の核実験を強行するとともに、日本上空を通過した2発を含め15発以上の弾道ミサイルを発射し、その核・ミサイル能力の増強は、日本及び国際社会の平和と安定に対するこれまでにない、重大かつ差し迫った脅威となっている。（外交青書 2018）

nuclear test：核実験　including X：Xを含む
flew：fly（飛行する）の過去形　grow：増える；成長する；高まる
unprecedented：前例のない；異例の
grave：重大な；重要な（gravity：重力）
imminent：差し迫った；切迫した

国連安保理でも、北朝鮮からの石炭輸入の全面禁止等の措置を含む決議第2371号が採択された。（外交青書 2018）

adopt：採択する；可決する；承認する；養子にする
import：輸入；輸入する
coal：石炭；炭

bargaining

[bɑ́ːrgəniŋ]

☐ 39

交渉；取り引き；駆け引き

☞ bargain 交渉する；駆け引きをする

Some people say that, in diplomatic **bargaining**, one should leave a “glue margin” and enter negotiations above the nonnegotiable line. However, he never did that.

barter

[bɑ́ːrtər]

☐ 40

物々交換；交換する；交易する

☞ barter transaction バーター取引

In April 6, Country A announced that it had finalized an agreement with Country B, where Country A shall receive oil exported from Country B in **barter**. This mode of trade was undertaken as a way to get around the embargo imposed by the U.S.

bestow

[bistóu]

☐ 41

与える；授ける；贈る

☞ bestowment 授与

The trade representative, the head of the Office of the U.S. Trade Representative (USTR), is a cabinet-level post directly under the president. He/She is **bestowed** with a diplomatic negotiating authority on trade.

betray

[bitréi]

☐ 42

裏切る；漏らす；騙す

☞ betrayal 裏切り；背信；密告

Peace agreements were reached in the early 1990s in Central America, Cambodia, South Africa, and other regions, reflecting the changing environment. In these regions, the return of refugees became a significant United Nations High Commissioner for Refugees (UNHCR) activity. However, the reality that followed **betrayed** our optimism (Sadako Ogata, United Nations Information Centres).

外交交渉では「のりしろ」を残し、譲れない線よりも上から交渉に入るべきと言う人もいる。しかし彼は決してそんなことはしなかった。

diplomatic bargaining：外交交渉
margin：余白；余地；縁；周辺
nonnegotiable：譲れない；交渉の余地がない

A 国は4月6日、アメリカが行った禁輸措置への回避策として、同国から輸出した原油の代金を支払う代わりに物々交換で受け取る方法で、B 国と最終合意したことを明らかにした。

announce：公表する；発表する
exported：輸出された（export：輸出する）
undertaken：undertake（引き受ける；請け負う；着手する）の過去・過去分詞形
get around：回避する；うまく避ける

米通商代表部（USTR）のトップである通商代表は、大統領直属の閣僚級ポストで、貿易に関する外交交渉権を与えられている。

trade：貿易；通商
Office of the United States Trade Representative (USTR)：米通商代表部

環境の変化を反映し、1990年前半には中米やカンボジア、南アフリカその他の地域で和平合意が成立しました。これらの地域では、難民の帰還が UNHCR の主要な活動となりました。しかし、その後の現実は、私達の楽観を裏切るものでした。（国際連合広報センター，緒方貞子による寄稿）

peace agreement：和平合意
reflect：反映する；反射する
return：帰還；返還（in return：見返りとして；代償として；引き換えに）
optimism：楽観；楽観（楽天）主義

bilateral

[bailǽtərəl]

□ 43

二国間の；双務的な；両側の

☞ bilaterally 二国間で；相互に

☞ trilateral 三カ国の；三者の

Through the Look East Policy, which serves as a foundation for the good **bilateral** relationship between Japan and Malaysia and was proposed by Prime Minister Mahathir in 1981, about 16,000 Malaysian people have studied or have been trained in Japan so far. (Diplomatic Bluebook 2019)

biological and chemical weapons

[bàiəlάdʒikəl ənd kémikəl wépənz]

□ 44

生物化学兵器

☞ biology 生物学

☞ chemistry 化学

Biological and chemical weapons, also known as the nuclear weapons of the poor, are capable of killing or injuring large numbers of people without destroying cities or other weapons.

bipolar

[baipóulər]

□ 45

二極の；両極端の；相反する

☞ multipolarization 多極化

One way to view the era is to think of it as a multipolar world that has now arrived. Such follows the **bipolar** world that divided East and West during the Cold War and the unipolar world of U.S. dominance.

bolster

[bóulstər]

□ 46

強化する；支援する；支持物

☞ bolster morale 士気を高める（上げる）

Rule-Making to **Bolster** Free and Open Global Economic Systems (Diplomatic Bluebook 2019)

マハティール首相が1981年に提唱した日・マレーシア間の友好関係の基盤である東方政策により、これまでに約1万6,000人のマレーシア人が日本で留学及び研修した。(外交青書2019)

和文ではbilateral（二国間の）が訳出されていないが、「友好関係」＝「良い（good）二国間の（bilateral）関係（relationship）」と解釈できる。

serve：役に立つ；(目的を）果たす
foundation：基盤

貧者の核兵器とも呼ばれる生物・化学兵器は、街や兵器を破壊することなく、人を大量に殺傷することを可能にする兵器である。

(be) known as X：Xとして知られる
nuclear weapon：核兵器
the poor：貧者（= poor people)
destroy：破壊する

1つの時代の捉え方として、冷戦時代の東西を分けた二極世界から、米国による一極世界を経て、現在は多極世界が到来していると考えることができるだろう。

"bi-/di-"を接頭辞として「2」を意味する。("uni-/mono-"は「1」、"tri-"は「3」、"multi-"は「多」など。)

自由で開かれた国際経済システムを強化するためのルール・メイキング(外交青書2019)

当該の引用箇所は『外交青書』中のタイトル(小見出し）として使われており、そのため（前置詞などを除いて）各単語の文頭が大文字になっている。

branch

[brǽntʃ | brɑ́ːntʃ]

□ 47

部門；府；支店

☞ executive branch 行政機関；行政府

☞ judicial branch 司法機関；司法府

Only the U.S. media and a reporter from Japan's Washington **branch** were invited to the press conference. However, the correspondents who accompanied the prime minister were not permitted to enter the hall.

bureaucracy

[bjuərɑ́krəsi | -rɔ́k-]

□ 48

官僚（主義）；官僚制；官僚組織

☞ bureaucrat 官僚；役人

☞ bureau 事務局；局；支局

There are inevitably those disappointing moments when collisions of national interests among Member States or **bureaucracy** limit the scope of what the UN can accomplish. (Diplomatic Bluebook 2019, Column)

calumniate

[kəlʌ́mnièit]

□ 49

中傷する；誹謗する；謗る

☞ calumniation 中傷；誹謗；謗り

In such a situation, allow me to express our distress at information that some people are being treated unjustly just because they are of East Asian origin, for example by being suspended from using facilities or by being **calumniated**. I would like to take this opportunity at the Human Rights Council to ask everyone to ensure that such actions do not occur. (Statement Parliamentary Vice-Minister for Foreign Affairs Omi at the High-Level Segment of the 43th Session of the Human Rights Council)

campaigner

[kæmpéinər]

□ 50

運動員；活動家；従軍者

☞ campaign（組織的）運動；選挙運動

In an editorial on the contents of the UN Special Rapporteur's human rights report on Japan, the A newspaper vehemently condemned the report as "a biased view of some **campaigners**."

記者会見場に呼ばれたのは米メディアと日本のワシントン支局の記者のみで、首相に同行した記者団は会場入りが許されなかった。

press conference：記者会見（press：記者団；マスコミ；出版物）
correspondent：担当記者；特派員

加盟国の国益の衝突や官僚主義を前に、国連として「できること」の幅を限定される時の無念さ。(外交青書 2019, コラム)

complex：複雑な
inevitably：必然的に；否応なく
disappointing：失望させる；期待外れの
collision：衝突；対立
accomplish：成し遂げる；達成する

そうした中、最近、東アジア系であることのみを理由として、施設の利用停止や心ない誹謗中傷が行われているとの情報に接しており、心を痛めています。そうした行為が起きないよう、人権理事会のこの場を借りて全ての人に呼びかけたいと思います。(第43回人権理事会ハイレベルセグメントにおける尾身外務大臣政務官ステートメント)

allow me to express X：X を言わせて下さい（allow：許す：許可する）
origin：生まれ；起源；先祖
suspend：一時的に止める；吊るす
opportunity：機会；好機
ensure：確かにする；確実にする

国連の特別報告者による対日人権報告書の内容について、A 新聞は社説で「一部の活動家らの偏った見解だ」と強く非難した。

report：報告書；報道；報告する；伝える
biased：偏った；偏見を抱いた（bias：偏見；先入観）
view：見方；見解

capability

[kèipəbíləti]

☐ 51

能力；可能性；性能

☞ (be) capable of X
X の能力がある；できる

Such broad and rapid expansion of military **capability** lacking transparency, and continued attempts to unilaterally change the status quo are common regional concerns. Japan intends to urge through dialogue for an improvement of China's transparency and encourage China to be positively involved in the international order based on the rule of law, in cooperation with the countries concerned. (Diplomatic Bluebook 2017)

capitalism

[kǽpətəlìzm]

☐ 52

資本主義；資本制；キャピタリズム

☞ capitalist 資本主義者；資本家

The Cold War was a confrontation between **capitalism** and liberalism in the West, with the U.S. as its leader, on the one hand and was also a confrontation between communism and socialism in the East, with the Soviet Union as its leader, on the other.

cease

[síːs]

☐ 53

終わる；中止する；終止

☞ cease fire 停戦；休戦

Such unilateral development actions are extremely regrettable, and every time such moves by China are recognized, Japan has strongly requested China to **cease** its unilateral development and to resume negotiations as soon as possible on the implementation of the "2008 Agreement" regarding the cooperation between Japan and China on the development of natural resources in the East China Sea. (Diplomatic Bluebook 2019)

このような透明性を欠いた軍事力の広範かつ急速な拡大や一方的な現状変更の試みの継続は、地域共通の懸念事項であり、日本としては関係国と連携しつつ、中国の透明性の向上について対話を通じて働きかけるとともに、法の支配に基づく国際秩序に中国が積極的に関与していくよう促していく考えである。（外交青書 2017）

broad：広汎な；幅の広い
expansion：拡大；拡張
transparency：透明性
attempt：試み
common：共通の
intend：するつもりである；意図がある
encourage：促す；励ます

冷戦とは、西側諸国のアメリカを盟主とする資本主義・自由主義陣営と、東側諸国のソ連を盟主とする共産主義・社会主義陣営との対立であった。

Cold War：冷戦
liberalism：自由主義（liberal：寛大な；自由な；自由主義の；リベラルな）
the West：西側諸国；欧米諸国
the East：東欧諸国

このような一方的な開発行為は極めて遺憾であり、日本としては、中国側による関連の動向を把握するたびに、中国側に対して、一方的な開発行為を中止するとともに、東シナ海資源開発に関する日中間の協力についての「2008年合意」の実施に関する交渉再開に早期に応じるよう強く求めてきている。（外交青書 2019）

extremely：極めて；極端に
regrettable：遺憾な；残念な；気の毒な（regret：後悔する；遺憾に思う；気の毒に思う）
resume：再開する；取り戻す；回復する
natural resource: 天然資源

circumstance

[sə́ːrkəmstæ̀ns | -stəns]

□ 54

状況；環境；境遇

☞通例複数形 (circumstances) で用いる

According to the Food and Agriculture Organization (FAO) of the UN, this is the first time in almost a decade that the **circumstances** have worsened. Such data is compared to the previous year (2016), where approximately 11% of the world's population is suffering from hunger and malnutrition.

citizen

[sítəzən]

□ 55

民間人；市民；国民

☞ citizenship 市民権；公民権

In any state of war, international law prohibits all hostilities against nonmilitary aircrafts and **citizens**.

claim

[kléim]

□ 56

主張する；要求する；苦情

☞ baggage claim（空港の）手荷物受取所

Country A's foreign ministry spokesman B condemned Country C's actions as unjustified. He/She warned that Country A's government will **claim** that Country C should withdraw its sanctions on the military sector and that it would "bear serious consequences" if it did not.

coercive

[kouə́ːrsiv]

□ 57

強制的な；威圧的な；強引な

☞ coerce 強要する；抑圧する

U.S. Customs officials are currently stepping up their crackdown on imports from Region B of Country A. The officials suspect these places of **coercive** labor. As such, the said officials have already conducted a significant amount of seizures.

国連食糧農業機関(FAO)によると、前年(2016年)に比べ状況が悪化するのは約10年ぶりのことで、世界の人口のおよそ11%が飢餓や栄養失調に苦しんでいることが明らかになった。

agriculture : 農業
decade : 10年
worsen : 悪化する ; より悪くなる
compared to X : Xと比較して
approximately : およそ ; 約

いかなる戦争状態にあろうとも、国際法は非軍用機や民間人に対するあらゆる敵対行為を禁止している。

international law : 国際法
against X : Xに対して ; 反対して
nonmilitary : 非軍事(の) ; 非軍事的な
aircaft : 航空機

A国外務省のB報道官は、C国の行動は不当だと非難した上で、A国政府はC国に軍事部門への制裁の撤回を要求し、撤回しない場合は「重大な結果を負うことになるだろう」と警告した。

spokesman : 報道官 ; 広報担当官 ; 代弁者
unjustified : 正当化できない ; 不当な ; 根拠のない
warn : 警告する
bear : 生み出す ; (責任を)負う

米税関当局は現在、強制労働の疑いがあるA国B地域からの輸入品に対する取り締まりを強化しており、既に相当量の差し押さえを行なっている。

currently : 現在は ; 目下
step up : 強化する ; 増す
crackdown : 取り締まり : 弾圧
suspect : 疑う
labor : 労働(力) ; 仕事
the said : 前述の ; 上記の　amount : 量 ; 額

collapse

[kəlǽps]

□ 58

崩壊（する）；倒壊させる；倒れる

☞ economic collapse 経済崩壊；経済破綻

In 1974, Portugal relinquished its colonial control of East Timor with the regime's **collapse** in a political coup that occurred in the country. Such significantly increased the momentum for independence in East Timor.

collateral

[kəlǽtərəl | kɔ-]

□ 59

二次的な；付帯的な；巻き添え

☞ collateral damage
付帯的損害；巻き添え被害

The **collateral** damage to civilians from the joint airstrikes carried out by the U.S. and other NATO forces is enormous. Further military action would not be justified.

collective

[kəléktiv]

□ 60

集合的な；集団の；共同の

☞ collect 集める；収集する

At the National Assembly convened from around March to April, President Quang (the head of state) and the Prime Minister Phuc were newly elected. However, in Viet Nam, which adopts a **collective** leadership, a significant change in policy on domestic and external affairs is unlikely to happen. (Diplomatic Bluebook 2017)

commerce

[kάməːrs | kɔ́məːs]

□ 61

商業；貿易；商科

☞ e-commerce 電子商取引；e コマース

The U.S. Secretary of **Commerce** is prepared to take far-reaching countermeasures, including sanctioned tariffs against the country if the negotiations with Country B break down.

ポルトガルは1974年、国内で発生した政治クーデターによる政権の崩壊で、東ティモールの植民地支配を放棄した。これにより東ティモールでは、独立への機運が大いに高まった。

relinquish：放棄する；断念する
colonial：植民地の；植民の
control：支配；制限；管理
momentum：勢い；機運

米軍を中心とするNATO軍が共同で行った空爆による民間人への巻き添え被害は甚大で、これ以上の軍事行動は正当化されないだろう。

civilian：一般人；文民；非戦闘員
airstrike：空爆；空からの攻撃
carry out：実行する；遂行する；執行する
enormous：非常に大きな；巨大な；莫大な

3月から4月頃にかけ招集された国会において、クアン国家主席（元首）やフック首相等が新たに選出されたが、集団指導体制をとるベトナムでは、内外政について大幅な方針の変更はないと見られる。（外交青書2017）

leadership：指導；統率力；リーダーシップ
significant：重大な；重要な
domestic and external affairs：内外政の（external：外の；外部の）
（be）likely to X：Xしそうである

米商務長官は、このままB国との交渉が決裂すれば、同国に対する制裁関税を含めた広範囲に及ぶ対抗措置をも辞さない構えだ。

prepare：準備する；構える
countermeasure：対抗策；対抗手段（counter-：敵対して；逆の）
break down：失敗に終わる；決裂する

compassion

[kəmpǽʃən]

□ 62

思いやり；同情；憐れみ

☞ compassionate
思いやりのある；情け深い

Before his death, Yukio Okamoto, a former advisor to the prime minister, always stressed that "kindness" and "**compassion** for the position of others" are the most essential qualities of a globally minded person.

compel

[kəmpél]

□ 63

強要する；強制する；強いる

☞ compulsion 無理強い

Some media reports said that Country A had stopped submitting a UN resolution to **compel** Countries B and C to make peace, but Country A strongly denied it.

compete

[kəmpíːt]

□ 64

競争する；競い合う；匹敵する

☞ competitive 競争の激しい；競合する

Twenty teams, consisting of the top twelve teams (including Japan) from the previous tournament and eight teams that won the preliminary competitions, will **compete** fiercely for the shiny gold "Webb Ellis Cup" over a period of seven weeks in 12 cities across Japan, from Hokkaido to Kyushu. (Diplomatic Bluebook 2019, Column)

complicated

[kάmpləkèitid | kɔ́m-]

□ 65

複雑な；交錯した；難解な

☞ complicate
複雑にする；分かりにくくする

Multilateral negotiations are **complicated** since each country's interests are intricately complicated. Moreover, the composition of the differences in positions on each issue also varies.

元首相補佐官の岡本行夫氏は、生前、国際人として最も大切な資質は「やさしさ」と「他人の立場への思いやり」だと常々説いていた。

stress：強調する；重視する
qualities：quality（質）の複数形
minded：心がある；志向がある

A国は、B国とC国に和平を強要する国連決議案の提出を止めたとの一部報道がなされたが、A国はそれを強く否定した。

submit：提出する；屈服する
strongly：断固として；強硬に；堅調に
denied：deny（否定する；拒否する）の過去・過去分詞形

（日本を含む）前回大会の上位12チームと世界各地域の予選を勝ち抜いた8チームの全20チームが、黄金に輝く「ウェブ・エリス・カップ」優勝トロフィーを目指し、日本全国、北海道から九州まで12都市で7週間にわたり熱戦を繰り広げます。（外交青書 2019）

consist：成る；構成する
previous：前の；以前の
preliminary：予選の；準備の
competition：競技；試合；競争
fiercely：激しく；猛烈に

多国間交渉は各国の利害が複雑に絡み合い、論点ごとに立場の相違の構図が異なるため大変難しい。

since X：Xのため；なので；以来
each：それぞれの；各々の
composition：構図；構成
position：立場；位置；配置；置く；配置する
vary：変わる；変化する

comply

[kəmplái]

□ 66

遵守する；従う；応じる

☞ compliance 遵守；コンプライアンス

Japan will continue to closely work with relevant countries, including the U.S. and the ROK, and urge North Korea to refrain from further provocations and **comply** with the Joint Statement of the Six-Party Talks and the relevant UN Security Council resolutions. (Diplomatic Bluebook 2017)

compromise

[kámprəmàiz | kɔ́m-]

□ 67

妥協（する）；和解（する）；折衷案

☞ without compromise 妥協なしに

Concerning the enactment of legislation and budgetary measures, factional conflicts sometimes forced President Trump to **compromise**, and slowed progress on certain measures. This is partly because the Republicans, although holding the majority in both Houses, have only a slight advantage in seats at the Senate. (Diplomatic Bluebook 2018)

concealment

[kənsíːlmənt]

□ 68

隠蔽；潜伏；隠匿

☞ conceal 隠蔽する；隠す

The Japanese government's response to crisis management has been repeatedly criticized by foreign media for the delays in communicating and **concealment** of information.

日本は、引き続き、米国、韓国を始めとする関係国と緊密に連携しつつ、北朝鮮に対し、挑発行動の自制、六者会合共同声明や累次の国連安保理決議の遵守を強く求めていく。(外交青書 2017)

closely：緊密に；接近して
relevant：関係する；関連のある
joint statement：共同声明

立法化や予算措置については、上下両院で共和党が多数を占めるものの、上院では民主党との議席数が僅差であることもあり、党派対立の影響で、トランプ大統領が妥協を迫られたり、停滞する案件も見られた。(外交青書 2018)

concerning X：X に関して；について
enactment：(法律の) 制定
legislation：法律；立法；立法行為
budgetary：予算の；予算上の
factional：党派の；党派的な
slow：遅くする；遅くなる；遅い

危機管理下の日本政府の対応については、諸外国のメディアから、情報伝達の遅れや情報隠蔽を度々指摘されてきた。

crisis management：危機管理
repeatedly：繰り返し；再三にわたり
delay：遅れ；遅滞
communicate：伝達する

concession

[kənséʃən]

□ 69

譲歩；容認；利権

☞ concession speech 敗北宣言

With President A in a hurry to achieve diplomatic success before next year's U.S. presidential elections, Country B's government aims to extract **concessions** by leading the negotiations.

condemnation

[kàndemnéiʃən | kɔ̀n-]

□ 70

非難；有罪判決；没収

☞ condemn 非難する；糾弾する

At the ministerial-level meeting before APEC, the U.S. and China exchanged **condemnation** as they sharply disagreed over their respective trade policies.

conflict

[kənflíkt]

□ 71

紛争；論争；対立（する）

☞ pre-conflict 紛争前の；紛争発生前の

Many regional **conflicts** and civil wars are rekindled even after the conflict has ended. Hence, it is extremely important to provide appropriate support in the post-conflict period. (Diplomatic Bluebook 2018)

conformity

[kənfɔ́ːrməti]

□ 72

符合；一致；服従

☞ overconformity 過度の服従

In Japan-U.S. economic relations, frictions tend to rise to the foreground, particularly in the commercial sector. However, given the importance of managing the overall bilateral relationship, it is important that any matter of friction not be unduly politicized, and that solutions be sought in **conformity** with international rules. (Diplomatic Bluebook 1996)

米大統領選挙を控え、外交成果を焦るA大統領を相手に、B国政府は交渉を主導することで譲歩を引き出す狙いがある。

in a hurry：急いで；焦って
presidential：大統領の
lead：先導する；リードする

APECに先立つ閣僚級会議では、米中の2カ国がそれぞれの通商政策を巡って激しく対立し、非難の応酬を繰り広げた。

ministerial-level：閣僚級（の）（minister：大臣）
sharply：鋭く；激しく
respective：各々の；個別の

地域紛争や内戦は終結後に再燃することが多いため、事後に適切な支援を行うことが極めて重要である。（外交青書 2018）

regional：地域の；地方の
rekindle：再燃する；よみがえらせる
hence：それ故に；したがって
post-conflict:紛争後（和文では「事後」となっており「有事の後」という意味が出ている）

日米経済関係の特に通商分野では、両国の対立が顕在化しがちであるが、両国関係の全体的な運営との観点からすれば、如何なる摩擦案件についても、徒に政治問題化させず、国際ルールに則った解決を目指すことが重要である。（外交青書 1996）

riction：摩擦
foreground：前景
particularly：特に；とりわけ
commercial：商業の；商売の
unduly：過度に；不当に（duly：正当に；期日通りに）
politicize：政治化する；政治問題化する

confrontation

[kɑ̀nfrəntéiʃən | kɔ̀nfrʌn-]

□ 73

対決；対立；衝突

☞ confront
直面する；対決させる；対立させる

Country A's strategy is avoiding **confrontation** through military force and using intelligence to build an advantageous situation for its nation.

congress

[kɑ́ŋgris | kɔ́ŋgres]

□ 74

国会；議会；大会

☞ Congress アメリカ連邦議会

The conflict over the passage of legislation on the A issue between the ruling and opposition parties in the U.S. **Congress** has not been resolved. As such, some federal agencies have been forced to shut down.

consent

[kənsént]

□ 75

同意(する)；承諾(する)；許可(する)

☞ consensus 意見の一致

In recent years, many cases of survey activities conducted without Japan's **consent** in the waters surrounding Japan have been confirmed, including the East China Sea, as well as survey activities of a nature that are different from that to which Japan has **consented**. (Diplomatic Bluebook 2017)

consequence

[kɑ́nsəkwèns | kɔ́nsikwəns]

□ 76

結果；帰結；重大性

☞ consequently (≒as a consequence)
その結果；それ故に

Japan takes the humanitarian **consequences** brought about by cluster munitions very seriously. Therefore, in addition to taking steps to address this issue by victim assistance and unexploded ordnance (UXO) clearance, Japan is continuing efforts to increase the number of States Parties on Cluster Munitions (CCM) for its universalization. (Diplomatic Bluebook 2018)

A 国の戦略は、軍事力による直接的な対決を避け、インテリジェンスを駆使して自国にとって優位な状況を築くというものである。

advantageous：有利な；好都合な（advantage：優位；利益；好都合）
nation：国家；国民

A 問題に関する法案成立をめぐり米連邦議会で与野党の対立が解消されず、一部の連邦政府機関が閉鎖に追い込まれている。

passage：（法案などの）通過；可決；成立
ruling：権力の座にある；優勢な（ruling party：与党）
opposition party：野党；反対派
shut down：閉鎖する；停止する

近年、東シナ海を始めとする日本周辺海域において日本の同意を得ない調査活動や同意内容と異なる調査活動が多数確認されている。（外交青書 2017）

英文中の "nature" は種類や性質を指し、"nature that are different from X" で、「X とは異なった種類（性質）の」となる。

surrounding：周囲の；囲む
confirm：確認する；承認する；確かにする

日本は、クラスター弾がもたらす人道上の問題を深刻に受け止め、被害者支援や不発弾（UXO）処理といった対策を実施するとともに、クラスター弾に関する条約（CCM）の締約国を拡大する取り組みを継続している。（外交青書 2018）

この場合の「問題」は consequence の直訳ではない。解釈としては（humanitarian） consequences で「（人道上の）帰結；結果」を表すと捉えられる。

bring about：引き起こす（brought は bring の過去形・過去分詞形）
munition：武器弾薬
seriously：深刻に；重く；真剣に
assistance：援助；支援
universalization：普遍化；一般化（この場合は締結国拡大を意味する）

conspiracy

[kənspírəsi]

☐ 77

陰謀；謀議；共謀

☞ in conspiracy 共謀して；徒党を組んで

☞ conspire 共謀する；たくらむ

In today's world of social networking services, fake news and **conspiracy** theories are becoming more easily used to manipulate public opinion.

constitute

[kɑ́nstətjùːt | kɔ́nstitjùːt]

☐ 78

構成する；制定する；任命する

☞ the Constitution of Japan 日本国憲法

Since ASEAN is situated in a geopolitically important location and **constitutes** important sea lanes, and its stability and prosperity relates to those of not only the East Asian region but also the international community, it is important for the entire international community that ASEAN is integrated in accordance with values such as the rule of law and democracy. (Diplomatic Bluebook 2017)

consulate

[kɑ́nsələt | kɔ́nsju-]

☐ 79

領事館；領事の職権；領事の任期

☞ consulate(-)general 総領事館

A broker from Country B was arrested by the prefectural police on suspicion of corruptly bribing a consular officer at the **Consulate** General of Country A, who was contracted to issue fraudulent residence-related certificates.

contemptuously

[kəntémptʃuəsli]

☐ 80

軽蔑して；見下して；小馬鹿にしたように

☞ contemptuous 軽蔑した；さげすんだ；見下した

Country B continues to overtly interfere with Country A in its internal affairs. Country A's people are **contemptuously** treated and subjected to unreasonable demands, including the imposition of Country B's language as the official one for Country A.

SNS（ソーシャル・ネットワーキング・サービス）が身近になった今日、フェイクニュースや陰謀論を使って世論操作をすることが容易くなってしまっている。

take：偽の；でたらめな
conspiracy theory：陰謀論
easily：容易に；たやすく；気軽に
manipulate：操作する；操縦する；操る

地政学的要衝に位置しており、重要なシーレーンを有しているASEANの安定と繁栄は、東アジア地域のみならず、国際社会の安定と繁栄にも大きく関わることから、ASEANが法の支配や民主主義といった価値に沿った統合を進めることは国際社会全体にとって重要である。（外交青書2017）

この場合の「有している」は直訳ではない。「シーレーンを構成する」の意訳であると考えられる。

prosperity：繁栄

在留関係証明書の不正発行を請け負っていたA国総領事館の領事に賄賂を渡したとして、B国人ブローカーが外国公務員への贈賄の疑いで県警に逮捕された。

broker：仲介業者；ブローカー；仲立ちする；調停する
arrest：逮捕する；拘束する
prefectural police：県警
corruptly：不正に（corrupt：買収された；腐敗した；堕落する）

A国は、B国によって公然と内政を干渉されたあげく、国民は蔑まれ、B国の言語を公用語として押し付けられるなど、理不尽な要求にさらされ続けている。

overtly：公然と；明らかに
treat；扱う；とらえる
（be）subject to X：Xにさらされる；支配下にある；左右される

contingent

[kəntíndʒənt]

□ 81

偶発的な；不測の；左右されて

☞ contingency 偶然性；偶有性；不測の事態

☞ contingent on X X次第で；を条件として

Although neither country wants an all-out war, there are concerns that the situation may deteriorate rapidly from **contingent** military conflicts, and such a situation is unpredictable.

contrary to X

[kάntreri tu]

□ 82

Xに反して；とは逆に；裏腹に

☞ on the contrary それどころか；むしろ

Country A has been conducting a series of nuclear tests and ballistic missile launches, **contrary to** UN resolutions. The international community is in no position to accept this.

controversy

[kάntrəvə̀ːrsi | kɔ́n-]

□ 83

論争；（対立点のある）議論；物議

☞ controversial
物議を醸している；論争を引き起こす

More than 70 years have passed since the promulgation of the current constitution. However, during this time, the status of the Self-Defense Forces and the scope of their activities have been a constant source of **controversy**.

convention

[kənvénʃən]

□ 84

協定；条約；慣習

☞ convene 開催する；召集する

The Biological Weapons **Convention** (BWC) is a multilateral legal framework that provides for a comprehensive ban on biological weapons. Japan has ratified this convention.

両国とも決して全面戦争は望んでいないものの、偶発的な軍事衝突から事態が急激に悪化する懸念があり、予断を許さない。

neither X：（双方とも）X でない
all-out：全面的な
concern：懸念；心配事；心配する；憂慮する
deteriorate：悪化する
rapidly：急速に；迅速に

A国は、国連の決議に反して核実験や弾道ミサイルの発射を続けざまに行っており、国際社会として到底承服できる状態にはない。

international community：国際社会（community：共同体；団体；地域社会）
accept：受け入れる；承服する；受諾する

現行憲法の公布から70年以上が経つが、この間、常に論争の的になってきたのが自衛隊の位置づけやその活動範囲である。

X years have passed since Y：Y 以来（から）X 年が経つ
promulgation：発布；普及
scope：範囲
constant：絶えず続く；継続的な

生物兵器禁止条約（BWC）とは、生物兵器を包括的に禁止するすることを定めた多国間の法的枠組みであり、日本も批准している。

legal：法的な
provide：与える；供給する
comprehensive；包括的な；理解のある

convert

[kənvə́ːrt]

□ 85

変更する；改心させる；改宗させる

☞ conversion 変更；転換；改宗

Reportedly, some A or B believers who **converted** to other religions faced intimidation and ostracism by the adherents of their former religion in 20XX.

convoy

[kɑ́nvɔi | kɔ́n-]

□ 86

護衛（する）；護送（する）；護衛隊

☞ in convoy（護衛のために）船団を組んで

In May, a **convoy** having completed a shipment of supplies to a US base in Hit, west of Baghdad, was attacked and a Japanese national working for a private security company guarding that **convoy** went missing. (Diplomatic Bluebook 2006)

counterpart

[káuntərpɑ̀ːrt]

□ 87

相当するもの（人）；対の片方；片われ

☞ counterparty 相手方；契約相手

For example, for the purpose of rapidly and efficiently providing assistance for Japanese companies that are suffering from counterfeit and pirated goods, Intellectual Property Officers are assigned at almost all of the diplomatic missions overseas, so that they can advise Japanese companies and make inquiries with or suggestions to their **counterpart** governments. (Diplomatic Bluebook 2017)

20XX年には、他の宗教へ改宗したA教徒又はB教徒の一部が、以前信仰していた宗教の信奉者による脅迫や村八分に直面していることが報道された。

reportedly：報道によると；伝えられるところでは
believer：信者；信じる人
religion：宗教
face：直面する
ostracism：追放；排斥
adherent：支持者；信奉者

5月には、バグダッド西方ヒート近郊において米軍基地に物資を輸送し終え帰路についていた車列が襲撃され、その車列を警備していた民間警備会社所属の邦人1名が行方不明となった。（外交青書 2006）

shipment：輸送；発送
supplies：supply（物資；支給物）の複数形
base：基地；ベース；土台
Japanese national：日本人；邦人

例えば、海外において模倣品・海賊版被害を受けている日本企業を迅速かつ効果的に支援することを目的として、ほぼ全ての在外公館で知的財産担当官を任命し、日本企業への助言や相手国政府への照会、働きかけなどを行っている。（外交青書 2017）

for the purpose of X：Xのために；の目的で（purpose：目的）
counterfeit：偽造の；偽の
assign：任命する；配属する；割り当てる
inquiries：inquire（問い合わせ；照会）の複数形

courier

[kə́:riər | kúr-]

□ 88

特使；密使；急使

☞ international courier service
国際宅配便

In January 1985, a "secret **courier**" of Israeli Prime Minister Peres visited Japan and met with Prime Minister Yasuhiro Nakasone to urge the former's involvement in achieving peace in the Middle East. Such was confirmed by a diplomatic document that was released on December 20, 2017 (December 20, 2017, Sankei Shimbun).

courtesy

[kə́:rtəsi]

□ 89

丁寧な行為；厚意；礼儀

☞ courtesy shuttle service
（無料の）シャトルサービス

This was India's Prime Minister Modi's third visit to Japan. Japan's Prime Minister Abe gave Modi an exceptional **courtesy** to manifest the "close relationship" between their two countries.

covert

[kóuvərt | kʌ́v-]

□ 90

隠れた；覆われた；暗に示した

☞ overt 明白な；公然の

Leaks from Country B's government revealed that Country A had been conducting **covert** negotiations through other channels. Such negotiations were apart from Country A's official meetings with Country B.

credential

[kridénʃəl]

□ 91

信任状；資格；信任の

☞ security credential
セキュリティー証明書

The Japanese government will not officially receive the Ambassador Extraordinary and Plenipotentiary of Japan until the head of state and other officials hand over their **credentials** to His Majesty the Emperor. Until then, it would be the Ambassador-elect.

1985年1月、イスラエルのペレス首相の「密使」が日本を訪れ、中曽根康弘首相と会談し、中東和平実現に向けた関与を働き掛けていたことが、2017年12月20日公開の外交文書で確かめられた。(産経新聞 2017年 12月20日)

Israeli : イスラエルの ; イスラエル人
involvement : 関与 ; 関係
Middle East : 中東
release : 公開する ; 発出する ; 解放する ; 公開 ; 解放

インドのモディ首相としては3度目の来日となった今回、日本の安倍首相はその"蜜月ぶり"をアピールするため、異例の厚遇でもてなした。

visit : 訪問 ; 訪れる
exceptional : 例外的な ; 異例の (exception : 例外)
close : 近い ; 親密な ; 閉じる ; 閉鎖する

A国はB国との公式会合とは別に、別ルートで内密な交渉を進めていたことがB国政府からのリークによって明るみになった。

leak : リーク ; 漏洩
channel : チャンネル ; ルート ; 手段
apart from X : X とは別に ; 離れて

日本政府が正式に「特命全権大使」として接受するのは、相手国の元首らによる信任状が天皇陛下に手渡されてからであり、それまでは「次期大使」の位置づけとなる。

hand over : 手渡す ; 引き渡す
His Majesty the Emperor : 天皇陛下 (majesty : 陛下 ; 尊厳 ; 威厳)

33

credibility

[krèdəbíləti]

□ 92

信憑性；信用（性）；確からしさ

☞ credible 信頼できる；信用できる

The chief cabinet secretary explained that "some reports and speculations are untrue and have no **credibility**." He/She reiterated that Japan has a historical friendship with Country A.

custom

[kʌ́stəm]

□ 93

関税；税関；慣習

☞ customary
慣習法の；慣習となっている

The Office of the USTR has begun considering special measures to lower **customs** duties under presidential authority. Such was done to bring the trade agreement with Japan into force as soon as possible.

de facto

[diːfǽktou]

□ 94

事実上；事実上の（は）；
実際にある

☞ de facto standard
デファクトスタンダード；業界標準

Country A demanded the journalists of a certain media in Country B to return their press cards within 10 days. As a result, the journalist in question is placed in **de facto** deportation as his/her visa cannot be renewed.

declaration

[dèkləréiʃən]

□ 95

宣言；布告；申告

☞ declare 宣言する；布告する

☞ the Declaration of Independence
米国独立宣言

The term "treaty" in the context of international law refers not only to "treaty" itself but also to charter, covenant, convention, agreement, protocol, statute, arrangement, exchange of notes, **declaration**, and statement (Nakauchi, 2012).

官房長官は「一部の報道や憶測は事実と異なり、信憑性に欠ける」と説明し、A国とは歴史的に友好関係であり続けていることを改めて強調した。

chief：長官；長；上司
explain：説明する；明らかにする
reiterate：反復して言う；繰り返す
historical：歴史的な
friendship：友好関係；友情

米通商代表部（USTR）は対日貿易協定を早期に発効するため、大統領権限で関税を引き下げる特例措置の検討に入った。

special measure：特別措置；特措；特例措置
lower：下げる；減じる
as soon as possible（ASAP）：できるだけ早く；すぐに；速やかに

A国はB国の特定メディアの記者に対し、10日以内の記者証の返還を求めた。これにより該当の記者はビザの更新ができず、事実上の国外退去処分となる。

de facto はラテン語
demand：要求する；求める
journalist：ジャーナリスト；記者
in question：問題の；問題になっている；当の
deportation：国外追放；国外退去（deport：追放する）

国際法でいう条約（treaty）とは、「○○条約（treaty）」に限らず、憲章（charter）、規約（covenant）、条約（convention）、協定（agreement）、議定書（protocol）、規程（statute）、取極（arrangement）、交換公文（exchange of notes）、宣言（declaration）、声明（statement）、などを含む。（中内, 2012）

term：用語；期間；条件
refer：言及する；参照する
charter：憲章
covenant：規約

deed

[dí:d]

☐ 96

行為；行動；偉業

☞ good deed 善行；善い行い

A spokesperson for Country A's foreign ministry expressed strong concerns in an interview with Reuters, saying that, "This type of **deed** has not been and will not be tolerated in the future."

delegation

[dèligéiʃən]

☐ 97

代表団；使節派遣；権限移譲

☞ delegate
代表として派遣する；委任する；使節；代表

Country A's Ministry of Foreign Affairs announced on the third of this month that they will send a **delegation** to the UN high-level meeting on counterterrorism.

deliberately

[dilíbərətli]

☐ 98

故意に；慎重に；計画的に

☞ deliberate 意図的な；計画的な

The Convention against Torture and Other Cruel, Inhuman or Degrading Treatment or Punishment defines "torture" as **deliberately** inflicting serious physical or mental pain on public officials and other people for gathering information and other purposes.

demise

[dimáiz]

☐ 99

死去；逝去：活動停止

☞ death（死）の婉曲的表現

As a consequence of the **demise** on October 13, 2016 of His Majesty King Bhumibol, who was loved and respected as figure of spiritual support for the people and led the development of Thailand over the course of a long reign of 70 years since acceding to the throne in 1946, the new king, His Majesty King Vajiralongkorn, acceded to the throne on the same day (the announcement of the accession was on December 1). (Diplomatic Bluebook 2017)

A 国外務省の報道官はロイターのインタビューに対し「このような行為はこれまでも、そして今後も許されることはない」と強い懸念を示した。

spokesperson：報道官；スポークスパーソン；代弁者
express：述べる；示す；表現する
interview：インタビュー；取材訪問；記者会見；面接する
tolerate：許容する；我慢する

A 国の外交部は今月3日、国連のテロ対策に関するハイレベル会合に代表団を派遣すると発表した。

high-level meeting：ハイレベル（局長級）会合
counterterrorism：テロ対策；テロへの対抗措置

拷問等禁止条約では、「拷問」を公務員等が情報収集等のために身体的、精神的な重い苦痛を故意に与える行為と定義している。

torture：拷問；激しい苦痛
cruel：残酷な；残忍な；無慈悲の
degrading：品位を下げるような；下劣な（degrade：品位を落とす）
treatment：待遇；扱い；手当て
define：定義する

2016年10月13日、1946年に即位されて以来、70年間の長きにわたり、国民の精神的支柱として敬愛され、タイの発展を主導されたプミポン国王陛下が崩御されたことに伴い、同日、ワチラロンコン新国王陛下が即位された（即位の発表は 12月1日）。（外交青書 2017）

figure：象徴；姿；形；図
spiritual：精神的な；崇高な
accede：即位する；就く；継承する；加盟する
throne：王位；王座

demographic

[dèməgrǽfiks]

□ 100

人口統計（学）の；人口動態；デモグラフィック

☞ demography 人口統計学；デモグラフィー

In addition, various changes in the social structure are now underway, including **demographic** shifts resulting from the increasing number of young people, changes in the balance between Sunnis and Shiites and between secularists and Islamists, and a heightening of anti-American sentiment. (Diplomatic Bluebook 2007)

denounce

[dináuns]

□ 101

非難する；糾弾する；告発する

☞ denunciation 非難；糾弾；告発

In Kyrgyzstan, run-off parliamentary elections produce on March 14 the sweeping victory of the pro-President Akaev bloc. This fuels rallies by opposition supporters to demand the resignation of the president and **denounce** the elections as invalid. (Diplomatic Bluebook 2006, References)

denuclearization

[dìːn(j)ùːkliərizéɪʃən]

□ 102

非核化；核武装をやめること；核兵器撤去

☞ nuke 核兵器；原子力

A historic U.S.-North Korea Summit was convened in Singapore in June 2018, where U.S. President Trump and Chairman of State Affairs Commission Kim Jong-un agreed on the complete **denuclearization** of the Korean Peninsula. The second U.S.-North Korea Summit was held in Hanoi, Viet Nam in February 2019. (Diplomatic Bluebook 2019)

また、若年層の増大による人口動態の変化、スンニー派とシーア派、世俗主義とイスラム主義との間の均衡の変化、政治的心情としての反米感情の高まりなど、社会構造の変化も見られる。（外交青書 2007）

various：様々な；多様な
social structure：社会構造
underway：進行中で；既に始まって
shift：変化；転換
secularist：世俗主義者
sentiment：心情；感情

キルギスで議会選挙の決選投票実施、3月14日までにアカエフ大統領支持の与党側候補の圧勝が判明し、大統領辞任と選挙の不正を訴える野党支持者による抗議行動が激化。（外交青書 2006, 資料）

和文中の「訴える」は直訳ではなく、denounce the elections as invalid で「選挙が無効であるとして非難する」と解釈できる。

run-off：決選投票；決勝戦
sweeping victory：圧勝；完全な勝利

2018年6月、シンガポールにおいて歴史的な米朝首脳会談が行われ、トランプ米国大統領と金正恩国務委員長は朝鮮半島の完全な非核化に合意し、2019年2月にはハノイ（ベトナム）において、第2回米朝首脳会談が開催された。（外交青書 2019）

Chairman（Chairperson）of State Affairs Commission：国務委員長（commission：委員会；職務；委託；委託する）

deploy

[diplɔ́i]

□ 103

（軍などを）展開する；配備する；配置する

☞ deployment 配置；展開；配備

As of the end of February 2017, 16 UN PKO missions were **deployed**, primarily in the Middle East and Africa, with a total of over 100,000 military, police and civilian personnel **deployed** to these missions. (Diplomatic Bluebook 2017)

designate

[dézignèit]

□ 104

指定する；任命する；指名を受けた

☞ designation 指定；任命

With the implementation of four autonomous measures between July and December 2017, Japan **designated** 104 organizations and 110 individuals subject to asset freezing measures. (Diplomatic Bluebook 2018)

determinate

[ditə́ːrmənət]

□ 105

決定的な；限定的な；明確な

☞ determine
決定する；決心する；終結させる

The U.S.-China relations, which have a **determinate** influence on Japan's foreign and security policies, have continued to deteriorate over the past few years.

deterrence

[ditə́ːrəns | -tér-]

□ 106

抑止（力）；戦争抑止；阻止

☞ deterrent
抑止する；引き止める；制止する

Ensuring the forward deployment of U.S. Forces under the Japan-U.S. Security Arrangements and thereby enhancing **deterrence** are indispensable not only for the peace and security of Japan but also for the peace and stability of the Asia-Pacific region. (Diplomatic Bluebook 2017)

2017年2月末時点で、16の国連PKOミッションが中東・アフリカ地域を中心に活動しており、ミッションに従事する軍事・警察・文民要員の総数は10万人を超えている。(外交青書2017)

deployの直接の訳語は和文には出ていないが、「16の国連PKOミッションが ... 活動しており(展開され = deployed)、ミッション(のため)に従事する(配置された = deployed)人員の総数は」と解釈できる。

2017年7月から12月までの4回の更なる措置の実施により、日本においては、合計で104団体・110個人が資産凍結等の措置の対象に指定されている。(外交青書2018)

individual : 個人 ; 個人の
asset freezing : 資産凍結(asset : 資産 ; 財産 ; 資源)

日本の外交・安全保障政策に、決定的な影響を及ぼす米中関係は、ここ数年で悪化の一途をたどっている。

influence on X : Xへの影響
security policy : 安全保障政策
over X : Xを通して ; にわたって

日米安全保障体制の下での米軍の前方展開を確保し、その抑止力を向上させていくことは、日本の平和と安全のみならず、アジア太平洋地域の平和と安定にとって不可欠である。(外交青書2017)

Japan-U.S. Security Arrangements : 日米安全保障体制 ; 日米安保
thereby : それによって ; したがって
enhance : 高める ; 強化する ; 向上させる

devastating

[dévəstèitiŋ]

□ 107

壊滅的な；圧倒的な；悲惨な

☞ devastated area 荒廃地；被災地

The international community needs to work together as a united force to avoid **devastating** situations for states that have been affected by conflict and weakened health and other services.

dialog/dialogue

[dáiəlɔ̀ːg, -lɑ̀g | -lɔ̀g]

□ 108

対話（する）；会話；協議

☞ dialog box ダイアログボックス

The MOFA regards nongovernment organizations (NGOs) as important partners in development cooperation. It strives to strengthen partnerships with NGOs through providing financial assistance, improving their operational environment, giving aid, and engaging in **dialog**.

diplomacy

[diplóuməsi]

□ 109

外交；外交関係；外交手腕

☞ diplomatic 外交（上）の；外交的手段による

☞ diplomat 外交官；外交家

In 2017, China engaged proactively in foreign **diplomacy** based on the "Belt and Road Initiatives" and 19th Party Congress. In May, Beijing hosted a high-level international cooperation forum, dubbed "One Belt, One Road," which was attended by leaders from 29 countries. (Diplomatic Bluebook 2018)

disarmament

[disɑ́ːrməmənt]

□ 110

武装解除；軍備縮小（撤廃）

☞ disarm
武装（を）解除する；武器を取り上げる

Disarmament, Demobilization, and Reintegration (DDR) refers to peace operations led by the UN, international organizations, or states for the purpose of post-conflict reconstruction and peace-building.

紛争の被害を受け、医療サービス等が弱体化した国家が壊滅的な状況に陥らないためにも、国際社会は団結して協力する必要がある。

work together：協力する；共に働く
affect：影響を与える；作用する
weaken：弱める；弱体化させる
health service：（公共）医療サービス

外務省は、NGOを開発協力における重要なパートナーと位置付け、資金協力、活動環境整備支援、対話などを通じて、連携強化に努めている。

development cooperation：開発協力
strive：努力する；励む
financial：財務の；財政的な；財政上の
aid：援助；支援；援助する；支援する

2017年には、「一帯一路」構想や第19回党大会を念頭に積極的な外交が展開された。5月には、北京で「一帯一路」国際協力ハイレベルフォーラムが開催され、29カ国のリーダーが参加した。（外交青書2018）

engage（in）：従事する；携わる
proactively：積極的に；先を見越して（proactive；積極的な；率先した）
dub：称する

武装解除・動員解除・社会復帰（DDR）とは、紛争後の復興と平和構築を目的に、国連、国際機関または国家が主体となって行う平和活動を指す。

disarmament は「dis-（否定の意味）＋ arm（武装する）＋ ment（名詞化する接尾辞）」と考えると意味が理解できる。

demobilization：動員解除；復員
reintegration：復帰
peace operation：平和活動

disastrous

[dizǽstrəs | -zɑ́:s-]

□ 111

破滅的な；災害の；悲惨な

☞ disaster drill 避難（災害）訓練

In particular, due to falling in commodity prices in recent years, as well as **disastrous** economic policies, countries that economically depend on commodity products such as crude oil or mineral resources, continue to face severe economic circumstances. (Diplomatic Bluebook 2016)

discern

[disə́:rn, -zə́:rn]

□ 112

識別する；見分ける；分かる

☞ discernible 識別できる；認識できる

In fact, in the battlefield, **discerning** between friend and foe is extremely difficult, and misfires by friendly forces occur frequently.

dismantlement

[dìsmǽntəlmənt]

□ 113

廃棄；解体撤去；撤収

☞ dismantle 廃棄する；取り壊す

It is crucial that the international community makes concerted efforts to fully implement the UN Security Council resolutions for the **dismantlement** of all weapons of mass destruction and ballistic missiles of all ranges in a complete, verifiable and irreversible manner by North Korea. (Diplomatic Bluebook 2019)

dispute

[dispjú:t]

□ 114

論争（する）；異議を唱える；抵抗する

☞ disputatious 論争的な；論争好きの

☞ indisputable
議論の余地のない；疑う余地のない

Country A **disputed** the UN Security Council's draft statement prepared by Country C, which calls on Country B to suspend its military operations. The release of the Security Council's statement requires the consent of all the Council members.

特に近年の一次産品価格の低下に伴い、経済を原油や鉱物資源などの一次産品に依存している国では、経済政策の不調もあり、厳しい経済事情が続いている。(外交青書 2016)

和文中には直接 disastrous の意味は出ていないが、「経済政策の不調＝悲惨な (disastrous) 経済政策 (economic policies)」と解釈できる。

due to X : X が原因で；のせいで
commodity : 一次産品；鉱物；農作物；商品；日用品
crude oil : 原油 (crude : 加工されていない；粗雑な)
mineral : 鉱物；採掘物

実際、戦地では敵味方の識別が極めて難しく、友軍による誤爆や誤射が頻発する。

in fact : 実際 (は)
battlefield : 戦場
foe : 敵
occur : 起こる；生じる；発生する
frequently : 頻繁に；しばしば

北朝鮮による全ての大量破壊兵器及びあらゆる射程の弾道ミサイルの完全な、検証可能な、かつ、不可逆的な廃棄に向け、国際社会が一致結束して、安保理決議を完全に履行することが重要である。(外交青書 2019)

complete, verifiable and irreversible dismantlement (CVID) で、「完全な (complete)、検証可能な (verifiable)、かつ、不可逆的な (irreversible) 廃棄 (dismantlement)」という意味の定型表現となる。

crucial : 決定的な；極めて重要な
range : 距離；範囲

A 国は B 国に軍事作戦の停止を求める C 国作成の国連安保理の声明案に異議を唱えた。安保理の声明発表には全理事国の同意が必要となる。

, which (コンマ +which) は前部分に書かれた内容 (直前の語とは限らない) に対し、追加的に説明を加える際に主として用いる。

draft statement : 声明案；声明の原案 (下書き)

disregard

[dìsrigɑ́ːrd]

□ 115

無視（する）；軽視（する）；度外視（する）

☞ regard 注視する；注意する；見なす；敬意

Leading newspapers in English-speaking countries have repeatedly criticized the government of Country A for allowing the country to enter into loans in infrastructure construction with a **disregard** for their ability to repay such loans.

dissident

[dísədənt]

□ 116

意見を異にする；反体制派；反体制の

☞ dissidence 不一致；相違；不同意；異議

Among the ASEAN countries, the Philippines moved toward stability through the election victories of President Aquino's government and by putting down the activities of **dissident** elements in the military. (Diplomatic Bluebook 1988)

doctrine

[dɑ́ktrin | dɔ́k-]

□ 117

方針；教義；主義

☞ Truman Doctrine
トルーマン・ドクトリン

Then-Prime Minister Fukuda proposed the "Fukuda **Doctrine**" in 1977, which would serve as a fundamental principle for subsequent diplomatic ties with ASEAN, moving postwar diplomacy which mainly focused on problem solving and offering a clear approach. (Diplomatic Bluebook 2019, Special Feature)

domestic

[dəméstik]

□ 118

国内の；自国の；家庭内の

☞ foreign
外国の；対外の（domestic の反意語）

As the public opinion on **domestic** politics grows increasingly harsh, the current administration is seemingly attempting to find a way to make the most out of diplomacy.

英語圏有力紙は、A国が関係国のインフラ建設において、返済能力を度外視する融資を結ばせているとして批判的な論調を繰り返し述べている

leading newspaper：主要紙；有力紙
infrastructure：基盤；インフラ
repay：返金する；報いる

ASEAN諸国のうち、フィリピンでは、選挙におけるアキノ政権側の勝利、国軍不満分子の活動の鎮圧等を経て、その安定化への動きが見られた。（外交青書1988）

和文中の「不満分子」に相当する英語が "dissident elements" で、直訳的表現は「反体制の要素（派閥；分子）」となる。
put down：鎮圧する；鎮める

1977年には、福田赳夫総理大臣（当時）が、その後の対ASEAN外交の原則となる「福田ドクトリン」を提唱し、戦後の懸案処理型の外交を離れ、明確な理念を掲げました。（外交青書2019, 特集）

fundamental：基本的な；根本的な
tie：絆；連携；関係；結ぶ；縛りつける
problem solving：問題解決の

国内政治に対する世論が厳しさを増す中、現政権は外交に活路を見出そうとしているようだ。

harsh：厳しい；辛辣な
make the most of X：Xを最大限活用する；できるだけ利用する

dominant

[dɑ́mənənt | dɔ́m-]

□ 119

支配的な；主要な；最も有力な

☞ dominate 支配する；最も重要である

The significance of the economic diplomacy to Japan, which has renounced the use of military force in accordance with Article 9 of the Constitution, is incomparably more **dominant** than that of any other country.

draft

[drǽft | drɑ́ːft]

□ 120

起草する；下書きをする；草案

☞ rough draft 草稿（大まかな原稿）

Following this sixth meeting in Geneva, the seventh working group, which met in Beijing from the 15th to the 30th of last month, served as the substantial **drafting** committee for the joint statement.

dysfunctional

[disfʌ́ŋkʃənəl]

□ 121

機能不全の；逆機能の；機能が損なわれた

☞ functional 機能的な；実用的な

Given the World Trade Organization's (WTO) serious **dysfunctional** nature, it is no wonder that countries are beginning to explore the FTA (Free Trade Agreement) and the EPA (Economic Partnership Agreement).

embargo

[imbɑ́ːrgou]

□ 122

禁輸；通商禁止；出入港禁止を命じる

☞ lift the embargo 輸出禁止を解く

With regard to U.S.-produced oil, an FY2016 omnibus spending bill was passed enabling the importation into Japan of U.S.-produced oil based on short-term contracts, with the first importation since the **embargo** was lifted occurring in May 2016. (Diplomatic Bluebook 2018)

憲法9条によって軍事力の行使を放棄した日本にとって、経済外交の意義は、他の国とは比較にならないほど重要である。

economic diplomacy：経済外交
incomparably：比較にならないほど（comparably：比較できるほどに；同程度に）

この第6回のジュネーブ会合を経て、先月15日から30日まで北京で開かれた第7回作業部会が、実質的な共同声明の起草委員会となった。

meeting：会合；会議
working group：作業部会；作業グループ
joint：共同の；共有の；結合；つなぐ

たしかにWTOが深刻な機能不全に陥っていることを考えれば、各国がFTA（自由貿易協定）やEPA（経済連携協定）を模索し始めるのは当然であろう。

given X：Xを前提とすると；仮定すると；考えると
serious：深刻な；重大な
it is no wonder X：Xは驚くに値しない；明らかだ
explore：探求する；探る

米国産原油については、2016年度オムニバス歳出法案が成立し、2016年5月に輸出解禁後初となる米国産原油の輸入が実現して以来、短期契約の形で断続的に日本に輸入されている。（外交青書 2018）

U.S.-produced：米国産の
FY2016：2016年度
omnibus：包括する；オムニバス形式の
spending bill：歳出（支出）法案
contract：契約；協定

embark

[imbɑ́ːrk]

□ 123

着手する；乗り込む；積み込む

☞ embarkation/embarkment
積み込み；乗船；搭乗

Moreover, to **embark** on an effective and efficient implementation of aid, it is necessary to step up efforts to foster those concerned with development assistance, including experts and private consultants, as well as to strengthen collaborations with local municipalities, private organizations and NGOs. (Diplomatic Bluebook 1993)

embassy

[émbəsi]

□ 124

大使館；使節団

☞ embassy official 大使館員

When a Turkish employee at the U.S. **Embassy** in Istanbul was arrested by the Turkish authority in October on suspicion of having connections with Fethullah Gulen, U.S. diplomatic offices in Turkey halted the issuance of visas. Turkey also took similar measures in response to this (visa issuance resumed at the end of December). (Diplomatic Bluebook 2018)

emigration

[èmigréiʃən]

□ 125

移住；移民

☞ emigrant 移民；移住者；移民の

According to reports, the EU has successfully reached a compromise and has agreed to the talks on the contentious refugee and **emigration** issue after this latest overnight summit.

emphatic

[imfǽtik]

□ 126

強調された；際立った；語気の強い

☞ emphatic no
強調された"ノー"；断固とした"否"

Voters have given an **emphatic** no to the government's further austerity policies in this general election.

また、援助の効果的、効率的な実施を図るために、開発専門家、民間コンサルタントなどの援助関係者の育成、地方公共団体、民間団体、NGOなどとの連携の強化を目指している。(外交青書 1993)

和文中の「図る」は直接的なembarkの訳には当たらないが、「(実施を)図る」が「着手する」に相当する。
effective：効果的に
efficient：効率的に
foster：育成する；養育する

10月に在イスタンブール米国総領事館のトルコ人職員がギュレン氏関係の容疑でトルコ当局に逮捕されると、米国はトルコ国内にある米国公館による査証発給を停止、トルコも同様の対抗措置を行った(12月末に査証発給は再開)。(外交青書 2018)

和文では総領事館となっており、いずれも在外公館であるが、大使館と領事館では機能が異なる。
employee：被雇用者；従業員；職員
halt：停止させる；中断させる
issuance：発行；支給

欧州連合(EU)は今次の徹夜に及んだ首脳会合の結果、歩み寄りに成功し、争点だった難民・移民問題の協議で合意に達したと報じられた。

successfully：成功裏に；うまく
contentious：議論を引き起こす；議論のある
overnight：夜通しの；徹夜の

有権者は政府のさらなる緊縮政策に対し、今回の総選挙で明らかなノーを突きつけた形だ。

voter：有権者；投票者 (vote：票；投票；投票する)
austerity：緊縮；緊縮経済
general election：総選挙

endorsement

[indɔ́ːrsmənt]

□ 127

支持；承認；保証

☞ endorse 承認する；支援する

To develop a proactive foreign policy that pursues Japan's national interests, gaining the understanding and **endorsement** of the people is extremely important.

enforcement

[infɔ́ːrsmənt]

□ 128

施行；執行；強制

☞ enforce 施行する；強制する；強化する

In addition, the organizational structure and equipment of the marine law **enforcement** agencies as exemplified by the China Coast Guard have been reinforced, while such agencies are not under the command and order of the People's Liberation Army (PLA). (Diplomatic Bluebook 2017)

enlargement

[inlɑ́ːrdʒmənt]

□ 129

拡大；拡張；増大

☞ enlarge 大きくする；拡大する；拡張する

The Intergovernmental Conference (IGC) also began to discuss institutional reforms of the EU in response to EU **enlargement**, with the agenda including the size and composition of the European Commission, the redistribution of votes within the qualified majority voting system, and the expansion of the scope of application of qualified majority voting. (Diplomatic Bluebook 2001)

entangle

[intǽŋgl]

□ 130

もつれさせる；巻き込む；からませる

☞ entanglement 紛糾；もつれ；鉄条網

One of the causes of the UK's highly **entangled** negotiations to leave the EU is the issue of border control in Northern Ireland.

日本の国益を追求した積極的な外交を展開するためにも、国民からの理解と支持を得ることが極めて重要である。

develop：発展する；開発する；発達する
pursue：追求する；追いかける
gain：得る；増加する

また、人民解放放軍（PLA）の指揮命令系統下にある組織ではないものの、海警局に代表される海洋法執行機関の組織体制と装備も強化されている。（外交青書2017）

equipment：装備；備品
marine law：海洋法；海法
People's Liberation Army：（中国）人民解放軍

EUの拡大に対応するためにEUの機構改革について協議するための政府間会合（IGC）が開始され、欧州委員会の構成、特定多数決票数配分、特定多数決適用範囲の拡大等について議論が行われた。（外交青書2001）

enlargementなどの語頭の"en"は名詞を動詞化させる働きがある。（例：rich〔豊かな〕→ enrich〔豊かにする〕）
institutional：制度の；組織の；機構の（institution：制度；組織；機構）
qualified：条件付きの；限定された；資格のある
redistribution：再配分；再分配
majority voting：多数決；多数決投票

イギリスのEUからの離脱交渉が大いにもつれている原因の1つが、北アイルランドの国境管理問題である。

cause：原因
highly：高く；大いに；非常に
leave：去る；離れる
border control：国境管理；出入国管理；国境検問所

43

entity

[éntəti]

□ 131

存在；実体；実在物

☞ legal entity 法人（合法的な実体）

Distributed ledger (database) technology enables the handling of important data transactions over the Internet and other open networks, which requires a high level of trust. Utilization of this technology makes it possible to prevent falsification and tampering without working through a third-party **entity** (intermediary), which incurs costs. (Diplomatic Bluebook 2019, Column)

envoy

[énvɔi]

□ 132

特命使節（特使）；（特命全権）公使；使者

☞ envoy extraordinary and minister plenipotentiary 特命全権公使

Political dialogues were conducted at all levels involving the Prime Minister, Minister of Foreign Affairs, and special **envoy** of the Government of Japan for the Middle East peace. Japan is also making an effort to contribute to confidence-building between Israel and Palestine by inviting relevant people from both sides to Japan. (Diplomatic Bluebook 2017)

establish

[istǽbliʃ]

□ 133

設立する；確立する；制定する

☞ establishment 設立；確立；樹立；制定

The Shimane Prefecture has made a stern protest to South Korea, seeking to turn Takeshima's territorial rights into a fact. It has proposed and requested a new round of negotiations to **establish** its territorial rights rapidly, including a resolution at the International Court of Justice.

インターネットなどオープンなネットワーク上で、高い信頼性が求められる重要データのやり取りなどを可能にする「分散型台帳（データベース）技術」。この技術を活用することで、コストのかかる第三者機関（仲介役）を介さずに偽装や改ざんを防ぐことが可能になる。（外交青書 2019, コラム）

和文中の「機関」はこの場合 "entity（存在）" に相当するが、entity に「機関」という直接的な意味はない。

distributed：分散型（の）（distribute：分配する；配布する）
falsification：偽造；改竄
incur：招く；負担する；被る

総理大臣、外務大臣、中東和平担当特使など、あらゆるレベルで関係者との政治対話を行ってきているほか、イスラエル・パレスチナ双方の関係者や若者を日本に招へいする等の当事者間の信頼醸成の推進に取り組んでいる。（外交青書 2017）

special envoy：特使
make an effort to：努力する
confidence-building：信頼醸成（の）

島根県は竹島の領土権に関して、既成事実化を狙う韓国に厳重なる抗議を重ねるとともに、国際司法裁判所における解決を含め、領土権の早期確立に向けた交渉の新展開を提案、要望している。

stern：強固な；容赦ない
protest：抗議；抗議行動；異議を申し立てる
request：依頼する；要請する；依頼；要請
territorial rights：領土権

eternal

[itə́:rnl]

□ 134

永遠の；不滅の；不変の

☞ the Eternal 神

In other words, Western countries have maintained their unity under the basic stance that progress must be made in all the areas of arms control and reduction, regional conflicts, human rights and bilateral issues in order to establish an **eternal** base to realize deterrence and dialogue as well as stable and constructive relations between Eastern and Western countries. These goals were reconfirmed in the "Statement of East-West Relations" adopted at the summit (of seven major industrial democracies) in Venice in June 1987 and again in the political declaration issued on the occasion of the Toronto Summit in June 1988. (Diplomatic Bluebook 1988)

exclusive

[iksklú:siv]

□ 135

排他的な；閉鎖的な；スクープ

☞ exclusive economic zone (EEZ) 排他的経済水域

However, in July, North Korea launched two ballistic missiles with an intercontinental ballistic missile (ICBM) range both of which landed within Japan's **exclusive** economic zone (EEZ). (Diplomatic Bluebook 2018)

executive

[igzékjutiv]

□ 136

行政府；重役；執行する

☞ execution 遂行；履行；処刑；死刑執行

The position of secretary of state in the U.S. is considered to be close to the number two position in the **executive** branch, next to the president.

即ち、西側は87年6月のヴェネチア・サミットで採択された「東西関係に関する声明」で再確認された抑止と対話、並びに東西諸国間の安定した建設的な関係のために永続的な基礎を構築するには、軍備管理・軍縮、地域紛争、人権問題、二国間問題の全分野にわたる進展が必要との基本的立場の下に結束を維持してきたが、この点は88年6月のトロント・サミット政治宣言においても再確認された。（外交青書 1988）

maintain：維持する；主張する
unity：結束；一致；単一性
stance：立場；姿勢
progress：進歩；進捗；進展
constructive：建設的な

しかしながら、北朝鮮は、7月には大陸間弾道ミサイル（ICBM）級弾道ミサイルを2回連続で発射し、2回とも日本の排他的経済水域（EEZ）に着弾させた。（外交青書 2018）

exclusiveの反意語はinclusive（包括的な；包摂的な）
land：着弾する；着地する；上陸する；陸地

アメリカ合衆国における国務長官の地位は、大統領に次ぐ行政府ナンバー2に近いもといえよう。

この場合、"executive branch"で「行政府」を意味する。
next to X：Xの次に（next to impossibleで「ほとんど不可能な；無理な」という意味になる）

exemplify

[igzémpləfài]

☐ **137**

例証する；実例を挙げて説明する；典型例となる

☞ example 例；例示

In addition, active and tireless negotiations spanning many long years have also borne fruit, as **exemplified** by the finalization of negotiations of the Japan-EU EPA in December 2017. (Diplomatic Bluebook 2018)

exert

[igzə́ːrt]

☐ **138**

行使する；働かせる；努力する

☞ exertion 行使；発揮；骨折り

ASEAN **exerts** its centrality and is the engine of various regional cooperation. Therefore, realizing a more stable and prosperous ASEAN is absolutely essential to the stability and prosperity of the region as a whole. (Diplomatic Bluebook 2019)

explicit

[iksplísit]

☐ **139**

明確な；明示的な；系統立った

☞ explicitly はっきりと；明白に

It is extremely inappropriate to include such reference without showing any substantial grounds. The GOJ requests the Committee to provide us the answers to the above question based on **explicit** legal grounds. (Diplomatic Bluebook 2019, References)

exploitative

[iksplɔ́itətiv]

☐ **140**

搾取的な；収奪的な；資源開発の

☞ exploit 搾取する；食い物にする

In a speech he/she gave yesterday, the secretary of Country A's Ministry of B, C, strongly condemned Country D for pushing irresponsible and **exploitative** economic policies toward African countries.

また、2017年12月には日EU・EPAが交渉妥結するなど、長年にわたる精力的な交渉が実を結んだ。(外交青書2018)

和文中の「など」はexemplifyの直接の訳ではない。解釈としては「(交渉妥結)に例証されるように」となる。

tireless : 休むことのない ; 不断の
span : わたる ; 及ぶ
borne : bear (生む・産む) の過去分詞形 (bornは生命が生まれる時にのみ用い、それ以外はborneを用いる)

ASEANは、様々な地域協力の中心かつ、原動力である。ASEANがより安定し繁栄することは、地域全体の安定と繁栄にとって極めて重要である。(外交青書2019)

和文中にはexertに相当する訳語は出ていない。解釈としては「(中心としての役割)を働かせている」となる。

prosperous : 繁栄している ; 豊かである
as a whole : 全体として ; 総じて

適切な根拠が示されることもなく、このような言及を総括所見に含めることは極めて不適切です。日本政府としては、以上に述べた疑問に、委員会からの法的な根拠を明記した回答を求めます。(外交青書2019, 資料)

inappropriate : 不適切な ; ふさわしくない
ground : 根拠 ; 理由 ; 立脚点
GOJ : 日本政府 (=government of Japan)

A国B省のC長官は昨日行った講演で、D国がアフリカ諸国に対して無責任で搾取的な経済政策を推し進めているとして強く非難した。

speech : 演説 ; スピーチ ; 発話
push : 推し進める ; 強要する ; 押す
irresponsible : 無責任な ; 責任のない ; 責任を負わない

facility

[fəsíləti]

□ 141

施設；設備；容易さ

☞ facilitate
促進する；円滑に進める；手助けする

For that reason, Japan has offered grant aid to construct new bridges and **facilities** (One-Stop Border Post: OSBP) to facilitate border procedures at the border between Rwanda and Tanzania and has provided support to improve the operational capability of the OSBP **facility** through technical cooperation. (Diplomatic Bluebook 2017)

fail to

[féil tu]

□ 142

し損なう；できない；しないで終わる

☞ failure 失敗；失敗したもの；落第点

It is still fresh in our minds that the Japanese mobile phone industry, despite its superior technology, missed out on the international standards and has **failed to** capture the global market.

force

[fɔ́ːrs]

□ 143

力；軍隊；強引に押し進める

☞ forcible 力づくの；強制的な

Furthermore, the international order based on fundamental values, such as freedom, democracy, human rights, the rule of law and respect for international law, which has underpinned the peace and prosperity of Japan and the world, is being challenged by unilateral attempts at changing the status quo by **force** and the spread of terrorism and violent extremism. (Diplomatic Bluebook 2019)

foresight

[fɔ́ːrsáit]

□ 144

先見性；展望；洞察力

☞ hindsight 後知恵（foresight の反意語）

Re-reading it now, I am again deeply moved by Tezuka's **foresight**. (Diplomatic Bluebook 2019, Column)

そのため、日本は、無償資金協力により、ルワンダとタンザニアの国境に新しい橋や国境手続円滑化のための施設(ワンストップボーダーポスト:OSBP)を建設し、技術協力によりOSBP施設の運用能力向上を支援してきた。(外交青書2017)

grant aid:無償資金協力;無償援助
operational capability:運用能力
technical cooperation:技術協力

日本の携帯電話産業がその優れた技術にもかかわらず、国際規格を逃し、世界市場をつかみ損ねたのは記憶に新しい。

fresh:新しい　industry:産業;工業;勤勉
despite X:Xにもかかわらず
superior:優れた;上質の;まさる
international standard:国際標準;国際規格;国際水準(standard:基準;標準)
global market:世界市場

さらに、力を背景とした一方的な現状変更の試みやテロ及び暴力的過激主義の拡大により、日本を含む世界の平和と繁栄を支えていた自由、民主主義、基本的人権、法の支配、国際法の尊重といった基本的価値に基づく国際秩序が挑戦を受けています。(外交青書2019)

order:秩序;命令;静粛にする
underpin:支える;支持する
challenge:挑む;挑戦する;異議を唱える
status quo:現状
extremism:過激主義;過激思想

それを今読み返してみると、手塚先生の先見性に改めて感動させられます。(外交青書2019, コラム)

re-read:再び読む;読み返す
deeply:深く;深刻に
move:感動させる;動く

friendly fire

[fréndli fáiər]

□ 145

友軍射撃（味方からの誤射）；誤爆；同士討ち

☞ fire 発砲する；燃やす

There is no shortage of incidents that appear to be caused by **friendly fire**, accidental bombing, or over-defense by the U.S. and NATO soldiers into conflict zones.

fundamentalism

[fʌ̀ndəméntəlìzm]

□ 146

原理主義；根本主義

☞ -ism 主義；学説；イズム

☞ fundamentalist 原理主義者；原理主義者の

In Algeria the activities of radical terrorist groups linked to Islamic **fundamentalism** are leading to a deterioration of public security and instability in domestic politics. (Diplomatic Bluebook 1995)

geopolitical

[dʒìːəupəlítikəl]

□ 147

地政学の；地政学的な；地政学に関する

☞ geopolitics 地政学

Today, when investment money also reaches across developing countries, developing country risks can immediately set off ripple effects on the entire world economy, including **geopolitical** risks, such as regional conflict and terrorism threat, and sovereign risks related to national credit. (Japan's Official Development Assistance White Paper 2013)

having said that

[hǝ́viŋ séd ðǽt]

□ 148

そうはいっても；そうかといって；それでもやはり

☞ nonetheless それでもなお；といっても

The legitimacy of U.S. military intervention is highly questionable. **Having said that**, it should be commended that the U.S. aimed to reach an agreement at the Security Council before deciding to carry out their airstrikes.

米・NATO 軍兵士による紛争地域での誤射、誤爆、または過剰防衛によると見られる事件は後を絶たない。

"friendly fire" は "collateral damage" などと共に、独特な婉曲表現を含む戦争用語である。日本語にも「玉砕」、「疎開」などがある。

shortage : 不足 ; 欠乏
over-defense : 過剰防衛

アルジェリアでは、イスラム原理主義の流れをくむ過激派テロ組織の活動が、治安の悪化及び内政不安をもたらしている。(外交青書 1995)

radical : 過激派の ; 急進的な ; 抜本的な
link : つながる ; 結びつく ; 関係づける
public security : 治安 ; 公安

投資マネーが途上国にも広く波及している現在、地域紛争やテロの脅威といった地政学的リスク、国家信用にかかわるソブリンリスクといった途上国発のリスクも世界経済全体に直ちに波及します。(2013年版 政府開発援助(ODA)白書)

ripple effect : 波及効果 (ripple : さざ波 ; 波紋)
entire : 全体の ; 全くの
world economy : 世界経済
sovereign risk : ソブリン (カントリー) リスク (sovereign : 主権者 ; 統治者 ; 国王)
national credit : 国家信用

今回の米軍の軍事介入の正当性には大いに疑義がある。とはいえ、空爆を断行する前段階で、安保理での合意を目指したことは一定評価すべきである。

questionable : 疑問の余地がある ; 疑わしい
commend : 褒める ; 称賛する
aim : 意図する ; 向ける ; 狙う

hegemony

[hidʒéməni | -gém-]

□ 149

覇権；主導権；ヘゲモニー

☞ regional hegemony 地域覇権

While setting store upon relations with the United States, China has become increasingly wary of developments such as U.S.-led North Atlantic Treaty Organization (NATO) handling of the Kosovo situation, and Japan's passing of laws related to the Japan-U.S. Defense Guidelines, regarding these as manifestations of U.S. **hegemony**. (Diplomatic Bluebook 2000)

homogeneous

[hòumədʒíːniəs | hɔ̀m-, hòum-]

□ 150

同種の；均質の；同質的な

☞ heterogeneous
異種の；異質の（homogeneous の反意語）

This characteristic of Japan, often referred to as one-nation state, was generally very much to Japan's advantage in the postwar years of reconstruction and development as the social network spread fine and far throughout this **homogeneous** and hard-working population to enable Japan to become a world-class competitor despite its lack of natural resources. (Diplomatic Bluebook 1985)

hostage

[hɑ́stidʒ | hɔ́s-]

□ 151

人質；抵当

☞ hostage release 人質解放

The G7 leaders agreed to severely condemn **hostage**-taking, the occupation of diplomatic and consular missions, and the confinement of their staff. These acts are in violation of fundamental norms of international law and practice.

中国は対米関係を重視する一方で、米国主導による北大西洋条約機構（NATO）のコソヴォ問題への対処や日本における日米防衛協力のための指針関連法等の成立などの動向を「米国の覇権主義」の現れとして警戒感を強めている。（外交青書 2000）

和文中には「覇権主義」と「主義」まで記されているが、正確には hegemony には「主義」の意味を含まない。覇権主義は hegemonism となる。

set store：尊重する；重視する；価値を置く
wary：慎重な；警戒する

この単一民族国家と称されている我が国の特質は、戦後40年、その復興と成長の過程において、総じて大きなプラスとして働いた。均質、勤勉なる単一民族国家において、その社会の網の目は相当に細かく発展し、資源に乏しい我が国の国際競争力を強いものとした。（外交青書 1985）

characteristic：特徴；特性；特徴のある
fine：細かい；立派な
hard-working：勤勉な；よく働く
lack：不足；欠乏；欠いている

G7の各国首脳は、国際法及び国際慣行の基本的規範に違反する人質行為、外交・領事公館の占拠及びその職員の監禁を厳しく非難することで一致した。

severely：厳しく；激しく
consular mission：領事公館
confinement：監禁；幽閉（confine：監禁する；制限する）

49

hostile

[hɑ́stl, -tail | hɔ́stail, -tl]

□ 152

敵意のある；敵の；反対して

☞ hostility 敵意；敵対心；反抗
（「戦闘〔行為〕」という意味で用いる場合は hostilities と複数形で用いることが通例）

Specifically, President Moon Jae-in announced “the Korean peninsula peace initiative” in his speech in Berlin in July 2017 and proposed (1) the resumption of the reunions of separated families and revisits to ancestral graves, and holding of Inter-Korean Red Cross talks to this end, (2) North Korea’s participation in the Pyeongchang Winter Olympic Games, (3) the mutual cessation of **hostile** action along the Military Demarcation Line, and (4) the resumption of inter-Korean exchanges and dialogue. However, North Korea did not respond immediately. (Diplomatic Bluebook 2018)

humanitarian

[hjuːmæ̀nətéəriən]

□ 153

人道的な；人道主義の；博愛の

☞ humanitarian aid 人道援助；人道支援

The issue of refugees and other displaced persons is a serious **humanitarian** problem and has brought about friction in the international community over responses to the issue, and there is a concern that it will be further prolonged and aggravated. (Diplomatic Bluebook 2019)

hypocrisy

[hipɑ́krəsi | -pɔ́k-]

□ 154

偽善；偽善的行為；見せかけ

☞ hypocritical 偽善の；偽善者の

The Ministry of Foreign Affairs of Country A vehemently condemned the government of Country B for its continued importation of high-technology weapons from the U.S. while calling for disarmament. Country A called this move both a **hypocrisy** and a double standard.

具体的には、文在寅大統領は同年7月に「ベルリン構想」を発表し、①離散家族再会・墓参事業の再開、そのための南北赤十字会談開催、②平昌冬季オリンピック競技大会への北朝鮮の参加、③軍事境界線における敵対行為の相互停止及び④南北間の接触と対話の再開を提案したが、北朝鮮はすぐには応じなかった。(外交青書 2018)

resumption：再開；回復
reunion：再会；再統合；同窓会
ancestral：先祖の；先祖から伝わる（ancestor：先祖；祖先）
Red Cross：赤十字社；赤十字章
cessation：停止；中止；中断

難民等の問題は、深刻な人道問題であるとともに、その対応をめぐって国際社会に軋轢をもたらしており、問題の更なる長期化・深刻化が懸念されている。(外交青書 2019)

displaced：住むところを失った；立ち退かされた
prolong：長くする；引き延ばす
aggravate：悪化させる；より重くする；悩ます

A 国外務省は、B 国政府が軍縮を訴えながらも、米国から先端兵器を導入し続けていることに対し、偽善的でダブルスタンダードであるとして強く非難した。

vehemently：強く；猛烈に（vehement: 激しく；猛烈な）
importation：輸入；輸入品
double standard：ダブルスタンダード；二重基準

hypothetical

[hàipəθétikəl]

☐ 155

仮定（上）の；仮説（上）の；仮言の

☞ hypothesis
仮説；仮定（複数形は hypotheses）

Although the session used **hypothetical** cases prepared by the organizer, it was highly appropriate and ignited an active exchange of views in each group. (Diplomatic Bluebook 2017, Column)

identity

[aidéntəti]

☐ 156

同一性；アイデンティティー；身元

☞ identification
身元確認；身分証明証；同一化

☞ identify
身元を明らかにする；同定する；同一化する

In order to prevent illicit acquisition of passports that may nurture these secondary or tertiary crimes, MOFA has been making further effort to enhance strict **identity** examination in issuing a passport, for example, by such means as designating a stringent examination period against illicit acquisition of passports through identity theft at passport offices located in each prefecture.(Diplomatic Bluebook 2018)

ideological

[àidiəlάdʒik, ìd- | -lɔ́dʒ-, -ikəl]

☐ 157

イデオロギーに基づく；
イデオロギー（上）の；非現実的な

☞ ideology
イデオロギー；価値（信念）体系

On the other hand, replacing **ideological** confrontation, a variety of problems based on ethnic and cultural differences have become apparent. (Diplomatic Bluebook 2000)

immediately

[imí:diətli]

☐ 158

即座に；直接に；すぐ近くに

☞ immediate 即時の；差し迫った；直接の

In February, **immediately** after President Trump's inauguration, Prime Minister Abe visited the U.S. to hold a Japan-U.S. Summit Meeting. (Diplomatic Bluebook 2018)

議論の題材は事務局が用意した架空の事例でしたが、これがとても適切で、いずれのグループでも活発な意見交換を誘っていました。(外交青書 2017, コラム)

case：事例；場合；問題
organizer：組織者；事務局；主催者 (organize：組織する；計画する)
ignite：点火する；燃え立たせる (ignition：発火；点火；着火)

こうした2次・3次の犯罪を助長するおそれのある旅券の不正取得を未然に防止するため、各都道府県にある旅券窓口では、なりすましによる不正取得防止のための審査強化期間を設けるなど、旅券の発給時の本人確認の強化に一層の力を入れている。(外交青書 2018)

illicit：違法な；不法な
acquisition：取得；買収
nurture：助長する；養育する；育む
tertiary：三次の；第三の
crime：罪；犯罪
stringent：厳しい；厳重な；緊縮の

その一方で、イデオロギーに基づく対立に代わり、民族や文化の違いに根ざした様々な問題が顕在化している。(外交青書 2000)

replace：取りかえる；取ってかわる
ethnic：民族の；民族的な
apparent：明らかな；明白な；見かけの

トランプ大統領が就任した直後の2月、安倍総理大臣は米国を訪問し、日米首脳会談を実施した。(外交青書 2018)

inauguration：就任；開始；落成
summit：首脳 (会談)；首脳級；頂上
hold：開催する；保留する

immunity

[imjúːnəti]

□ 159

特権；免除；免疫

☞ immune
免疫がある；免除された；免れる

Turning to Central and South America, in Chile former President Augusto Pinochet was charged with violations of human rights during Chile's martial law era after court rulings removed the **immunity** he had enjoyed as a senator-for-life. (Diplomatic Bluebook 2001)

impeach

[impíːtʃ]

□ 160

弾劾する；告発する；問題にする

☞ impeachment 弾劾；告発

The president of the U.S. may be **impeached** by Congress and may be dismissed from his position. However, there has never been a case of impeachment and removal from office. The only U.S. president to resign was Richard Nixon, the 37th president of the U.S.

imperial

[impíəriəl]

□ 161

帝国の；皇室の；荘厳な

☞ imperialism 帝国主義（体制）；帝制；
領土拡張主義

Prime Minister Abe visited Darwin, Australia, a target of air raids of the **Imperial** Japanese Army during World War II. Prime Minister Abe visited a memorial dedicated to the war dead with Prime Minister Morrison and sent out a message regarding the successful postwar reconciliation between the two countries. (Diplomatic Bluebook 2019)

implement

[ímpləmənt]

□ 162

実施する；実装する；用具

☞ implementation 遂行；執行；実施

Country A's foreign minister has announced that he/she will continue to urge Country B to "steadily **implement**" the recent agreement.

中南米ではチリにおいて、ピノチェト元大統領が軍政時代の人権侵害問題で、チリ国内での議員特権剥奪の上、起訴された。(外交青書 2001)

charge : 起訴する ; 請求する ; 責める
court ruling : 判決 (court : 裁判所)
for-life : 終身 (の)

米国大統領は議会の弾劾により罷免される可能性があるが、これまでに弾劾が成立し罷免された事例はない。また唯一、歴代米国大統領の中で辞任した大統領は第37代米国大統領リチャード・ニクソンである。

dismiss : 解雇する ; 免職する
removal : 解任 ; 除去 ; 廃止 (remove : 取り除く ; 取り去る ; 廃絶する)

安倍総理大臣のオーストラリア訪問は、第二次世界大戦において旧日本軍が空爆したダーウィンを訪問するものであり、モリソン首相と共に、戦没者慰霊碑を訪問し、日豪間の戦後和解成功のメッセージを発信した。(外交青書 2019)

和文中の「旧日本軍」は「帝国陸軍」のことを指し、これが Imperial Japanese Army の訳語となる。

raid : 空襲 ; 襲撃 ; 奇襲
memorial : 記念碑 ; 記念館
dedicated to X : X のために尽くす ; 捧げる

A 国外務大臣は B 国に対し、先般の合意の「着実な履行」を引き続き求めていく方針を明らかにした。

steadily : 着実に ; 絶え間なく (steady : 安定した ; 揺るぎない)
recent : 最近の ; 近頃の、先般の (recently : 最近)

implication

[ìmplikéiʃən]

□ 163

ほのめかし；含意；連座

☞ imply ほのめかす；暗示する

At the Fifth Ministerial Meeting in Manila in July, a frank and lively exchange of views took place on the regional situation, including the security **implication** of the Asian economic crisis, the Myanmar situation and the situation in Cambodia. (Diplomatic Bluebook 1999)

implicit

[implísit]

□ 164

暗に示された；暗黙の；潜在的な

☞ implicitly
暗に；それとなく（explicitly の反意語）

There are so many “**implicit** threats” in today’s cyberspace. However, it is likely to be too late for them to manifest themselves such as when they are already the victims of a cyberattack.

impose

[impóuz]

□ 165

課す；負わす；押し付ける

☞ imposition 押し付け；強制；義務

The public notice issued by Country A unilaterally **imposes** an obligation on civilian aircraft flying in airspace over the high seas to follow its procedures, which is unacceptable.

in accordance with X

[in əkɔ́ːrdns wəð]

□ 166

X にしたがって；一致して；則って

☞ accord 一致する；調和する

In addition, MOFA has been engaged in efforts to facilitate the public use of the diplomatic documents **in accordance with** the Public Records and Archives Management Act. (Diplomatic Bluebook 2018)

7月にマニラで開催された第5回閣僚会合においては、アジア経済危機の安全保障上の影響、ミャンマー情勢、カンボディア情勢等、地域情勢につき率直かつ活発な意見交換が行われた。(外交青書 1999)

和文中では implication を「(安全保障上の) 影響」と遠回しに表現しており、経済危機が安全保障上の問題へと派生する可能性を示している。

今日のサイバー空間において「潜在的な脅威」は非常に多いが、それらが顕在化してから、つまりサイバー攻撃の被害に遭ってからでは手遅れになる可能性が高い。

cyberspace : サイバー空間 ; サイバースペース
too X : X 過ぎる ; あまりに X 過ぎて (できない)
such as X : 例えば X ; X などの
victim : 被害者 ; 犠牲者

A 国が発表した公告は、公海上の空域を飛行する民間航空機に対し一方的に自国の手続に従うことを義務を課したものであり、到底容認できない。

public notice : 公告 ; 公示
airspace : 空域
(the) high sea (s) : 公海 ; 外洋
unacceptable : 容認できない ; 受け入れられない (acceptable : 容認できる ; 受け入れられる)

また、公文書管理法にのっとり外交史料利用の利便性向上にも努めている。(外交青書 2018)

effort : 努力 ; 尽力 ; 骨折り
public use : 公用 ; 公共用途
record : 記録 ; 登録 ; 記録する

in behalf of X/ on behalf of X

[in/ən bihǽf əv]

□ 167

X を代表して；代理として；のために

☞ behalf 利益；支持

"Kibo" is capable of releasing nanosatellites and is also used to release nanosatellites **on behalf of** many emerging and developing countries with the aim of providing support for capacity building in the space field. (Diplomatic Bluebook 2017)

incompatible

[ìnkəmpǽtəbl]

□ 168

相いれない；両立しない；互換性のない

☞ incompatibility 不適合；不一致

Such a move is extremely regrettable and **incompatible** with the position of the Government of Japan. (Diplomatic Bluebook 2018)

incorporate

[inkɔ́ːrpərèit]

□ 169

取り入れる；取り込む；合併する

☞ incorporation
組み込み；合併；法人設立

To **incorporate** vigorous economic growth abroad, mainly in Asia, into the Japanese economy, support for Japanese companies by the Government has become more important. (Diplomatic Bluebook 2019)

induce

[indjúːs | -djúːs]

□ 170

誘導する；説得する；帰納する

☞ induction 誘導；導入；帰納

(e) Assist, encourage or **induce**, in any way, anyone to engage in any activity prohibited to a State Party under this Treaty (Diplomatic Bluebook 2018, Special Feature)

「きぼう」は超小型衛星の放出機能を有しており、宇宙分野における能力構築支援を目的として、数多くの新興国・開発途上国の衛星の放出にも利用されている。（外交青書 2017）

和文中には直接的に on behalf of の訳は出ていないが、「「きぼう」は…数多くの新興国・開発途上国を代表して（の利益のために）」と解釈できる。

nanosatellite：（超）小型衛星
emerging country：新興国（emerge：出現する；現れる）

このような動きは日本政府の立場と相いれない、極めて残念なものである。（外交青書 2018）

incompatible の反意語である compatible は「互換性のある；両立可能な；相性がよい」という意味になる。

アジアを中心とする海外の経済成長の勢いを日本経済に取り込む観点からも、政府による日本企業支援の重要性は高まっている。（外交青書 2019）

incorporate X into Y：X を Y に取り入れる；組み込む
vigorous：活気のある；活発な
economic growth：経済成長
mainly：主として；大部分は

(e) この条約が禁止する活動に対する援助、奨励又は勧誘（外交青書 2018）

assist：援助；援助する
in any way：決して；いかなる形であっても
state party：締約国（party：〔行動を共にする〕団体；関係者；政党）

inflict

[inflíkt]

□ 171

押し付ける；負わせる；与える

☞ infliction 苦しみ；刑罰

The decisions clearly violate Article II of the Agreement and **inflict** unjustifiable damages and costs on the Japanese companies. Above all, the decisions completely overthrow the legal foundation of the friendly and cooperative relationship that Japan and the ROK have developed since the normalization of diplomatic relations in 1965. (Diplomatic Bluebook 2019)

infringement

[infríndʒmənt]

□ 172

違反（行為）；侵害；抵触

☞ infringe 侵害する；破る；違反する

The U.S. is considering invoking sanctions under Section 301 of the Trade Act in response to China's alleged **infringement** of intellectual property rights and coercive technology transfer policies against U.S. companies.

initiative

[iníʃətiv, -ʃiə-]

□ 173

主導権；進取の気性；取り組み

☞ government-led initiative
政府主導の（による）イニシアチブ

These issues cannot be solved by one country alone, and require a united response by the international community, and the **initiatives** for these issues are one critical part of Japan's "Proactive Contribution to Peace" **initiative**. (Diplomatic Bluebook 2017)

insult

[insʌ́lt]

□ 174

侮辱（する）；辱める；無礼

☞ add insult to injury
泣きっ面に蜂の状態にさせる；
踏んだり蹴ったりにさせる

Perhaps the government had neither the right nor the obligation to try to stop them, and instead, were our unwanted efforts to protect Japanese nationals an **insult** to their ideals and a waste of tax money? (Diplomatic Bluebook 2004, Topic)

これらの大法院判決は、日韓請求権・経済協力協定第2条に明らかに反し、日本企業に対し不当な不利益を負わせるものであるばかりか、1965年の国交正常化以来築いてきた日韓の友好協力関係の法的基盤を根本から覆すものであって、極めて遺憾であり、断じて受け入れられない。(外交青書 2019)

violate：違反する；犯す；破る
overthrow：転覆させる；ひっくり返す；屈服させる
normalization：正常化

米国は、中国による知的所有権の侵害や、米国企業に対する強制的な技術移転政策の疑いに対し、通商法301条による制裁措置の発動を検討している。

section：条；部分
intellectual property right：知的所有権；知的財産権
technology transfer：技術移転（technology：技術；科学技術）

これらの課題は、一国のみで対処できるものではなく国際社会が一致して対応する必要があり、これらの課題への取り組みは「積極的平和主義」の取り組みの重要な一部分となっている。(外交青書 2017)

solve：解決する；解く
alone：単独で；孤立して
critical：重要な；批判的な；危機的な

政府としては止める権利も義務もないのではないか。むしろ、求められていない邦人保護活動は、彼らの理想に対する侮辱であり、税金の無駄遣いではないか。(外交青書 2004, トピック)

instead：その代わりに
unwanted：求められない；不必要な
ideal：理想；極致
waste：無駄；浪費する

55

integrated
[íntəgrèitid]
□ 175

統合した；一体の；人種差別をしない

☞ integrate 統合する；調和させる

☞ integration 統合；融合

At the fourth meeting of the SDGs Promotion Headquarters held in December 2017, the SDGs Action Plan 2018 was decided. This Action Plan incorporated the key initiatives that the Government of Japan aims to advance in an **integrated** manner. (Diplomatic Bluebook 2018)

intelligence
[intélədʒəns]
□ 176

諜報（機関）；機密情報；インテリジェンス

☞ counter intelligence 防諜；対敵情報活動

The organizations responsible for Japan's **intelligence** include the Cabinet Intelligence and Research Office, the National Police Agency Security Bureau (Public Security Police), and the Public Security Intelligence Agency.

intensify
[inténsəfài]
□ 177

強める；強化する；激しくする

☞ intensive 集中的な；激しい；強い

The Democratic Party has also set its sights on the 2020 presidential election, and it is predicted that the Democrats will **intensify** their criticism of the Trump administration by advancing investigations, including those on "Russia-gate," by utilizing their Congressional authority. It has been pointed out that the progress of the investigation concerning "Russia-gate" could greatly affect President Trump's political base. (Diplomatic Bluebook 2019)

2017年12月の第4回 SDGs 推進本部会合では、「SDGs アクションプラン 2018」を発表し、日本政府が一体となって進める主要な取り組みを盛り込んだ。(外交青書 2018)

SDGs : "Sustainable Development Goals" の略で「持続可能な開発目標」
promotion : 推進 ; 促進 ; 昇進
advance : 前進させる ; 進展させる

日本のインテリジェンスを担う組織としては、内閣官房内閣情報調査室、警察庁警備局(公安警察)、公安調査庁などがある。

the Cabinet Intelligence and Research Office : 内閣官房内閣情報調査室
the National Police Agency : 警察庁
Public Security Intelligence Agency : 公安調査庁

民主党は、2020年の大統領選挙も視野に入れ、議会の権限を活用して「ロシア疑惑」等に関する調査を進め、トランプ政権への批判を強めると予測されている。また、「ロシア疑惑」をめぐる捜査の進展次第では、トランプ大統領の政権基盤に大きな影響が及ぶ可能性があるとの指摘もある。(外交青書 2019)

Democratic Party : (米国) 民主党 (democratic : 民主的な ; 民主制の ; 民主主義の)
sight : 視野 ; 視力
criticism : 批判 ; 非難
investigation : 調査 ; 捜査
utilize : 利用する ; 活用する
point out : 指摘する ; 注目させる

intercession

[ìntərséʃən]

□ 178

仲裁；斡旋；調停

☞ intercede 仲裁する；とりなす

The international community expects Country A to continue its efforts as a future ideal diplomatic **intercession** state.

interdependent

[ìntərdipéndənt]

□ 179

相互依存の；相互依存的な；互いに頼り合う

☞ interdependence 相互依存；持ちつ持たれつの関係

As countries have become more **interdependent** on the economic front, the importance of the military aspect of security appears to have diminished.

interfere

[ìntərfíər]

□ 180

妨げる；干渉する；邪魔をする

☞ interference 干渉；妨害；邪魔

Russia, and the European countries and the U.S. remained in confrontation because of the Ukrainian situation as well as suspicions that Russia **interfered** with the U.S. election. (Diplomatic Bluebook 2018)

intervention

[ìntərvénʃən]

□ 181

干渉；介入；仲裁

☞ intervene 干渉する；介在する；調停する

Simultaneously, examples of state actors themselves utilizing military means by methods that are difficult to identify definitely as “armed attack” and cases involving **intervention** in democracy from foreign countries through the manipulation of information and other methods are also being pointed out. (Diplomatic Bluebook 2018)

A 国には今後も理想的な外交的仲裁国として、その努力を続けることが国際社会から期待されている。

スペル違いの intersession は「学期（session）と学期の間；学期間休暇」である。
expect：期待する

経済面での各国の相互依存関係が深まったことで、安全保障における軍事面での重要性は減少したかにみえる。

economic front：経済面；経済前線
aspect：側面；向き；相
diminish：少なくする；減少させる

ロシアと欧米諸国との間では、ウクライナ情勢、ロシアによる選挙介入疑惑等をめぐり、対立関係が続いた。（外交青書 2018）

because of X：X のために；せいで
Ukrainian：ウクライナの；ウクライナ人（語）の
suspicion：疑い；疑念

同時に、国家主体自身が、武力攻撃と明確には認定し難い形で軍事手段を用いる事例や、情報操作等を通じた外国からの民主主義への介入などの事例も指摘されている。（外交青書 2018）

simultaneously：同時に（e.g. simultaneous interpretation：同時通訳）
definitely：確かに；厳密に；はっきりと
involve：関与する；巻き込む：関わる

57

intimidation

[intìmədéiʃən]

□ 182

威嚇；脅し；脅迫（行為）

☞ intimidate 脅す；威嚇する；怖がらせる

Hard power against soft power is accompanied by physical pressure and coercion, including **intimidation** and economic sanctions, underpinned by military force.

intricate

[íntrikət]

□ 183

複雑な；入り組んだ；込み入った

☞ extricate 解放する；自由にする；脱出させる

While globalization is accelerating, countries struggle to find ways to maximize their national interests in an **intricate** environment.

intrigue

[intríːg]

□ 184

陰謀（を企てる）；術策をめぐらす；好奇心をそそる

☞ intriguer 陰謀者；策士

Regarding the recent killing of a diplomat, the government of Country A pointed out the possibility of political **intrigue** in Country B. However, Country B brushed it off as a “false accusation.”

intrude

[intrúːd]

□ 185

侵入する；押し入る；立ち入る

☞ intruder 侵入者；乱入者；邪魔者

In the East China Sea, Chinese Government-owned vessels continue to **intrude** into Japanese territorial waters around the Senkaku Islands. Also, the Chinese military has been rapidly expanding and increasing its activities in quality and quantity in the area. (Diplomatic Bluebook 2018)

ソフトパワーに対するハードパワーには、軍事力を背景とした威嚇や経済制裁などの物理的な圧力や強制力が伴う。

accompany : 伴う ; 同行する
physical : 物理的な
coercion : 強制 (力); 抑圧

世界のグローバル化が加速する一方で、各国は複雑に入り組んだ情勢の中、国益を最大化させる方略に苦慮している。

accelerate : 加速する ; 前倒しする
maximize : 最大化する ; 極大化する
environment : 環境 ; 周囲 (の状況); 情勢

先般の外交官殺害の件について、A 国政府は B 国の政治的陰謀の可能性を指摘したが、B 国は「誤った非難」だと一蹴した。

killing : 殺害 ; 致死の
possibility : 可能性
brush off : はねつける ; 無視する ; 一蹴する
false : 間違った ; 誤った ; 偽りの

東シナ海では、尖閣諸島周辺海域における中国公船による領海侵入が継続しており、また、中国軍もその海空域での活動を質・量とも急速に拡大・活発化させている。(外交青書 2018)

-owned : 所有されている
territorial waters : 領海
expand : 拡大する ; 拡張する ; 膨張させる
quality and quantity : 質と量

investor

[invéstər]

□ 186

投資家；出資者；資本主

☞ invest 投資する；出資する

On the economic front, close cooperation continues, as shown by the fact that Japan is the largest **investor** for Malaysia and the number of Japanese-affiliated companies operating in Malaysia amounts to as many as 1,400. (Diplomatic Bluebook 2017)

ironically

[airɔ́nikəli]

□ 187

皮肉なことに；皮肉にも；反語的に

☞ irony 皮肉；アイロニー

Ironically, the more domestic support Country A gains from populism, the more its international standing will continue to decline.

isolate

[áisəlèit]

□ 188

孤立させる；分離する；隔離する

☞ isolated 孤立した；隔絶された

☞ isolation 孤立；分離；隔絶

North Korea's move to engage in direct dialog with the U.S. could change the nature of negotiations and **isolate** Japan diplomatically.

justify

[dʒʌ́stəfài]

□ 189

正当化する；弁明する；正当だと理由づける

☞ justification 正当化；弁明

North Korea sees the aggressive stance of the U.S. as a threat. Thus, North Korea is trying to **justify** its nuclear program as a self-defense measure.

経済面では、日本はマレーシアに対する最大の投資国であるほか、マレーシアへの進出日系企業数は1,400社にも上るなど、引き続き緊密な協力関係にある。（外交青書 2017）

和文中には「投資国」と「国」の表記があるが、この場合投資する主体が国であるため、「投資者」ではなく「投資国」となっている。

as many as X : X もの数の ; X と同じ数だけ多くの

皮肉なことだが、A 国がポピュリズムで国内の支持を得れば得るほど、国際的な地位は低下し続けるであろう。

populism : ポピュリズム ; 大衆迎合主義
decline : 減少する ; 辞退する ; 拒否する

米国との直接対話に北朝鮮が動くことによって交渉のあり方が変わり、その結果日本は外交的に孤立する可能性がある。

direct dialog : 直接対話
nature : 本質 ; 特質 ; 性質 ; 自然
diplomatically : 外交的に

北朝鮮は米国の強硬姿勢を脅威とみなし、自衛措置として自国の核開発を正当化しようとしている。

aggressive : 攻撃的な
thus : それゆえに ; だから ; 結果として
try to X : X しようとする
self-defense : 自衛（の）; 自己防衛（の）

59

lame duck

[léim dʌ́k]

□ **190**

死に体；レームダック；役立たずな人

☞ lame 正常に歩けない；歩行が困難な

After the mid-term elections, so-called a **lame-duck** session, attended by the members of the 113th Congress, was held from November 12 until the end of the second session of the 113th Congress. Attention was paid to how the Obama Administration and the Republican Party would cooperate with each other during the session as the results of the midterm elections. (Diplomatic Bluebook 2015)

launch

[lɔ́ːntʃ]

□ **191**

着手する；発射する；進水させる

☞ launch a missile ミサイルを発射する

Launched in 2005, the EAS is a premium forum of the region, which aims to facilitate candid dialogue among leaders on issues of importance to the region and the international community, and to promote leaders-led cooperation in politics, security and economy. (Diplomatic Bluebook 2019)

legitimacy

[lidʒítəməsi]

□ **192**

正統（性）；合法性；嫡出

☞ legitimate 合法の；合法的な

☞ legitimately 合法的に

☞ illegitimate 違法の；非合法の

The **legitimacy** of the reelected president of Country A is strongly questioned by the G7 and many Latin American countries.

中間選挙後の11月12日から第113議会第2会期末までの間、改選前の議員構成で開催されるいわゆる「レームダック・セッション」が開かれ、選挙結果を受けたオバマ政権と共和党の協力姿勢の有り様が注目された。（外交青書 2015）

mid-term election：中間選挙
so-called：いわゆる
Republican Party：共和党

EASは、地域及び国際社会の重要な問題について首脳間で率直に対話を行うとともに、首脳主導で政治・安全保障・経済上の具体的協力を進展させることを目的として、2005年に発足した地域のプレミア（主要な）・フォーラムである。（外交青書 2019）

premium：高品質の；プレミア付きの；主要な
candid：率直な；偏見のない
promote：進展させる；促進させる；昇進させる
politics：政治

A国大統領の再選について、G7や中南米の多くの国がその正統性に強い疑問を持っている。

reelect：再選する
question：問題として取り上げる；疑問を持つ；質問
G7：Group of Seven (Countries)

Part I

Part II

Part III

Part IV

lift

[líft]

☐ 193

解禁する（禁止を解く）；
持ち上げる；向上させる

☞ lift off 離昇する；打ち上がる

In terms of relations with the U.S., the relationship is developing, as U.S. President Obama visited Viet Nam in May and announced the full **lifting** of the arms embargo on Viet Nam, etc. (Diplomatic Bluebook 2017)

limitation

[lìmətéiʃən]

☐ 194

限界；制限；制約

☞ limit 制限する；限る

With regard to the global warming issue, the Third Session of the Conference of the Parties to the United Nations Framework Convention on Climate Change (COP3) was held in Kyoto in December 1997, adopting the Kyoto Protocol, which provides for greenhouse gas reduction and **limitation** obligations on developed countries and countries with economies in transition. (Diplomatic Bluebook 2000)

loyalty

[lɔ́iəlti]

☐ 195

忠実；忠誠（心）；誠実

☞ loyal 忠実な；誠実な

"These, then, are the qualities of my ideal diplomatist. Truth, accuracy, calm, patience, good temper, modesty and **loyalty**. They are also the qualities of an ideal diplomacy." (Harold Nicolson)

米国との関係では、5月にオバマ米国大統領がベトナムを訪問し、ベトナムへの武器禁輸の完全解除を表明するなど、米・ベトナム関係は発展傾向にある。(外交青書 2017)

in terms of X : X に関して
relation : 関係
arms embargo : 武器禁輸 ; 武器輸出禁止

地球温暖化問題に関しては、97年12月の京都における気候変動枠組条約第3回締約国会議(COP3)で、具体的な数値目標を挙げ温室効果ガスの削減を先進国などに対し義務づける「京都議定書」が採択された。(外交青書 2000)

和文中には直接的に limitation の訳は出ていないが、limitation obligations で「(制限 = limitation を) 義務付ける = obligation (s)」と解釈できる。

economies in transition : 経済移行国

「というわけで、以下のものが私の理想とする外交官の資質である。すなわち、誠実、正確、平静、忍耐、よい機嫌、謙虚及び忠誠。そして、それらはまた理想的外交の資質でもある。」(ハロルド・ニコルソン、斎藤眞・深谷満雄訳)

diplomatist : diplomat (外交官) と同義
truth : 真実
accuracy : 正確さ
patience : 我慢強さ
modesty : 謙虚 ; 慎み深さ

manifest

[mǽnəfèst]

□ 196

明白な；はっきり表れた；表明する

☞ manifestation 示威運動；示威行動

For countries all over the world, building up new markets to ensure that the effects of the outstanding technological advances achieved in recent years become fully **manifest** has now become an urgent priority. (Diplomatic Bluebook 2001)

marginal

[mɑ́ːrdʒinl]

□ 197

周辺的な；取るに足りない；ぎりぎりの

☞ peripheral 周囲の；周辺的な；末梢の

The additional sanctions imposed by Japan have a substantial **marginal** effect.

maritime

[mǽrətàim]

□ 198

海の；海事の；船員特有の

☞ maritime insurance 海上保険

The Exclusive Economic Zone (EEZ) and the continental shelf in the East China Sea have not yet been delimited. Japan takes a position that **maritime** delimitation should be conducted based on the geographical equidistance line between Japan and China. (Diplomatic Bluebook 2017)

martial law

[mɑ́ːrʃəl lɔ́ː]

□ 199

戒厳令

☞ martial 軍の；戦争の

Amid a violent confrontation between the Country A’s government and the rebels, the president suddenly imposed a 60-day **martial law** and banned the people from going out at night.

近年の目覚ましい技術進歩の便益が十分な効果を発揮する新しい市場を作り上げることは、各国にとって緊急の課題となっている。(外交青書 2001)

和文中の「効果を発揮する」という箇所が "manifest" に相当するが、解釈としては「十分に(= fully)明らかとなる〔ような〕(= manifest)」となる。

build up : 築き上げる ; 確立する
outstanding : 極めて優れた ; 目立った

日本が独自に行った追加制裁措置は、実質的にはほとんど効果が見込めない。

"have a marginal effect" で「ほとんど効果がない」という意味になる。
additional : 追加の ; 付加的な

東シナ海における日中間の排他的経済水域(EEZ)及び大陸棚の境界は未画定であり、日本は日中中間線を基に境界画定を行うべきであるとの立場である。(外交青書 2017)

和文中には直接的に maritime の訳語が出ていない。この場合 "maritime delimitation(海の限界の決定)" で「(EEZ や大陸棚の)海洋境界の画定」となり、前文で既に海洋に関するトピックが出ているため、「海の(= maritime)」という表現が省略されている。

A 国政府と反政府組織が激しく対立する中、大統領は突如 60日間の戒厳令を出し、夜間の外出も禁止した。

violent : 激しい ; 暴力的な (violence : 暴力 ; 猛威 ; 激しさ)
go out : 外出する ; 公にされる ; 消える

mediation

[mìːdiéiʃən]

□ 200

調停；仲裁；媒介

☞ mediate 仲裁する；調停する

The U.S. did not have a specific position on the content of the proposed **mediation** filed unilaterally by Country A. According to the U.S., Country A should reopen its dialog with Country B and resolve the issue through their diplomatic efforts.

memorandum

[mèmərǽndəm]

□ 201

覚書；備忘録；メモ

☞ MOU (=memorandum of understanding) 覚書；基本合意書

During this visit, a wide-ranging exchange of views regarding bilateral relations, the regional affairs, etc., was held, and in addition, the **Memorandum** of Intent on deepening the cooperation in agriculture and its related areas was signed. (Diplomatic Bluebook 2017)

mercy

[məːrsi]

□ 202

慈悲；容赦；情け

☞ at the mercy of X Xのなすがままに；に翻弄されて

71 years ago, in Hiroshima and in Nagasaki respectively, a number of innocent citizens were lost to a single atomic bomb without any **mercy**. (Diplomatic Bluebook 2017, References)

military

[mílitèri | -təri]

□ 203

軍事的な；軍（人）の；軍隊

☞ military government 軍事政権；軍政

☞ demilitarize 非武装化する；武装解除された

The question is whether or not the U.S. will move its **military** on behalf of Japan in an emergency situation.

米国は、A 国が一方的に申し立てた仲裁案の内容に特定の立場を持たないとし、A 国が B 国と再び対話を再開し、外交努力によって問題を解決すべきだとした。

mediation には「仲裁」という意味はあるが「仲裁案」のように「案」の意味は厳密にはない。この場合「案」は propose（提案する）から出ていると解釈できる。

同訪問中、二国間関係、地域情勢等につき幅広い意見交換が行われたほか、農業分野の協力に関する覚書が署名された。（外交青書 2017）

deepen：深める
related：関連する；関係する
sign：署名する；記入する；サインする

71年前、広島、そして長崎では、たった一発の原子爆弾によって、何の罪もない、たくさんの市井の人々が、そして子供達が、無残にも犠牲となりました。（外交青書 2017, 資料）

この場合、「without any mercy（いかなる慈悲もなしに）」の意味で「無残にも」という和文が相当する。

innocent：純真な；無罪の；無害の

論点は、有事の際、米国が日本のために本当に自国の軍隊を動かすかどうかという点に尽きる。

whether X：X かどうか；いずれにせよ
emergency situation：緊急事態；有事（emergency：緊急；非常；突発）

mission

[míʃən]

□ 204

任務；派遣団；布教

☞ missionary 布教の；伝道の

As the only country to have ever suffered atomic bombings in war, Japan has a **mission** to lead the international community's efforts concerning nuclear disarmament and non-proliferation, with the aim of realizing a world free of nuclear weapons. (Diplomatic Bluebook 2019)

mitigate

[mítəgèit]

□ 205

軽減する；緩和する；鎮静する

☞ mitigation 緩和；軽減

In such circumstances, Japan should proactively work to **mitigate** military tensions in the Middle East region.

monarchy

[mάnərki | mɔ́n-]

□ 206

君主制；君主国；王政

☞ constitutional monarchy
立憲君主制；立憲君主国

Bhutan peacefully shifted from a monarchy to a constitutional **monarchy** in 2008. Currently, efforts are being made to establish a democracy under the Tobgay administration. (Diplomatic Bluebook 2018)

morality

[mərǽləti]

□ 207

道徳（性）；倫理；教訓

☞ moral 道徳上の；良心の

"We believe that no nation is responsible to itself alone, but that laws of political **morality** are universal; and that obedience to such laws is incumbent upon all nations who would sustain their own sovereignty and justify their sovereign relationship with other nations." (Diplomatic Bluebook 1991, the Preamble of the Constitution)

日本は、唯一の戦争被爆国として、核兵器のない世界を目指し、国際社会の核軍縮・不拡散に関する取り組みを主導していく使命を有している。（外交青書2019）

atomic bombing：原爆投下（atomic：原子力の；原子の）
non-proliferation：不拡散；拡散防止の

このような状況を踏まえ、日本は中東地域の軍事的緊張緩和のために積極的に努力するべきである。

military tension：軍事的緊張（tension：緊張；緊張状態）
region：地域；地方；領域

ブータンは2008年に王制から立憲君主制に平和裏に移行し、現在はトブゲー政権の下で民主化定着のための取り組みが行われている。（外交青書 2018）

peacefully：平和（的）に；平和裏に（peaceful：平和な；平和的な）
constitutional：憲法（上）の；合憲の；構成上の

「われらは、いづれの国家も、自国のことのみに専念して他国を無視してはならないのであって、政治道徳の法則は、普遍的なものであり、この法則に従うことは、自国の主権を維持し、他国と対等関係に立とうとする各国の責務であると信ずる」（外交青書 1991, 憲法前文）

universal：普遍的な
political morality：政治道徳
incumbent：行う義務のある；現職の

64

mounting

[máuntiŋ]

□ 208

高まる；台；据えつけ

☞ mount 登る；据えつける；開始する

On the other hand, **mounting** protectionist and inward-looking trends in the U.S. and major countries in Europe run counter to globalization, and these tendencies remain pronounced. (Diplomatic Bluebook 2018)

multilateral

[mʌ̀ltilǽtərəl]

□ 209

多国間（参加）の；多面的な；多角的な

☞ multilaterally 多国間で；多面的に

The EU and European countries share with Japan fundamental values and principles such as freedom, democracy, rule of law, and human rights, and continue to be proponents of free trade and **multilateral**ism. (Diplomatic Bluebook 2019)

multinational

[mʌ̀ltinǽʃənəl]

□ 210

多国籍の；多国間の；多国籍企業

☞ multinational force 多国籍軍

In this field, Japan proactively participates in bilateral dialogues and a number of **multinational** fora such as the UN and makes contributions including constructive dialogue with the UN human rights mechanisms in order to improve the human rights situation globally. (Diplomatic Bluebook 2017)

mutual

[mjúːtʃuəl]

□ 211

相互の；共通の；相互的な

☞ mutuality 相互関係；相互依存

☞ mutually お互いに；相互に

Cooperative relations between Japan and member states of the Association of Southeast Asian Nations (ASEAN) are being further enhanced in broad fields through **mutual** VIP visits including by leaders and summit meetings between Japan and the ASEAN. (Diplomatic Bluebook 2016)

一方、グローバル化に逆行する動きとして、欧米の主要国内で高まった保護主義や内向きの傾向があり、この動きは引き続き顕著である。（外交青書 2018）

protectionist：保護主義論者（protection：保護）
run counter to X：X に逆行する；反対の行動を取る
pronounced：目立った；顕著な

EU 及び欧州各国は、自由、民主主義、法の支配及び人権等の基本的価値や原則を日本と共有しており、自由貿易や多国間主義の推進者であり続けている。（外交青書 2019）

share：共有する；共同使用する
rule of law：法の支配；法治
free trade：自由貿易；自由貿易の

日本はこの分野において、世界の人権状況の改善に向けた取り組み、二国間での対話や国連など多数国間のフォーラムへの積極的な参加、国連人権メカニズムとの建設的な対話等の取り組みを行っている。（外交青書 2017）

participate：参加する
a number of：多数の；多くの
fora：forum（フォーラム；公開討論会）の複数形

東南アジア諸国連合（ASEAN）各国とは、首脳レベルを含めた要人往来や日・ASEAN 首脳会議等を通じて、広範な分野で協力関係が一層強化されている。（外交青書 2016）

和文中の「要人往来」の解釈としては、「相互〔日本と ASEAN〕の（mutual）」「要人（VIP）の」「行き来（訪問：visits）」となろう。mutual そのものには「往来」という意味はない。

nation-state

[nèiʃən-stéit]

□ 212

国民国家；民族国家

☞ national state 国民国家

The occasion of its 20th session in 2018 recorded participation from 65 universities in 19 countries. Here, university students from 15 countries (Japan, Bangladesh, China, India, Indonesia, the ROK, Malaysia, Mongolia, Nepal, Pakistan, the Philippines, Russia, Singapore, Thailand, and Viet Nam) took part in oral proceedings round held in Tokyo. They competed in written and oral pleadings in English on the themes of fictional international disputes on exercising the right of self-defense versus non-**nation-state** actors and the law of the sea. (Diplomatic Bluebook 2019)

national interest

[nǽʃənl íntərəst]

□ 213

国益；国の利益

☞ interest 利益；関心；興味を持たせる

Japan has continued to proactively and strategically utilize ODA in ways that contribute both to the development of Japanese companies' businesses overseas and to the recipient countries' economic and social development, in order to contribute to the peace, stability and prosperity of the international community and to secure Japan's **national interests**. (Diplomatic Bluebook 2019)

national security

[nǽʃənl sikjúərəti]

□ 214

国家安全保障；国家の安全

☞ National Security Council (NSC) 国家安全保障会議

In recent years, there are an increasing number of cases where interests of countries clash with each other from the perspective of securing resources and **national security**. (Diplomatic Bluebook 2016)

20回目となった2018年には、非国家主体に対する自衛権の行使及び海洋法に関する架空の国家間紛争を題材に、19カ国65校から参加登録があり、15カ国（日本、バングラデシュ、中国、インド、インドネシア、韓国、マレーシア、モンゴル、ネパール、パキスタン、フィリピン、ロシア、シンガポール、タイ及びベトナム）の大学生が東京で開催された口頭弁論（本戦）に参加し、英語による書面陳述・弁論能力等を競った。（外交青書 2019）

fictional：架空の；フィクションの
oral proceeding：口頭弁論；口頭審理
exercise：行使する；用いる；鍛える
law of the sea：海洋法

国際社会の平和、安定及び繁栄並びにそれを通じた日本の国益確保に取り組むべく、日本企業の海外展開と相手国の経済社会開発の双方に資する形で、引き続き積極的かつ戦略的なODAの活用に努めている。（外交青書 2019）

strategically：戦略的に
contribute：貢献する；寄与する
recipient：受益者；受容者

近年、資源の確保や安全保障の観点から各国の利害が衝突する事例が増えている。（外交青書 2016）

和文中の「安全保障」には「国の（= national）安全保障（= security）」という、「国の（国家の）」という意味を含んでいると考えられる。

naval

[néivəl]

□ 215

海軍の；海軍に属する；軍艦の

☞ navy 海軍；艦隊

The deployed destroyers protected 147 merchant ships on 78 escort operations between January and December 2015, while the P-3C maritime patrol aircrafts carried out 227 mission flights, in which they conducted surveillance, information gathering and provided information to **naval** vessels of other countries. (Diplomatic Bluebook 2016) ▶

negotiation

[nigòuʃiéiʃən]

□ 216

交渉；折衝；克服

☞ negotiate 交渉する；協議する

A parliamentary election was held in New Zealand in September, and the National Party failed to attain the majority of seats on its own, resulting in **negotiations** for the forming of coalitions between different parties. This led to the forming of a coalition between the New Zealand Labour Party and New Zealand First Party, which was inaugurated in October. It was the first time in nine years, since 2008, for a change in Government. (Diplomatic Bluebook 2018) ▶

non(-) governmental

[nάn gʌvərnméntl]

□ 217

非政府（の）；民間の；政府と無関係の

☞ non-governmental organization (NGO) 非政府組織

In the past, the primary mission of Peacekeeping Operations (PKOs) was to monitor the cease-fire. However, in recent years, the military and private sectors have been working together to carry out activities that were traditionally led by the **non-governmental** organizations. These activities include disarmament and humanitarian and reconstruction assistance. ▶

北朝鮮派遣された護衛艦は、2015年1月から12月まで78回の護衛活動で147隻の商船を護衛し、P-3C哨戒機は、227回の任務飛行を行い、警戒監視や情報収集、他国艦艇への情報提供を行った。（外交青書 2016）

「艦艇」の解釈として、艦艇が海軍のものであることは明白であるため、あえて和文では「海軍の（= naval）」とは訳出していないと考えられる。この場合、naval vessel (s) で「艦艇」となる。

ニュージーランドでは、9月、議会選挙が実施され、与党国民党の獲得議席が単独過半数に達せず、各党間で連立交渉が行われた結果、10月に労働党・NZファースト党連立政権が発足し、2008年以来9年ぶりに政権が交代した。（外交青書 2018）

parliamentary：議会の（parliament：議会；国会）
attain：達成する；獲得する
coalition：連立；連合

これまでのPKOは停戦監視などが主な任務であったが、近年では武装解除や人道復興支援など、従来非政府組織が主導した活動を、軍民が連携して実施している。

primary：最上位の；初等の；一次の
private sector：民間部門
traditionally：伝統的に

nullify

[nʌ́ləfài]

□ 218

無効にする；無価値にする；取り消す

☞ nullification 無効化；取り消し

Country A's immigration authorities stressed that diplomatic privileges are **nullified** when a diplomat applies for asylum in Country B.

obedience

[oubíːdiəns | əb-]

□ 219

服従；従順；忠実

☞ obey 従う；服従する

Furthermore, ISIL's growing power has led to a large-scale outflow of refugees and internally displaced persons. In the areas under its control, humanitarian crises have arisen, including the enforcement of **obedience** upon the people by severe means. (Diplomatic Bluebook 2015)

obligation

[ɑ̀bləgéiʃən | ɔ̀b-]

□ 220

義務（感）；義理；債務

☞ oblige 強いる：余儀なくさせる

Along with nuclear disarmament and non-proliferation, the peaceful uses of nuclear energy are considered to be one of the three pillars of the NPT. According to the Treaty, it is the "inalienable right" for any country that meets its **obligations** to nuclear disarmament and non-proliferation to develop nuclear research, production and use for peaceful purposes. (Diplomatic Bluebook 2017)

occasion

[əkéiʒən]

□ 221

機会；場合；行事

☞ occasionally 時々；時折

On this **occasion**, Japan announced it would extend 200 million US dollars to support quality education for girls, adolescent girls and women in developing countries and human resources development. (Diplomatic Bluebook 2019)

A国の出入国管理局は、外交官がB国に亡命を申請した場合、外交特権は無効化されることを強調した。

immigration authorities:出入国管理局;入国監査官(immigration:移住;入国管理)
diplomatic privilege：外交特権；外交官特権

さらに、その勢力拡大により大規模な難民、国内避難民が発生し、加えて支配地域においては、苛烈な手段を用いて住民に服従を強制するなど、人道危機が発生している。(外交青書 2015)

outflow：流出
internally displaced：国内避難した(国内で住む場所を追われた)
arisen：arise(起こる；生じる)の過去分詞形

原子力の平和的利用は、核軍縮・不拡散と並んでNPTの三本柱の1つとされており、核軍縮・不拡散を進める国が平和的目的のために原子力の研究、生産及び利用を発展させることは「奪い得ない権利」であるとされている。(外交青書 2017)

和文中の「進める」は厳密なobligationの対訳ではない。“any country that meets its obligations”で「その義務を満たすいかなる国にとっても」と解釈できる。

日本はこの機会に、途上国の女児・思春期の少女・女性に対する質の高い教育、人材育成支援のために2億ドルの支援を発表した。(外交青書 2019)

extend：延ばす；拡張する；延長する
adolescent：思春期の
human resources(HR)：人的資源；人材

occupy

[ɑ́kjupài | ɔ́k-]

□ 222

占領する；占有する；占める

☞ occupation 占領；占有；職業

Anti-whaling countries **occupy** the majority at the IWC, and while the international situation regarding whaling still remains difficult, Japan is making persistent efforts to deepen understanding among the international community based on scientific evidence and international law. (Diplomatic Bluebook 2019)

offensive

[əfénsiv]

□ 223

攻撃態勢；攻撃的な；攻撃側の

☞ defensive 防御の；守勢の

In response to the use of chemical weapons in April amidst the strengthening **offensive** by the Syrian government in the East Ghouta district, the U.S., the UK, and France carried out a missile attack on April 14. (Diplomatic Bluebook 2019)

official

[əfíʃəl]

□ 224

当局者；公式の；公務員

☞ officially 公式に；正式に；当局の発表では

When interviewed by the A, a senior U.S. government **official** indicated that there is “almost no doubt that the military regime used the germ weapon on its part.”

on the verge of X

[ən ðə vəːrdʒ əv]

□ 225

今にもXしようとして；Xの間際に

☞ verge 瀬戸際；ふち

In other words, Country B’s aim was to manipulate public opinion to give the impression that Country A was **on the verge of** commencing nuclear uranium enrichment. Such a move was likewise made to incite a military attack on the country.

IWCでは反捕鯨国が締約国の過半数を占めており、捕鯨をめぐる国際的な状況は依然厳しいが、日本は、科学的根拠及び国際法に基づき、国際社会の理解が深められるよう粘り強く取り組んできた。(外交青書 2019)

anti-whaling : 反捕鯨の ; 捕鯨に反対の
persistent : 粘り強い ; 持続的な
evidence : 証拠 ; 形跡

なお、4月に東グータ地区に対するシリア政府の攻勢が強化される中で化学兵器が使用された事案を受け、4月14日に米国・英国・フランスによるミサイル攻撃が行われた。(外交青書 2019)

in response to X : X に応えて ; 応じて
district : 地区 ; 地域 ; 地方
attack : 攻撃

A の取材に対し、米国政府高官は「細菌兵器が軍事政権側によって使用されたことはほぼ疑いがない」との見方を示している。

この場合 senior official で「高官（地位の高い官職にある人）」という意味となっている。
germ weapon : 細菌兵器 (germ : 細菌)

つまり今にも A 国が核ウラン濃縮を始めるかのような印象を与え、B 国に対する軍事攻撃を煽る世論操作が B 国の狙いであった。

in other words : つまり ; 言い換えれば
impression : 印象
commence : 開始する ; 始める
uranium enrichment : ウラン濃縮 (enrichment : 濃縮 ; 豊かにすること ; 強化すること)

69

operation

[àpəréiʃən]

☐ 226

軍事行動（作戦）；運転；作業

☞ operational 軍事行動の；操作の

The U.S. military, which led this military **operation**, deployed a variety of high-technology weapons to show the B regime the overwhelming difference in their military strengths.

opponent

[əpóunənt]

☐ 227

敵対者；競争相手；敵対する

☞ oppose 反対する；敵対する

In the United States, President Reagan defeated his Democratic **opponent**, Walter Mondale, by a decisive margin to win reelection in the November 6 Presidential election. (Diplomatic Bluebook 1985)

opposition

[àpəzíʃən | ɔ̀p-]

☐ 228

反対；対立；野党

☞ opposed 反対した；対立した

Although it was made clear that President Trump's announcement did not forejudge the final status of Jerusalem, many Arabic/Islamic countries expressed their **opposition** to the announcement as they saw it as being a violation of the established principles of the international community regarding its status. (Diplomatic Bluebook 2018)

outrageous

[autréidʒəs]

☐ 229

とんでもない；法外な；奇抜な

☞ outrage 激怒；激しい怒り

Country A's Secretary B issued the following statement: "Such an act of terrorism is an **outrageous** and inexcusable offense that we are extremely indignant about. We condemn it unreservedly."

今回の軍事作戦を指揮した米軍は各種ハイテク兵器を投入し、B 政権に圧倒的な軍事力の差を見せつけた。

high-technology：ハイテク（high-tech）の；先端技術の
overwhelming：圧倒する；圧倒的な

米国では、11月6日大統領選挙で、レーガン大統領が民主党のモンデール候補を大差で破り、再選を果たした。（外交青書 1985）

「候補」は文脈上の訳。「対立する候補者」という意味で "opponent" と表現されている。

defeat：打ち負かす；勝つ；破る
decisive：決定的な（decide：決定する）
reelection：再選

トランプ米国大統領の声明は、エルサレムの最終的地位を予断するものではないことを明確にするものであったが、エルサレムの地位に関する国際社会のこれまでの原則に反するものと受け止められたため、アラブ・イスラム諸国を始めとする多くの国が、この発表に異を唱えた。（外交青書 2018）

和文中の「異」の解釈は、"expressed their opposition" で「反対の意思を表明した」＝「異を唱えた」となる。

forejudge：予断する

A 国の B 長官は次のように声明を出した。「このようなテロ行為は言語道断の許しがたい暴挙であり、強い憤りを覚える。断固として非難する。」

outrageous の語源は「out-（「外に」を意味する接頭辞）＋ rage（怒り）＋ -ous（形容詞を作る接尾辞）」ではなく、「outra-/ultra-（「超えて / 越えて」を意味する接頭辞）＋ age」で、「常軌を逸して;一線を越えて」が原義となる。ただし一見すると out ＋ rage と混同されやすいため、現在では「怒り」をニュアンスとする意味も含まれるようになっている。

inexcusable：許せない；弁解の余地のない(in-：否定の接頭辞、excusable：許される；申し訳の立つ）
indignant：怒った；憤慨した

override

[òuvərráid]

□ 230

優先する；無効にする；くつがえす

☞ overridden override の過去分詞形

Tax treaties principally **override** domestic law. Article 98, paragraph 2 of the Japanese Constitution provides basis for the previous statement.

overseas

[òuvərsíːz]

□ 231

海外の（で）；海外へ；外国へ

☞ overseas affiliated firm 現地法人；現地関連会社

In this way, the foundation of incorporating the vitality of **overseas** markets leading to the growth of the Japanese economy has been being steadily built. (Diplomatic Bluebook 2016)

partisan

[pάːrtizən | pὰːtizǽn]

□ 232

ゲリラ（の）；パルチザン（の）；党派心の強い

☞ guerrilla ゲリラ；ゲリラ兵

Partisans, in particular, are said to use all types of weapons, which not only prolongs and intensifies conflicts but also hinders humanitarian aid and reconstruction and development activities after the end of the conflict. This effect shall in turn encourage the recurrence of conflicts.

peninsula

[pənínsjulə]

□ 233

半島

☞ peninsular 半島（状）の

At the first ever U.S.-North Korea Summit on June 12, a joint statement of the U.S. and North Korean leaders was issued, in which Chairman Kim directly promised President Trump the “complete denuclearization” of the Korean **Peninsula** in a written document with his signature. (Diplomatic Bluebook 2019)

租税条約は基本的に国内法に優先して適用される。その根拠は日本国憲法第98条第2項に見出せる。

principally：主に；主として；第一に（principal：主な；主要な；校長）
domestic law：国内法

こうして海外市場の活力を取り込み、日本経済の成長につなげる基盤が着実に構築されている。（外交青書2016）

vitality：活力；持続力
market：市場；需要
built：build（築く；建設する）の過去形・過去分詞形

小型武器、特にパルチザン等はあらゆるタイプのものを使用していると言われているが、紛争を長期化、激化するだけではなく、紛争終了後、人道援助や復興開発活動を阻害し、紛争の再発等を助長する原因となっている。

hinder：妨げる；妨害する
in turn：今度は；順番に
recurrence：再発；再帰（recur：再発する）

6月12日の史上初となる米朝首脳会談では、米朝首脳共同声明が発出され、金正恩国務委員長がトランプ大統領に対して、朝鮮半島の「完全な非核化」について、自ら署名した文書の形で直接約束した。（外交青書2019）

promise：約束（する）；誓う；誓約
written document：文書
signature：署名；サイン

peremptory

[pərémptəri]

□ 234

絶対の；横柄な；有無を言わせない

☞ peremptory rule
確定的決定；確定命令

Regarding the specifics of a **peremptory** norm, some have argued for prohibitions on aggression, slave trade, piracy, and genocide. However, there is still much debate about the matter, and it has not been clearly determined.

periodically

[pìriádikli | pìriádikəli]

□ 235

定期（的）に；周期的に

☞ period 期間；時代；時期

From this perspective, Japan **periodically** releases a comprehensive report through the IAEA, covering matters including the progress of decommissioning, contaminated water management at the Fukushima Daiichi Nuclear Power Station, results of the monitoring of air dose rate and radioactivity concentration in the sea water, and food safety. Information is also provided through diplomatic missions overseas and briefing sessions held for diplomatic corps. (Diplomatic Bluebook 2017)

permanent

[pə́ːrmənənt]

□ 236

恒久的な；永続する；常置の

☞ perpetual 永遠の；永久の

Immanuel Kant’s theory of **permanent** peace is said to have had a significant ideological influence on establishing the League of Nations, the predecessor of the UN.

強行規範の具体的内容については、侵略、奴隷取引、海賊行為、ジェノサイドの禁止などを定める主張もあるが、未だ議論も多く、はっきりと確定していない。

peremptory norm：強行規範（norm：規範；標準）
aggression：侵略；攻撃
slave：奴隷；奴隷の
piracy：海賊行為；著作権侵害
genocide：集団虐殺

この観点から、日本は、福島第一原発の廃炉作業・汚染水対策の進捗、空間線量や海洋中の放射能濃度のモニタリング結果、食品の安全といった事項について、IAEA を通じて包括的な報告を定期的に公表しているほか、外交団に対する説明会の開催や在外公館を通じた情報提供などを行っている。（外交青書2017）

perspective：見方；考え方；眺望
decommission：廃止する；閉鎖する
contaminated：汚染された（contaminate：汚染する；汚す）
dose rate：線量率
concentration：集中；濃度
briefing：説明（会）；概況；ブリーフィング

イマヌエル・カントの永久平和論は、国際連合の前身である国際連盟の設立に大きな思想的影響を与えたと言われている。

Immanuel Kant：イマヌエル・カント（1724-1804）
League of Nations：国際連盟
predecessor：先行したもの；前任者

permission

[pərmíʃən]

□ 237

許可；認可；承諾

☞ permit 許可する；認める；許可証

In the month of Y, 20XX, the president of Country A held a press conference and declared a state of emergency. Due to this, foreigners, except for diplomats and those with **permission** to stay in the country, are not allowed to enter country A.

perseverance

[pə̀ːrsəvíərəns]

□ 238

忍耐（力）；根気；辛抱強さ

☞ perseverant 忍耐強い；我慢強い

This law set out provisions for an official apology for the internment from the U.S. Government, as well as the payment of 20,000 US dollars in compensation to survivors. The **perseverance** and efforts of Nikkei members of the U.S. Congress including the U.S. Senator, the late Daniel Inouye, and the member of the House of Representatives, Norman Mineta, were instrumental for the enactment of this law. (Diplomatic Bluebook 2019, Special Feature)

persuade

[pərswéid]

□ 239

説得する；説得してさせる；確信させる

☞ persuasion 説得（力）；信条；宗派

Japan prioritizes the early entry into force of the CTBT, as it is a key pillar of the international nuclear disarmament and non-proliferation regimes based upon the NPT. Japan continues its diplomatic efforts to **persuade** those countries that have not yet ratified it to do so. (Diplomatic Bluebook 2017)

20XX年Y月、A国大統領は記者会見を開き、自国への非常事態宣言を発令した。これにより外交官及び滞在許可のある者を除く外国人はA国へ入国できなくなった。

state of emergency：非常事態；緊急事態
except：除いて；以外は
enter：入る；出場する

強制収容に対する米国政府の公式謝罪や、生存する収容経験者への補償金2万ドルの支払い等を定めたこの法律の成立の背景には、故ダニエル・イノウエ上院議員やノーマン・ミネタ下院議員（いずれも肩書は当時）といった日系連邦議員の粘り強い活動がありました。（外交青書2019, 特集）

和文中の「粘り強い（活動）」は“perseverance and efforts”をまとめて訳したものと解釈できる。

official apology：公式謝罪；正式な謝罪（apology：謝罪）
internment：抑留；収容
payment：支払い；納入

日本は、NPTを基礎とする核軍縮・不拡散体制を支える重要な柱であるCTBTの早期発効を重視し、未批准国への働きかけなどの外交努力を継続している。（外交青書2017）

和文中の「働きかけ」は文脈を反映した表現になっており、厳密にはpersuadeに「働きかける」という意味はない。

key pillar：重要な柱（pillar：柱）

plague

[pléig]

□ 240

悩ます；伝染病；ペスト

☞ catch the plague 疫病にかかる

In addition, as harsh economic conditions **plague** the former socialist countries, among others, there is an increasing danger of the proliferation of weapons of mass destruction, such as nuclear weapons accumulated during the Cold War. It is of critical importance to further improve the international non-proliferation regime. (Diplomatic Bluebook 1995)

pledge

[plédʒ]

□ 241

誓う；誓約（する）；公約

☞ (a) verbal pledge 口約束

Regarding Japan's assistance to Ukraine, Japan **pledged** additional aid of approximately 1.5 billion yen in January and in addition dispatched a Japanese expert to Ukraine as an advisor to the finance minister of Ukraine. (Diplomatic Bluebook 2017)

plot

[plɑ́t | plɔ́t]

□ 242

たくらむ；陰謀；構想

☞ plot an assassination 暗殺を謀る

It is very clear that Conuntry A was **plotting** a broad, large-scale attack against American interests.

policy

[pɑ́ləsi | pɔ́l-]

□ 243

政策；方針；手段

☞ fiscal policy 財政政策

Public understanding and support of Japan's **policy** and initiatives both domestically and abroad are indispensable for the implementation of Japan's foreign policy. (Diplomatic Bluebook 2019)

また、旧社会主義諸国等の厳しい経済状況を背景として、冷戦期に蓄積された核兵器等の大量破壊兵器が拡散する危険があり、国際的な不拡散体制の整備が重要な課題となっている。（外交青書 1995）

伝染病の「ペスト」はドイツ語の発音に由来しており、英語では plague になる。和文中には plague の直接的な意味は出ていないが、"harsh economic conditions plague the former socialist countries" で、「厳しい経済状況が旧社会主義国を苦しめる」となる。

対ウクライナ支援では、1月に約 15 億円の追加支援を決定したほか、財務相アドバイザーとして日本人専門家をウクライナへ派遣した。（外交青書 2017）

和文中の「決定した」が pledge に相当し、厳密には「誓約した」という意味になる。

dispatch：派遣する；急送する
finance：財政；財務

A 国が米国の権益に対し、広範で大規模な攻撃を画策していたことは明らかだ。

clear：明らかな；確実な；はっきりした；疑う余地のない
large-scale：スケールの大きい；大規模な（scale：規模）

外交政策を展開していく上では、国内及び国際社会における日本の政策・取り組みについての理解と支持が必要不可欠である。（外交青書 2019）

domestically：国内で；国内的に
abroad：海外で（に）；広く
indispensable：不可欠な；なくてはならない（dispensable：なくても済む；必ずしも必要でない）

power

[páuər]

☐ 244

力；大国；強国

☞ power of attorney 委任状；委任権

Now that China has become a **power**, it will be essential for Japan to have strategic diplomacy that does not solve problems bilaterally with China but seeks an alternative framework.

pragmatic

[prægmǽtik]

☐ 245

実用的な；現実的な；実際的な

☞ pragmatism プラグマティズム；実用主義

Japan's stance is that it is undesirable to isolate Iran, and Japan continues to strongly urge Iran to take concrete action to dispel the international community's concerns and to adopt **pragmatic** policies. (Diplomatic Bluebook 1996)

precedence

[présədəns, prisíːdns]

☐ 246

優先（権）；先行；先立つこと

☞ precede 先行する；先んじる

In the general laws that define the powers of local governments in the U.S. and the scope to which they extend, the **precedence** of the "home rule" is strictly guaranteed by the U.S. Constitution.

predominance

[pridɑ́mənəns | -dɔ́m-]

☐ 247

優勢；卓越：支配

☞ predominate 優位に立つ；支配する

In the current international affairs, the military **predominance** of Country A has resulted in a situation of diplomatic dominance. As such, the neighboring countries are suffering a unilateral disadvantage.

中国が大国化した今、日本は中国と二国間で問題を解決しようとせず、別の枠組みを模索する戦略的外交が不可欠となるだろう。

now that X：今や X なので（X には that 節の文が来る）
essential：必須の；本質的な

日本の立場は、イランの孤立化は望ましくなく、国際社会に存在する懸念を具体的行動をもって払拭するようイランに強く申し入れつつ現実的政策を助長する必要があるというものである。（外交青書 1996）

和文中では「現実的」を pragmatic としているが、より適した日本語のニュアンスとしては「（理想論や強がりではなく）現実的な状況を踏まえ、考えられうる最善の」といったものに近い。

dispel：払いのける；晴らす

米国の地方政府の権限とそれが及ぶ範囲を規定した一般法では、「ホームルール」の優先権が合衆国憲法によって厳格に保障されている。

general law：一般法；一般法則
local government：地方自治体；地方政府
guarantee：保証する；請け合う

今次の国際問題においては、A 国の軍事的優勢が、結果的に外交的に優位な状況を生み出しており、周辺国は一方的な不利益を被っている。

result in X：X という結果になる；に終わる
dominance：優位；優越；支配
as such：その結果；そうすることで；それ自体（は）；そのようなものとして

prerequisite

[prìːrékwəzit]

□ 248

前提条件；あらかじめ必要な；不可欠の

☞ prerequisite course 前提（必修）科目

The two men, both renowned as tough negotiators, agreed to begin bargaining in earnest – this time without needing any **prerequisites** for each other.

prevail

[privéil]

□ 249

普及する；優勢である；（打ち）勝つ

☞ Justice will prevail. 正義は勝つ

(In answer to the questions from Mr. Bruun,) Japan shall faithfully observe the treaties concluded by Japan and established rule of international law, based on Article 98-2 of the Constitution of Japan and considers that such treaties **prevail** over domestic laws. (Diplomatic Bluebook 2019, References)

principle

[prínsəpl]

□ 250

原理；主義；原則

☞ principle of Archimedes アルキメデスの原理

Monroeism was a fundamental American foreign policy **principle** that aimed for a mutual non-interference with Europe.

prior to X

[práiər tu]

□ 251

Xに先立って；より前に

☞ priority 優先すること；重要度が高いこと；優先順位

Prior to the release of a 1953 diplomatic document on the U.S. military presence in Japan, the Japanese and U.S. governments held a joint U.S.–Japan committee meeting on the 13th of April to discuss the matter.

共にタフ・ニゴシエーターとして名高い二人だが、今回は互いにいかなる前提条件もつけずに、本格的な交渉を始めることで一致した。

renowned：有名な；高名な
tough negotiator：手強い交渉人；タフ・ネゴシエーター
in earnest：本気で；本格的に

（ブルン委員からの質問に応え、）我が国は、日本国憲法第98条第2項に基づき、我が国が締結した条約及び確立された国際法規を誠実に遵守することとしており、条約は国内法に優位するものと考えられている。（外交青書 2019, 資料）

和文中の「優位する」とは、「勝る」という意味の prevail であると解釈できる。
faithfully：忠実に；誠実に
observe：遵守する；観察する（observer：オブザーバー；〔議決権を持たない〕会議参加者）

モンロー主義とは、ヨーロッパとの相互不干渉を目的としたアメリカの基本的外交原理だった。

Monroeism：モンロー主義
mutual non-interference：相互不干渉（non-interference：不干渉）

米軍駐留に関する1953年の外交文書の公表に先立ち、日米両政府は13日、この件を巡って日米合同委員会を開いた。

diplomatic document：外交文書
military presence：軍の駐留；軍事的存在（presence：存在；駐留）
matter：問題；問題である

prisoner-of-war

[prízənər-əv-wɔ́ːr]

☐ 252

（戦争）捕虜；俘虜

☞ prisoner-of-war camp
（戦争）捕虜収容所

During the First World War, some German soldiers taken captive by Japanese troops in Qingdao of China, a concession of Germany, were held at the Bando **Prisoner-of-war** Camp in today's Naruto City, Tokushima Prefecture. (Diplomatic Bluebook 2019, Column)

privileged

[prívəlidʒd]

☐ 253

特権の（ある）；光栄で；免責された

☞ privilege 特権；名誉；光栄

A large amount of aid from developed countries has not helped the country's development at all. Such aid has only enriched a few **privileged** groups in country A.

procedure

[prəsíːdʒər]

☐ 254

手続き；方法；手順

☞ proceed 続行する；進む

The CCW seeks to prohibit or restrict the use of certain conventional weapons which are considered excessively injurious or whose effects are indiscriminate. It contains a framework treaty, which sets out **procedure** and the basic agenda, and five protocols that regulate specific conventional weapons. (Delegation of Japan to the Conference on Disarmament 2018)

proclaim

[proukléim | prə-]

☐ 255

宣言する；公布する；示す

☞ proclaim an amnesty 恩赦を布告する

By **proclaiming** that Japan's economic sanctions are a "de facto declaration of war," Country A is trying to extract concessions from Japan by creating a diplomatic bargaining chip.

第一次世界大戦中、ドイツの租借地であった中国の青島で日本軍の捕虜となったドイツ兵の一部は、徳島県鳴門市にあった板東俘虜収容所に収容されました。(外交青書 2019, コラム)

俘虜＝捕虜（第二次世界大戦以前、日本では「捕虜」とは呼ばず「俘虜」と呼んだ。）
German：ドイツ人の；ドイツ（語）の
soldier：軍人；兵士
captive：捕虜；人質

先進国からの多額の援助も、A 国では一部の特権階級を潤すのみで、国の発展には全く役に立っていない。

not X at all：全く X ではない；全然 X でない（肯定文の at all は「仮にも；いやしくも」と条件節で用いる）

特定通常兵器使用禁止制限条約（CCW）とは、過度に障害を与え又は無差別に効果を及ぼすことがあると認められる通常兵器の使用を禁止又は制限するもので、手続等基本的事項を定めた枠組条約及び個別の通常兵器等について規制する 5 つの附属議定書から成る。(軍縮会議日本政府代表部／外務省 2018)

conventional：従来（型）の；慣習的な
excessively：過度に；過剰に
injurious：傷つける；有害な
indiscriminate：無差別の；見境のない

A 国は日本からの経済制裁を「事実上の宣戦布告である」と宣言することで、外交的駆け引きの材料を作り、こちらから譲歩を引き出そうとしている。

declaration of war：宣戦布告
extract：引き出す；抜粋する
bargaining chip：交渉の切り札；交渉を有利にする材料

profound

[prəfáund]

☐ **256**

深い；深刻な；深遠な

☞ profoundly 深く；大いに

The UN secretary-general expressed **profound** concerns on North Korea's suggestion of resuming its nuclear tests and test-firing of ICBMs.

prohibition

[pròuhəbíʃən]

☐ **257**

禁止；禁（止）令；差し止め

☞ prohibit 禁止する；差し止める；妨げる

As they are concerned about the human rights issues in Country A, the EU unanimously decided on the **prohibition** of arms exports, a ban on ministerial contact, and the postponement of economic cooperation plans.

prominent

[prάmənənt | prɔ́m-]

☐ **258**

卓越した；目立った；著名な

☞ prominence 卓越；傑出；名声

For Japan's diplomacy to lead the international community, producing many people with **prominent** language skills and a wealth of experience is essential.

proponent

[prəpóunənt]

☐ **259**

提唱者；支持者；擁護者

☞ proposition 提案；計画；案

Furthermore, emphasizing the importance of promoting quality infrastructure for enhancing connectivity, Japan, as a **proponent** of the "Free and Open Indo-Pacific" and organizer of the Pacific Islands Leaders Meeting (PALM), announced that it would secure and strengthen Japan's presence in the Asia-Pacific region. (Diplomatic Bluebook 2019)

国連事務総長は、北朝鮮が核実験や ICBM の試射再開を示唆したことについて深い懸念を表明した。

secretary general：事務局長；事務総長
test-firing：試射（firing：発射；発砲；点火）

EU は A 国における人権問題を憂慮し、武器輸出の禁止、閣僚レベルの接触禁止、経済協力計画の延期などを全会一致で決定した。

arms export：武器輸出
ministerial：閣僚級の；閣僚レベルの
postponement：延期；先送り

国際社会を牽引する日本外交を実現するためには、卓越した語学力と豊富な経験を併せ持つ人材を数多く輩出することが不可欠である。

prominent を用いたその他の例に "prominent diplomatic achievement" があり、「突出した外交（的）成果；卓越した外交成果」となる。
wealth of experience：豊富な経験

さらに、連結性強化のための質の高いインフラ促進の重要性を強調し、「自由で開かれたインド太平洋」の提唱者、太平洋・島サミット（PALM）の主催者として、アジア太平洋地域における日本のプレゼンスを確保、強化すると表明した。（外交青書 2019）

ディベートなどで見られる pro/con (pros and cons) にあるように、pro は賛成という意味を持つ。ponent の pon の語根は「置く」という意味で、賛成側に（= pro）置く（= pon）ため、「支持者」や「擁護者」などの意味になる。また opponent になると「反対側」に「置く」ため「敵対者」「競争相手」などの意味になる。さらに、component になると「共に(com)」「置く」ため、「構成要素」や「成分」といった意味になる。

protectorate

[prətéktərət]

□ 260

保護国；保護関係；保護領

☞ protect 保護する；庇護する

Although the **protectorate** recognizes formal independence, there have been many examples throughout history where countries are being deprived of their internal affairs through puppet regimes by the suzerain state.

protocol

[próutəkɔ̀ːl | -kɔ̀l]

□ 261

（外交）儀礼；（国家間）協定；手続き

☞ Kyoto Protocol（気候変動に関する国際連合枠組条約の）京都議定書

Concerning Syria's implementation of the IAEA security measures, little progress has been achieved, partly due to the Syria crisis. To clarify the facts, it is important for Syria to cooperate fully with the IAEA, sign and ratify the Additional **Protocol**, and implement it. (Diplomatic Bluebook 2018)

provincial

[prəvínʃəl]

□ 262

地方の；偏屈な；州（省・県）の

☞ province 地方；州（省・県）；田舎

The 8th National Parliamentary elections in March were held in conjunction with the restored **provincial** council elections, the first in 25 years. (Diplomatic Bluebook 2017)

provocative

[prəvάkətiv | -vɔ́k-]

□ 263

挑発的な；怒らせる；刺激的な

☞ provocation 挑発；憤激

North Korea has continuously taken **provocative** actions, disregarding the strong will of the international community towards peaceful solution. (Diplomatic Bluebook 2018)

保護国においては形式上の独立が認められているものの、歴史を遡れば、宗主国による傀儡政権によって、実質的に内政まで奪われる例が後を絶たなかった。

formal：形式上の；公式の；儀礼的な
throughout X：X の間中ずっと；あらゆる場所に
deprive：奪う；取り上げる

シリアによる IAEA 保障措置の履行については、シリア危機の影響もあって事態は進展していないが、シリアが IAEA に対して完全に協力し、事実関係が解明されるためにも同国が追加議定書を署名・批准し、これを実施することが重要である。（外交青書 2018）

「外交儀礼」としての protocol とは、国家間の儀礼上のルールのことを指し、外交を推進するための潤滑油である。外務省によれば、その精神は、ア. 国の大小に関係なくすべて平等に扱う、イ. 誰もが納得するルールに従う、とされている。

3 月の第 8 期国民議会議員選挙は、25 年ぶりに復活した県議会議員選挙と併せて実施された。（外交青書 2017）

in conjunction with X：X とあわせて；同時に (conjunction：接続；結合)
council：地方議会；評議会；審議会

北朝鮮は、国際社会の平和的解決への強い思いを踏みにじり挑発行動を継続している。（外交青書 2018）

continuously：継続的に
will：意思；決意；意向
towards X：X に向かって；を目指して (= toward)

prudently

[prúːdəntli]

□ 264

慎重に；手堅く；用心深く

☞ prudence 慎重さ；慎ましさ；用心深さ

As the fierce back-and-forth between Country A and Country B over the attack on the tanker continues, the Japanese government, which aims to act as a mediator, is **prudently** assessing the situation.

punishment

[pʌ́niʃmənt]

□ 265

処罰；刑罰；懲罰

☞ punish 罰する；罰則を科す

To put an end to non-**punishment** for perpetrators and to support victims of violence are important. Thus, Japan continues to attach great importance to build partnerships with international organizations such as UN Action and the UN Special Representative of the Secretary-General on Sexual Violence in Conflict and participate in discussions at various international forums. At the same time, Japan is engaging in more proactive efforts in this field to make the 21st century a world with no human rights violations against women. (Diplomatic 2017)

purge

[pə́ːrdʒ]

□ 266

粛清（する）；一掃（する）；追放する

☞ Red Purge レッドパージ；赤狩り

After the attempted coup, the B regime in Country A embarked on a massive **purge** of military and judicial personnel, civil servants, and the press.

タンカーへの攻撃を巡ってA国とB国の激しい応酬が続く中、仲介者としての役割を目指す日本政府は事態を慎重に見極めている。

back-and-forth：堂々巡りの；行ったり来たりの
tanker：タンカー；油槽船
assess：評価する；査定する

加害者不処罰の終焉及び被害者を支援していくことが重要であるという観点から、国連アクションや紛争下の性的暴力担当国連事務総長特別代表事務所といった国際機関との連携や国際的な議論の場への参加を重視しつつ、21世紀こそ女性の人権侵害のない世界にするため、日本はこの分野に一層積極的に取り組んでいる。(外交青書2017)

put an end to：終わらせる；終止符を打つ；決着をつける
perpetrator：加害者；犯罪者；犯人

クーデター未遂の後、A国B政権は軍部や司法関係者、公務員、報道機関など大規模な粛清に着手した。

coup：政変；クーデター
massive：大規模な；大量の；巨大な
personnel：職員；社員；隊員；人事部；人事の
civil servant：公務員

quarantine

[kwɔ́ːrəntìːn | kwɔ́rən-]

□ 267

検疫（する）；隔離（する）；隔離期間

☞ quarantine certificate 検疫証明書

Minister of Agriculture, Forestry and Fisheries Yuji Yamamoto also visited China in July to meet Minister of General Administration of Quality Supervision, Inspection and **Quarantine** Zhi Shuping, and Vice Minister for the Ministry of Agriculture and Rural Affairs Yu Xinrong. Then in August, Minister of Agriculture, Forestry and Fisheries Ken Saito attended a food expo in Hong Kong. (Diplomatic Bluebook 2018)

ransom

[rǽnsəm]

□ 268

身代金；受け戻し；取り戻す

☞ ransom demand 身代金（の）要求

Ransomware cyberattacks, for example, show that the world is now beginning to be exposed to new threats.

ratify

[rǽtəfài]

□ 269

批准する；承認する；追認する

☞ ratification 批准；承認；裁可

As well as calling on countries in the Asia-Pacific region to **ratify** or accede to the Convention, Japan has, since 1998, provided support worth over 71 billion Japanese yen to 51 countries and regions to assist them in dealing with the consequences of land mines (for example, landmine clearance and victim assistance). (Diplomatic Bluebook 2018)

また7月、山本有二農林水産大臣が訪中し、支樹平中国質検総局長及び余欣栄農業部副部長との会談を行い、8月には、齋藤健農林水産大臣が香港で行われたフードエキスポに参加した。(外交青書 2018)

和文中の「検」は quarantine に相当し、「検疫」の意味を持つ。
fisheries : fishery (漁業 ; 水産業) の複数形

例えばランサムウェア(身代金要求型ウィルス)によるサイバー攻撃は、今世界が新たな脅威にさらされ始めたことを物語っている。

cyberattack : サイバー攻撃 ; サイバーアタック
expose : さらす ; 暴く ; 露呈する

A氏のアジア太平洋地域各国への(オタワ)条約締結の働きかけに加え、1998年以降、51カ国・地域に対して約710億円を超える地雷対策支援(地雷除去、被害者支援等)を実施している。(外交青書 2018)

本例文では、「締結」に相当する英語を "ratify or accede" としているが、ratify は実際の条約を「批准する(こと)」、accede は条約へ「加盟する(こと)」を意味しておりニュアンスは異なる。

rebellion

[ribéljən]

□ 270

反乱；暴動；謀反

☞ rebel 反逆者；反抗者；反抗する；反政府の

Foreign Minister A vehemently condemned the B government's brutal crackdown on **rebellion** and, moreover, insisted that the B government no longer had any legitimacy.

reciprocal

[risíprəkəl]

□ 271

相互の；互恵的な；相互的な

☞ reciprocity 相互依存；互恵主義

These **reciprocal** visits symbolized the strength of the Japan-U.S. Alliance, and served as an opportunity to demonstrate the power of tolerance and peace between countries which had previously been at war. (Diplomatic Bluebook 2017)

recognition

[rèkəgníʃən]

□ 272

認識；認知；見覚え

☞ recognize 識別する；認める；承認する

Based on the **recognition** that securing a stable supply of energy is directly related to national security, Japan is striving to maintain friendly relations with the energy-producing and energy-consuming countries of the world.

reconnaissance

[rikɑ́nəsəns | -kɔ́n-]

□ 273

偵察（隊）；（予備）調査；踏査

☞ reconnoiter 偵察する

The security importance of space is increasing. Japan should actively utilize space for its national security, using **reconnaissance** satellites and other means more than ever before.

A 外相は、B 政府の反乱軍に対する残虐な弾圧を激しく非難し、B 政府にはもはや何の正当性もないことを主張した。

rebellion には「反乱」という意味しかないが、反乱は当然「軍」もしくはそれに類する組織を伴うため、「反乱軍」として rebellion が用いられている。

この相互訪問は、日米同盟の強さを象徴するとともに、かつて戦火を交えた国同士が寛容と和解の力を示す機会となった。（外交青書 2017）

symbolize : 象徴する ; 表す
demonstrate : はっきり示す ; 実演する ; デモをする
previously : 以前に ; 前に

エネルギーの安定供給を確保することは、国家の安全保障に直結するという認識に基づき、我が国（日本）は世界のエネルギー生産国及び消費国双方との友好関係の維持に努めています。

based on X : X に基づいて ; を踏まえて
friendly relation : 友好関係
consuming : 消費する ; 消費しつくす（consume : 消費する ; 浪費する）

宇宙空間における安全保障上の重要性が高まっており、日本もこれまで以上に偵察衛星などを活用し、自国の安全保障のための宇宙利用を積極的に行うべきである。

space : 宇宙（空間）; 間隔 ; 場所
satellite : （人工）衛星 ; 衛星都市
more than ever before : かつてないほどに ; これまで以上に

refugee

[rèfjudʒíː]

□ 274

難民；亡命者；避難者

☞ refuge 避難；保護；避難所

The UNHCR has been encouraging countries to accept **refugees** through third-country resettlement.

regime

[rəʒíːm | rei-]

□ 275

（政治）体制；政権；制度

☞ regime change 政権交代；体制変革

Initially, the economic downturn was caused by the turmoil of the **regime** change. However, the economy has since turned around due to the economic support from other countries around the world and financial assistance from the International Monetary Fund (IMF).

relegate

[réləgèit]

□ 276

左遷する；格下げする；追いやる

☞ relegation 左遷；追放；格下げ

Foreign Minister A issued a personnel order **relegating** Deputy Minister B of the MOFA to the Deputy Assistant Minister position. Such is generally perceived as a retaliatory move by the foreign minister.

renunciation

[rinʌ̀nsiéiʃən]

□ 277

放棄；棄権；拒否

☞ renounce 放棄する；破棄する；断念する

When discussing constitutional amendments in Japan, the main focus will be on the revision of Article 9, which stipulates the **renunciation** of war.

国連難民高等弁務官事務所（UNHCR）は、第三国定住による難民の受入れを各国に推奨してきた。

UNHCR : the Office of the United Nations High Commissioner for Refugees
third-country : 第三国
resettlement : 再定住 ; 再植民

当初は体制転換の混乱により経済の低迷が続いたが、世界各国からの経済支援や国際通貨基金（IMF）の資金援助によってその後経済が好転した。

initially : 当初は ; 最初に
turmoil : 騒動 ; 混乱 ; 動揺
turn around : 好転する ; 回復する ; 方向転換する

A 外相は外務省の B 官房長に対し、官房審議官に降格する人事を発令した。これは外相による報復人事との受け止め方が一般的だ。

Deputy Minister : 官房長
Deputy Assistant Minister : 官房審議官
retaliatory : 報復的な ; 仕返しの（retaliate : 仕返しする ; 報復する ; 応酬する）

日本において憲法改正を議論する際、最も焦点となるのは、やはり戦争放棄を規定した 9 条の改正であろう。

constitutional amendment : 憲法（の）修正 ; 改憲
stipulate : 規定する ; 明記する
renunciation of war : 戦争放棄

repatriate

[riːpéitrièit | -pǽt-]

□ 278

(本国へ) 送還する；送り返す；帰還者

☞ forced repatriation 強制送還

In 2015, Japan cooperated in an asset recovery initiative, mainly within the context of the G7 framework, seeking to confiscate and **repatriate** to the country of origin the proceeds of corruption that have found their way overseas. (Diplomatic Bluebook 2016)

represent

[rèprizént]

□ 279

代表する；象徴する；表現する

☞ present
存在する；出席している；現在の；提示する

Diplomatic missions overseas, such as Embassies and Consulates General, not only **represent** Japan but also play a key role in areas such as information gathering on the frontline of diplomacy, strategic communication to the public overseas, promotion of diplomatic relations, and international contribution. (Diplomatic Bluebook 2018)

representative

[rèprizéntətiv]

□ 280

代表の；（下院）議員；代議士

☞ representation
代表を務めること；代議制度；表現

The U.S. Congress is divided into two houses, the Senate and the House of **Representatives**. The Senate has a flat number of two members for each state, while the House of **Representatives** allocates a number of members based on the population of the state.

reputation

[rèpjutéiʃən]

□ 281

評判；名声；好評

☞ repute 評する；評判

By cooperating with the Japanese Space experts and earning an excellent **reputation** worldwide, we have been conducting “Space diplomacy” proactively. (Diplomatic Bluebook 2017, Column)

2015年、日本はG7の枠組みを中心に、海外に流出した腐敗収益の没収や元の国への返還を図る「財産回復」の協力を進めた。(外交青書 2016)

asset recovery：資産(財産)回復
within the context of X：Xの脈略(文脈)の中で
confiscate：没収する；差し押さえる
proceeds：収益：売上高

大使館や総領事館などの在外公館は、海外で国を代表するとともに、外交の最前線での情報収集・戦略的な対外発信・外交関係促進・国際貢献などの分野で重要な役割を果たしている。(外交青書 2018)

diplomatic missions overseas：在外公館(diplomatic missions abroadと表記されることも多い)
frontline：最前線；第一線

米国連邦議会は上院と下院の2つに分けられており、上院は各州で一律2名の、下院は人口に応じた数の議員が割り振られている。

和文中の「院」は直接representativeを指しておらず、"House of Representatives" で「(米国)下院」を表す。
divide：分ける；分割する
allocate：割り当てる；配分する

このように、日本が世界に誇る宇宙の専門家の方々から様々な形で協力を得て、積極的な「宇宙外交」の展開が実現されています。(外交青書 2017, コラム)

expert：専門家；熟達者
excellent：極めて良い；優秀な
worldwide：世界的に見て；世界的な

resentful

[rizéntfəl]

□ 282

憤って；憤慨して；腹を立てて

☞ resent 憤慨する；腹を立てる

☞ resentment 憤り；腹立たしさ

While Prime Minister A described President B's actions as an "unforgivable outrage," State C issued a statement saying that it was **resentful** of the expression, further worsening the relations between the two countries.

resign

[rizáin]

□ 283

辞職する；断念する；身を任せる

☞ resignation 辞職；退陣；辞表

Country A's B cabinet was finally forced to **resign**, taking responsibility for the chaos caused by the anti-regime protests.

resolution

[rèzəljúːʃən]

□ 284

決議；解決；解像度

☞ draft resolution 決議草案

Ambassador B of Country A to the UN, which is chairing the Council this month, told reporters that North Korea's actions were a "clear violation of Security Council **resolutions**." He/She said the Council will take serious action.

restoration

[rèstəréiʃən]

□ 285

回復；復元；返還

☞ Meiji Restoration 明治維新

In addition, Japan is contributing to the **restoration** of Iraq's infrastructure through yen loan projects in areas such as electricity. Furthermore, based on the announcement at the G7 Ise-Shima Summit in 2016, Japan is supporting the **restoration** of Iraq's finances, which have suffered from factors such as falling oil prices and increased war-related costs. (Diplomatic Bluebook 2018)

A 総理は、B 大統領の行為を「許し難い暴挙」であると述べる一方、C 国はこの表現に対し憤慨している旨の声明を発表し、両国関係は一段と悪化した。

unforgivable：許されない；容赦できない（forgivable：許せる；容赦できる）
further：さらに深く；さらに遠く

反政権デモによる混乱の責任を取り、A 国の B 内閣はとうとう総辞職に追い込まれた。

resign には和文中にある「総辞職」の「総」の意味までを厳密には含まない。この場合、内閣が辞職するわけであり、文脈上「総辞職」となる。

chaos：混乱；混沌；カオス

理事会で今月議長国を務める A 国の B 国連大使は記者団に対し、北朝鮮の行為は「安保理決議の明白な違反」であると指摘。理事会は重大な措置を講じるとした。

chair：議長を務める；議長
Security Council resolution：安保理決議（Security Council：安全保障理事会、安保理）

加えて、日本は、電力分野等における円借款事業を通じてイラクのインフラ復興に貢献しているほか、2016 年の G7 伊勢志摩サミットでの表明を踏まえ、油価下落や戦費拡大等を受けて深刻化したイラク財政の建て直しを支援している。（外交青書 2018）

yen loan project：円借款事業
electricity：電気；電力
war-related：戦争関連の；戦争に関連する

restrain

[ristréin]

☐ 286

制限する；抑制する；拘束する

☞ restraint 抑制；制止；拘束

Currently, the size of Country A's military force and the cooperation of its allies are not enough to **restrain** the actions of Country B. If Country A is perceived as having little intention to intervene with respect to its military, its deterrence strategy against Country B will be ineffective.

restriction

[ristríkʃən]

☐ 287

制限；制約；限定

☞ restrict 制限する；限定する

The JCPOA imposes **restrictions** on Iran's nuclear activities while ensuring that they serve peaceful purposes, and clearly sets forth the procedures for lifting the sanctions that have been imposed until now, alongside the implementation of measures by Iran. (Diplomatic Bluebook 2017)

revoke

[rivóuk]

☐ 288

無効にする；廃止する；取り消す

☞ revocable 取消可能な

The Government of Japan has expressed its concerns about these issues by issuing a statement by the Minister for Foreign Affairs, and immediately made strong protests to China, demanding that China **revoke** all measures interfering with the freedom of flight in international airspace. (Diplomatic Bluebook 2014)

ruthless

[rúːθlis]

☐ 289

情け容赦ない；無慈悲な；残忍な

☞ ruthlessly 情け容赦なく

As more and more of society changes online, the rules will be so **ruthless** that traditional strengths will suddenly become useless.

現状、A 国の軍事力の規模と同盟国の協力だけでは B 国の行動を抑制することはできない。A 国が軍事介入する意思が乏しいと見透かされれば、B 国に対する抑止戦略に効果はない。

military force : 軍事力
perceive : 気づく ; 見抜く ; 知覚する
intention : 意図 ; 意向
with respect to X : X に関しては ; については（respect : 点 ; 尊敬〔する〕）
ineffective : 効果がない ; 役に立たない

JCPOA では、イランの原子力活動に制約をかけつつ、それが平和的であることを確保した上で、イラン側の措置の実施に伴い、これまでに課された制裁が解除される手順が明記された。（外交青書 2017）

nuclear activities : 原子力活動
set forth : 表明する ; 明記する
alongside : 並行して ; 同時に ; 横に

日本側からは、こうした懸念を表明する外務大臣談話を発出するとともに、直ちに中国側に対して強く抗議し、公海上空における飛行の自由を妨げるような一切の措置を撤回するよう求めた。（外交青書 2014）

freedom : 自由 ; 解放
flight : 飛行 ; 飛行便 ; 飛行距離
measure (s) : 法案 ; 対策 ; 措置

オンラインによる社会変化がより一層進むことでこれまでのルールが無慈悲に変わり、従来の強みは突如役に立たなるなるだろう。

more and more : ますます
online : オンラインで ; オンラインの ; オンライン
useless : 役に立たない ; 無益な

sanction

[sǽŋkʃən]

□ 290

制裁（を加える）；認可（する）；拘束力

☞ trade sanction 貿易制裁

Economic **sanctions** have long been used as an intermediate measure between diplomatic pressure and the use of force, either as a single country's foreign policy or as a joint multilateral act.

screening

[skríːniŋ]

□ 291

選考；ふるい分け；遮蔽

☞ screen 隠す；覆う；遮断する

MOFA is responsible for the application and **screening** process, pre-departure orientation, and support for the activities of the JET Alumni Association (JETAA in 18 countries with about 23,000 membership). (Diplomatic Bluebook 2019)

secure

[sikjúər]

□ 292

確保する；保証する；安全な

☞ secure network
安全な（セキュリティーで確保された）ネットワーク

Japan cannot **secure** its own peace and security by itself, and the international community expects Japan to play a more proactive role for peace and stability in the world, in a way commensurate with its national capabilities. (Diplomatic Bluebook 2019)

seize

[síːz]

□ 293

つかむ；差し押さえる；逮捕する

☞ seizure 掌握；拿捕；押収（物）

Country A once unilaterally **seized** Country B's territory C. For Country B, the primary purpose of the current war is to retake the same territory.

経済制裁は、外交的な圧力と武力行使との中間的な措置として、一国の対外政策や、多国間の共同行為として古くから利用されてきた。

intermediate：中間の；中間的な；中級の
pressure：圧力；（圧力をかけて）無理強いさせる
single：1つの；単独の

外務省は、在外公館における募集・選考や渡日前オリエンテーション、18カ国に存在する元JET参加者の会（JETAA、会員数約2万3,000人）の活動を支援している。（外交青書2019）

application：応募；申請；出願
departure：出発；出国
orientation：方向づけ；オリエンテーション

日本の平和と安全は我が国一国では確保できず、国際社会もまた、日本がその国力にふさわしい形で、国際社会の平和と安定のため一層積極的な役割を果たすことを期待している。（外交青書2019）

by itself：それ自体で；単独で；自然に
play a role：役割を果たす
commensurate：釣り合った；等しい；同等の
national capability：国力；国の能力

A国はB国の領土Cをかつて一方的に奪った。B国にとって、今次の戦争はその奪還が主目的である。

once：かつて；ひとたび；一旦
retake：取り戻す；再び受ける（re-：再び、take：受ける）

self-restraint

[sélf-ristréint]

□ 294

自制；自主規制；自粛

☞ self- 自己の；自分を

In the past, **self-restraint** export controls were often imposed at the request of the importing country. Now, they are explicitly prohibited in the Agreement on Safeguards, including their requirements.

session

[séʃən]

□ 295

会期；会議；学期

☞ legislative session
立法府の（今次の）会期

This was one passage in the policy speech by Prime Minister Abe in the 183rd **Session** of the Diet in February 2013. (Diplomatic Bluebook 2017, Column)

settlement

[sétlmənt]

□ 296

植民地；解決；精算

☞ settle 落ち着く；定住する；解決する

Sierra Leone is a former British **settlement** and has been a member of the Commonwealth since independence.

shuttle

[ʃʌ́tl]

□ 297

定期往復便；折り返し運転；往復する

☞ shuttle bus 近距離往復バス

During the 1980s, when the Iran–Iraq war broke out, Japan was actively involved in resolving the conflict through “**shuttle** diplomacy” toward Iraq.

かつては、輸入国からの要求によって輸出の自主規制を行うことがしばしばあった。しかし現在は、セーフガード協定においてその要求も含めて明確に禁止されている。

in the past : 従来は ; かつて (昔) は
at the request of X : X の依頼を受けて ; 要求により
importing country : 輸入国

これは、2013年2月の第183回国会における安倍総理大臣施政方針演説の一節です。(外交青書 2017, コラム)

国会の会期に関して session を用いる場合、慣例的に「(第 XX) 回」と表記する。
policy speech : 施政方針演説
Diet : 国会

シエラレオネはかつてのイギリスの植民地であり、独立以後も英連邦の加盟国である。

British : イギリスの ; 英国の
the Commonwealth : 英連邦 ; イギリス連邦 (commonwealth : 連邦 ; 共和国 ; 団体)

イラン・イラク戦争が起きた80年代は、日本はイラクに対して「シャトル外交」を行い紛争解決に積極的に関与してきた。

during X : X の間中 ; 間ずっと
break out : 勃発する ; 突発する ; 起こる (broke は break の過去形)

significantly

[signífikəntli]

□ 298

かなり；意義深いことに；有意に

☞ signify 示す；意味する；表す

The result of the referendum in June 2016 on the withdrawal of the UK from the EU caused a major shock and tough withdrawal negotiations are expected, while the importance of Europe described above will not **significantly** change even after the withdrawal of the UK from the EU. (Diplomatic Bluebook 2017)

socialism

[sóuʃəlìzm]

□ 299

社会主義

☞ socialist 社会主義者；社会主義（の）

The report on the 19th Party Congress described the “Xi Jinping thought on **socialism** with Chinese characteristics for a new era” as a guiding principle to “achieve the Chinese dream of great rejuvenation of the Chinese nation,” which was laid down in the party protocol. (Diplomatic Bluebook 2018)

solution

[səlúːʃən]

□ 300

解決（策）；解答；溶液

☞ diplomatic solution 外交的解決

Based on the basic recognition that the normalization of diplomatic relations with North Korea is impossible without resolving **solution** of the abduction issue, Japan has positioned its resolution as the most important foreign policy issue. Accordingly, Japan urges North Korea to ensure the safety of all abductees and their immediate return to Japan, to provide a full account of all the abduction cases, and to hand over the perpetrators. (Diplomatic Bluebook 2017)

2016年6月の英国のEU離脱に関する国民投票の結果は、大きな驚きを与えるものであり、今後厳しい離脱交渉が予想されるが、以上のような欧州の重要性は、英国のEU離脱後も，大きく変わるものではない。（外交青書2017）

referendum：国民投票；住民投票
major：大きい；主要な；専攻
tough：厳しい；難しい；屈強な

第19回党大会の報告では、「中華民族の偉大な復興」を実現するための指導理念として「習近平による新時代の中国の特色ある社会主義思想」が打ち出され、党規約に明記されることとなった。（外交青書2018）

describe：述べる；記述する；描写する
rejuvenation：復活；若返り；活性化（juvenile：若い；未熟な；年少者の）
lay down：制定する；横たえる（laid は lay の過去形・過去分詞形）

日本としては、拉致問題の解決なくして北朝鮮との国交正常化はあり得ないとの基本認識の下、その解決を最重要の外交課題と位置付け、全ての拉致被害者の安全の確保と即時帰国、拉致に関する真相究明、拉致実行犯の引渡しを北朝鮮側に対し強く要求している。（外交青書2017）

abduction issue：拉致問題（abduction：誘拐；拉致）
abductee：拉致被害者；誘拐された被害者

sovereignty

[sάvərənti | sɔ́v-]

□ 301

主権（国家）の；統治権；独立国

☞ national sovereignty 国家主権

The security environment has become complicated with concerns regarding the increase of "Grayzone" situations that are neither pure peace time nor contingencies over territorial **sovereignty** and interests in the context of a shift in the balance of power and insufficient institutionalization of cooperative security frameworks. (Diplomatic Bluebook 2017)

stability

[stəbíləti]

□ 302

安定（性）；着実；確固

☞ stable 安定した；変動のない

Poverty threatens the survival, daily life, and dignity of each person and becomes a source of social injustice, political **instability** and violent extremism, and its eradication is vital also from the perspective of "human security." (Diplomatic Bluebook 2019)

stagnant

[stǽgnənt]

□ 303

よどんでいる；不景気な；停滞した

☞ stagnancy 停滞；よどみ

Unemployment rate in October, at 4.1%, reached the lowest level since the mid-1970s, but growth in real wages stays **stagnant**. (Diplomatic Bluebook 2019)

strategic

[strətíːdʒik, -dʒikəl]

□ 304

戦略的な；戦略（上）の；戦略上重要な

☞ strategist 戦略家；ブレイン

Japan's diplomatic, **strategic** move to use international law as a shield to make a breakthrough is now at a significant turning point.

パワーバランスの変化や安全保障に関する協力の枠組みの制度化が不十分であることを背景として、領域主権や権益をめぐって、純然たる有事でも平時でもないグレーゾーン事態の増加が懸念されており、安全保障環境が複雑化している。(外交青書 2017)

grayzone : グレーゾーン (=gray zone)
insufficient : 不十分な ; 不足して
institutionalization : 制度化 ; 組織化 ; 慣行化 ; 収容

貧困は、一人ひとりの生存・生活・尊厳を脅かし社会的不公正・政情不安や暴力的過激主義の根源となっており、その撲滅は「人間の安全保障」の観点からも極めて重要である。(外交青書 2019)

和文中の「安」がこの場合の stability の訳に相当するが、解釈としては "political instability" で「政治的(な)不安定(さ)」の意味となる。instability は stability の反意語で、「不安定 (性)」を表す。

dignity : 威厳 ; 高位 ; 品格

10月の失業率は4.1%と70年代中盤以降で最も低水準となっているが、実質賃金は伸び悩んでいる。(外交青書 2019)

unemployment rate : 失業率 (employment rate : 就職率 ; 就業率)
real wage : 実質賃金 (wage : 賃金、wage war で〔戦争を〕仕掛ける ; 行う)

国際法を盾に突破口を開こうとする日本の外交戦略は、今や大きな転換点に差し掛かっている。

shield : 盾 ; 防御物 ; 盾となる
turning point : 転換点 ; 岐路 ; ターニングポイント

strengthen

[stréŋkθən, stréŋθən]

□ 305

強化する；丈夫にする；増強する

☞ strength 力；強み；強さ

In May 2020, an amended Foreign Exchange and Foreign Trade Act was enacted to **strengthen** the oversight of foreign investors' direct investments in industries related to national security.

structure

[strʌ́ktʃər]

□ 306

構造；体制；構成

☞ structural 構造（上）の；構築物の

As we face diplomatic issues that are becoming more complex and diverse, MOFA must enhance its foreign policy implementation **structure** in order to build a stronger foundation for policy execution. (Diplomatic Bluebook 2019)

struggle

[strʌ́gl]

□ 307

もがく；争う；努力（する）

☞ struggle against X
Xとの（に対する）抗争

Although they **struggle** with the plunge of the price of natural resources, Latin America and the Caribbean (LAC) region is enhancing its profile with its free trade policy among the global value chain, especially the countries promoting economic reform and an open market. (Diplomatic Bluebook 2018)

subsequent

[sʌ́bsikwənt]

□ 308

その次の；その後の；それに続く

☞ subsequently その後；それ以降

Japan has been cooperating actively with Cambodia, including through the Cambodian peace process in the late 1980s and in its **subsequent** reconstruction and development process. In 2013 the relations between the two countries were elevated to a "Strategic Partnership." (Diplomatic Bluebook 2018)

2020年5月には、国の安全保障に関わる産業に対して、外国人投資家が行う直接投資の監視を強化する改正外為法が成立している。

amended : 修正された ; 補正された
Foreign Exchange and Foreign Trade Act : 外為法（外国為替及び外国貿易法）
enact : 制定する ; 上演する
oversight : 監視 ; 監督 ; 見落とし ; 過失

外交課題がますます難しく多様化する中、外交の実施を支える足腰を強固にすることは不可欠である。(外交青書 2019)

和文中には直接 "structure" に相当する表現は出ていないが、"implementation structure" で「実施（体制）」として、structure の意味が含まれていると解釈できる。

国際資源価格の影響を受けながらも、経済改革や市場開放を推進する国々を中心に、中南米地域は、グローバル・バリューチェーンの中で自由貿易体制における地位を高めつつある。(外交青書 2018)

"struggle with the plunge of" で「急落の影響を受けながら」となる。文意の解釈としては「国際的な価格の急落に（もろに影響を受け）悪戦苦闘しながら（苦しみながら ; もがきながら)」となる。

plunge : 下落 ; 急落 ; 急落する

日本は、1980年代後半のカンボジアの和平プロセスやその後の復興・開発に積極的に協力しており、2013年に両国関係は「戦略的パートナーシップ」に格上げされた。(外交青書 2018)

peace process : 和平プロセス
late 1980s : 1980年代後半
elevate : 高める ; 上げる ; 昇進させる

subsidiary

[səbsídièri | -diəri]

□ 309

補助の；従属の；付属物

☞ subsidiary organization
下部組織；補助組織

Public and private sector lobbying for the California High-Speed Rail Project is continuing. Support is also being provided for realization of the Texas Central Railway Project, with the private U.S. company working on the project, Texas Central Partners (TCP), concluding a technology transfer agreement with HTeC, a **subsidiary** of the Central Japan Railway Company. (Diplomatic Bluebook 2018)

substantial

[səbstǽnʃəl]

□ 310

実質的な；相当な；しっかりした

☞ substance 物質；実質；重要性

☞ substantially 大幅に；実質的には

The December 12 meeting in Hawaii between the Secretary of State B of Country A and the Communist Party Politburo member D of Country C ended in failure. The said meeting yielded little **substantial** results.

substitute

[sʌ́bstətjùːt | -tjùːt]

□ 311

代用する；代理をする；代替

☞ substitution 代理；代用；代理出席

Prime Minister A met with former Prime Minister B at the headquarters of his political party on September 4. Prime Minister A asked Mr./Ms. B to attend an international conference scheduled to be held in Russia in late October as a **substitute**, which Mr./Ms. B agreed to do.

subversion

[səbvə́ːrʒən, -ʃən]

□ 312

（国家）転覆；打倒；破壊

☞ subvert 倒す；転覆させる；滅亡させる

Regarding social affairs, Mr. Liu Xiaobo, a Nobel Laureate who had been incarcerated for inciting **subversion** of state power, passed away in July. (Diplomatic Bluebook 2018)

カリフォルニア高速鉄道計画では引き続き官民で働きかけを実施するとともに、テキサス高速鉄道計画では米国民間企業（TCP）が JR 東海子会社である HTeC と技術支援契約を締結する等、同計画の実現に向け支援が行われている。（外交青書 2018）

realization：実現；成就；認識
conclude：締結する；結論を下す
technology transfer agreement：技術移転契約（協定）

12月12日にハワイで行われた、A 国の B 国務長官と C 国の D 共産党政治局委員との会談は物別れに終わり、実質的な成果はほとんど得られていない。

politburo member：政治局員（politburo：政治局）
yield：生む；産出する；もたらす

A 首相は9月4日、所属する政党本部で B 前首相と会い、10月下旬にロシアで開催予定の国際会議に代理出席するよう要請し、B 氏は了承した。

headquarters：本部；司令部；本社
attend：出席する；参列する；随行する
schedule：予定する；予定に入れる

社会情勢では、7月、国家政権転覆を扇動した罪で服役中であったノーベル平和賞受賞者の劉暁波氏が死亡した。（外交青書 2018）

Nobel Laureate：ノーベル賞受賞者
incarcerate：投獄する；監禁する；幽閉する
incite：扇動する；駆り立てる；奮い立たせる
pass away：死亡する；逝去する

superpower

[sú:pərpàuər]

☐ 313

超大国

☞ military superpower 軍事大国

Canada is located next to the U.S., a **superpower**. It has dared to maintain its independent diplomacy despite various pressures from the U.S.

suppress

[səprés]

☐ 314

抑圧する；鎮圧する；隠す

☞ suppression 抑圧；鎮圧；隠蔽

Country A plotted to overthrow the local regime C on the back of military support for armed force B. However, B was immediately **suppressed** by a multinational force that was led by the U.S. military.

surreal

[sərí:əl | -ríəl]

☐ 315

非現実的な；現実離れした；超現実主義の

☞ surrealism 超現実主義；シュールレアリズム

The statement by the leader of Country A is mere wishful thinking that ignores current social circumstances. Country B has been chilly about this statement as almost **surreal**.

surrender

[səréndər]

☐ 316

降伏（する）；放棄（する）；明け渡す

☞ unconditional surrender 無条件降伏

In a three-year battle between Country A's rebel group B and the UN-backed Country A government forces, B made it clear on the 14th of this month that it would **surrender** in full.

カナダは、超大国アメリカの隣に位置し、これまでもアメリカによって様々な圧力をかけられながらも、あえて自主外交を貫いてきた。

(be) located : 位置する
dare : あえてする ; 大胆にもする ; 思い切ってする (dare は同様の意味で助動詞として用いることも可能)

A 国は武装勢力 B による軍事支援を背景に、現地政権 C の転覆を謀ったが、米軍を中心とした多国籍軍によって B は直ちに鎮圧された。

local : その地域の ; 現地の
on the back of X : X を背景に ; という経緯があって
military support for X : X への軍事支援 (support : 支援 ; 援助 ; サポート)

A 国首脳の発言は、今日の社会情勢を無視した単なる願望に過ぎず、この発言に対しては、B 国側もおよそ非現実的なこととして冷ややかに見ている。

mere : 単なる ; ほんの
wishful thinking : 希望的観測 (wishful : 望んでいる)
chilly : 冷淡な ; 冷ややかな

A 国の反政府武装勢力 B と、国連軍の支援を受けた A 国政府軍が 3 年にわたって繰り広げてきた戦闘で、今月14日、B が全面的に降伏することを明らかにした。

backed : 支援を受けた ; 後援された (back : 支援する ; 後押しする)
government forces : 政府軍 ; 官軍
make it clear : はっきりさせる ; 明らかにする

93

surveillance

[sərvéiləns]

□ 317

偵察；監視；査察

☞ survey 調査する；見渡す；調査；検査

The UN PKOs are required to perform a variety of tasks, including not only the cease-fire **surveillance** to support the parties' cease-fire agreement, but also the protection of civilians and long-term peace-building.

sustain

[səstéin]

□ 318

維持する；持続させる；耐える

☞ sustainable 持続可能な；維持できる

☞ unsustainable 持続不可能な；維持できない

Japan supports the "open, stable and self-**sustained** development" of Central Asia, and is promoting diplomacy, which aims at contributing to the peace and stability of the region. The three pillars of Japan's diplomacy in Central Asia are as follows: (1) steadily strengthening of bilateral relationships; (2) encouraging regional cooperation and contribution to the common issues of the region through the "Central Asia plus Japan" Dialogue; and (3) cooperating in the global arena. (Diplomatic Bluebook 2019)

tactic

[tǽktik]

□ 319

戦術（の）；作戦；戦略

☞ tactical 戦術的な；戦術（上）の；巧妙な

The apparent possession of nuclear weapons by Country A forced a complete review of Country B's diplomatic **tactics**.

tariff

[tǽrif]

□ 320

関税（を課す）；関税率；税率表

☞ tariff barrier 関税障壁

After Country B imposed unfair additional **tariffs** on their products, country A has indicated that it will consider filing a lawsuit with the WTO.

国連 PKO にも、当事者の停戦合意を支える停戦監視のみならず、文民の保護や長期的な平和構築など多様な任務が求められている。

PKO：平和維持活動（peacekeeping operations の略）
cease-fire agreement：停戦（休戦）合意（協定）
long-term：長期の；長期間にわたる

日本は、中央アジアの「開かれ、安定し、自立的な発展」を支え、同地域の平和と安定に寄与することを目的とした外交を推進しており、①二国間関係の着実な強化、②「中央アジア＋日本」対話を通じた地域協力の促進・地域共通の課題への貢献及び ③グローバルな舞台での協力を中央アジア外交の三本柱としている。（外交青書 2019）

和文中の「自立的な発展」における「立」は sustain の直訳とは言えないが、解釈としては「自ら（self-）維持 / 持続させられる（sustained）発展（development）」と捉えることができる。

A 国の核保有が明白になったことで、B 国の外交戦術は全面的な見直しを迫られることになった。

possession：保有；所有；所持
review：再検討；見直し；評価；再調査する；見直す

A 国は自国の産品に対し、B 国が不当な追加関税を課したことを受け、WTO への提訴を検討する姿勢を示した。

unfair：不公平な；不当な
indicate：示す；指し示す；示唆する
file a lawsuit：訴訟を起こす；告訴する；提訴する（file：申し立てる；提訴する）

territory

[térətɔ̀ːri | -təri]

☐ 321

領土；領域；縄張り

☞ territorial 領土の；領土に関する

Since 1885, Japan had conducted repeated investigations and, having confirmed that there were no traces to suggest that the islands were under the control of the Qing dynasty, incorporated them into Japanese **territory** in January 1895. (Diplomatic Bluebook 2017)

testify

[téstəfài]

☐ 322

証言する；証拠となる；立証する

☞ testimony 証言；証明

In Country A, those who **testify** in favor of former regime officials are not expected to come forward for the fear of an asset freeze or sanctions being imposed by the U.S.

threatening

[θrétəniŋ]

☐ 323

威嚇的な；脅迫的な；険悪な

☞ threaten 脅す；脅迫する；脅威を与える

☞ threat 脅し；脅迫；威嚇

Country A urged Countries B and C to refrain from using **threatening** words and actions against each other and to seek a peaceful resolution to the conflict through diplomatic efforts.

trace

[tréis]

☐ 324

形跡；痕跡；追跡する

☞ traceability 追跡可能性；履歴管理

Although Country B immediately congratulated Country A on the presidential reelection results, there was no **trace** of at least some “statement” from other Southeast Asian countries, which brought to light Country B’s own foreign policy strategy.

日本は、1885年以降再三にわたる現地調査を行い、清朝の支配が及んでいる痕跡がないことを確認の上、1895年1月に尖閣諸島を日本の領土に編入した。（外交青書 2017）

repeated：度重なる；繰り返した
under the control of X：Xの支配を受けて；Xの制御下で
dynasty：王朝；王家

A国では元政権高官などに有利な証言をする者は、米国による資産凍結や制裁を恐れて名乗り出ないとみられている。

those who：人々
in favor of X：Xに賛成して；利益になるように
fear：恐れ；恐怖；懸念

A国はB国とC国に対し、互いに威嚇的な言動を慎み、外交的努力により紛争の平和的解決を図るよう促した。

words and actions：言動；言行
peaceful resolution：平和的解決
diplomatic efforts：外交（的）努力

A国大統領再選の結果に対し、B国は直ちに祝意を示したが、少なくとも他の東南アジア諸国が何らかの「声明」を出した形跡はなく、B国独自の外交戦略が浮き彫りになった。

congratulate：祝う；祝いの言葉を述べる
at least：少なくとも
bring to light：暴露する：明るみに出す；表沙汰にする

trade-off

[tréid-ɔ́ːf]

☐ 325

両立しないこと；（相殺）取引；交換

☞ political trade-off 政治的取引

In diplomatic negotiations, especially in recent years, domestic and foreign policy issues are often **trade-offs** that are increasingly difficult to determine.

tragic

[trǽdʒik]

☐ 326

悲劇的な；悲惨な；痛ましい

☞ tragedy 悲劇；惨事

☞ tragically 悲劇的に；あえなく

Ways to minimize the impact of U.S. military activities in Japan on residents living in the vicinity of U.S. military facilities and areas have been important issues for ensuring smooth implementation of the Japan-U.S. security arrangements. As a result of the **tragic** incident in Okinawa at the beginning of September 1995, in which a school girl was raped by three U.S. servicemen, there has been a growing concern focused on various issues related to the stationing of U.S. forces in Okinawa. (Diplomatic Bluebook 1996)

transfer

[trænsfə́ːr | trænsfə́ː]

☐ 327

移す；移動させる；伝達する

☞ transferee 転任者；被譲渡人

The Ministry of Foreign Affairs of Country A has decided to temporarily close the Embassy of Country A in Pyongyang. The report said that the MOFA plans to **transfer** the ambassador and his family to C in Country B.

transition

[trænzíʃən, -síʃ-]

☐ 328

移行；変遷；過渡期

☞ transitionally 過渡的に

The cease-fire agreement of YY 20XX was reached in response to the severe **transitions** in the situation. It was followed by the peace agreement that was signed three months later.

外交交渉において、内政問題と外交問題がトレードオフになる場合が多く、特に最近では判断が難しいケースが増えている。

diplomatic negotiation：外交交渉
especially：特に；とりわけ
increasingly：ますます；次第に

在日米軍の活動が米軍施設・区域の周辺の住民に与える影響等をいかに小さくするかという問題は、従来より、日米安保体制を円滑に運用していく上で大きな課題であったが、95年9月初めに沖縄県で女子小学生が3名の米軍兵によって暴行されるという不幸な事件が発生し、沖縄県における米軍の駐留に伴う諸問題に対する関心が大きく高まった。（外交青書 1996）

minimize：小限に抑える；最小化する
vicinity：周辺；周辺地
smooth：円滑な；順調な；速やかな
servicemen：serviceman（軍人）の複数形
stationing：駐留

A国外務省は駐平壌A大使館を一時閉鎖することを決め、大使と家族をB国のCに移動させる予定だと報じた。

temporarily：一時的に；当座のところ；当面は（temporary：一時的な；仮の）
plan：計画する；するつもりである；計画；企画

深刻な事態の推移を受けて成立したのが20XX年YY月の停戦合意であり、それに引き続き3ヶ月後に調印された和平合意である。

severe：厳しい；深刻な
situation：状況；状態；場面
followed by X：続いてXがある；後にXが続いて

transnational

[trænznǽʃənəl]

□ 329

多国籍の；国を跨いで；多国籍企業

☞ transnationally 国境を越えて

Globalization also had the effect of increasing the influence of non-state actors such as NGOs and **transnational** corporations.

treaty

[tríːti]

□ 330

条約（文書）；協定（書）；契約

☞ peace treaty 講和条約；平和条約（協定）

North Korea called on the U.S. to hold a dialogue to change the armistice agreement into a peace **treaty** but the U.S. did not accept this and has enhanced its pressure on North Korea. (Diplomatic Bluebook 2017)

trigger

[trígər]

□ 331

引き金（を引く）；きっかけ（となる）；起こす

☞ triggering device 起爆装置

The execution of Mr./Ms. C by the Country A's government and the attack on the Embassy of Country A by angry citizens of Country B were the direct **triggers** for the break of diplomatic relations. However, the two had long been known to be antagonistic.

tripartite

[traipɑ́ːrtait]

□ 332

三者（間）の；三者加盟の；3 つに分かれた

☞ trinity 三つ組；三位一体

The Government of Japan engages in **tripartite** cooperationwith Asian nations under the framework of the "Cooperation among East Asian Countries for Palestinian Development (CEAPAD)" aiming to mobilize Asian countries for practical assistance to Palestine. (Diplomatic Bluebook 2017)

グローバル化は、NGO（非政府組織）や多国籍企業といった国家以外の主体の影響力を増大させる効果も生んでいる。

globalization : グローバル化 ; グローバリゼーション
corporation : 民間企業 ; 法人

北朝鮮は米国に対し、休戦協定を平和協定に変えるための対話を求めたが、米国はこれを受け入れず、北朝鮮に対する圧力を強化している。

hold a dialogue : 対話をする ; やり取りする（dialogue = dialog）
change X into Y : X を Y に変える

国交断絶の直接的な引き金となったのは、A 国政府による C 氏の処刑と、それに憤った B 国市民による A 大使館の襲撃であるが、両者はかねてより対立関係にあったことで知られていた。

angry : 怒って ; 憤慨して
break : 断絶 ; 中止 ; 破損 ; 壊す ; 破る
antagonistic : 敵対（対立）関係にある

アジア諸国からの支援を動員すべく日本が開始した「パレスチナ開発のための東アジア協力促進会合（CEAPAD）」の枠組みの下で、アジア諸国との三角協力を通じた対パレスチナ支援が進んでいる。（外交青書 2017）

tripartite cooperation : 三角協力
Palestinian : パレスチナの ; パレスチナ人（の）
mobilize : 動員する ; 結集する

troop

[trúːp]

□ 333

軍隊；一団；群をなして動く

☞ overseas dispatch of troops 海外派兵

Country A's government has indicated that it will cut **troops** deployed in the Middle East and Europe. Moreover, they shall reposition the reduced forces primarily to the Asia-Pacific region following the new national defense strategy.

trustworthiness

[trʌ́stwə̀rðinés]

□ 334

信頼性；信用性；頼りがい

☞ trustworthy 信頼できる；信用できる

It is crucial to develop and strengthen an effective international justice system in general, to ensure honest compliance with international law, and to enhance the justice system's **trustworthiness** in the international legal system.

ultimatum

[ʌ̀ltəméitəm]

□ 335

最後通牒；最後通告；最終的申し入れ

☞ ultimata ultimatum の複数形

Country A issued an **ultimatum** for a pre-emptive strike on Country B. Country A likewise advised all foreigners in Country B, including media personnel and UN inspectors, to leave immediately.

unanimously

[juːnǽnəməsli]

□ 336

満場一致で；全員異議なく；全会一致で

☞ unanimous 全員一致の；全会一致の；同意見で

Country A's Upper House **unanimously** passed a law to counter the regional hegemony of Country B. At the same time, Senator C, the representative of the legislative delegation submitting the bill, stressed that the passage of the bill is only the first step in the effort.

A 国政府は中東や欧州に展開する部隊を削減し、新たな国防戦略に基づき、削減された部隊を主にアジア太平洋地域に再配置する方針を示した。

reposition：再配置；再配置する
Asia-Pacific region：アジア太平洋地域
defense strategy：防衛戦略

国際法の誠実な遵守を確保し、国際法体系に対する信頼性を高めるためにも、実効的な国際司法制度全般の整備、強化が重要である。

justice system：司法制度（justice：正義；司法）
in general：一般の；概して
honest：誠実な；率直な
legal system：法制度；法体系；法律制度

A 国は B 国への先制攻撃に向けた最後通告をし、B 国内にいる報道関係者や国連査察官らすべての外国人に即時退去を勧告した。

pre-emptive strike：先制攻撃（pre-emptive：先制の；先取りの）
likewise：同様に；同じように

A 国上院は、B 国の地域覇権に対抗するための法律を満場一致で可決したが、法案提出の議員団の代表である C 氏は、法案通過は取り組みの第一歩に過ぎないことを強調した。

Upper House：上院
pass：通過する；可決する；合格する
bill：法案；請求書；紙幣

undergo

[ʌ̀ndərgóu]

□ 337

経験する；受ける；耐え忍ぶ

☞ underwent undergo の過去形

In addition, at the Summit Meeting in October, Prime Minister Abe requested Cambodia to **undergo** democratization and conveyed his intention to expand governance support including invitations to Japan to young, politics-oriented Cambodians. (Diplomatic Bluebook 2019)

underneath

[ʌ̀ndərníːθ]

□ 338

下（部）に；底面に；背後に

☞ beneath 下に；下方に；真下に

The intentions **underneath** the diplomat's words were not easy to grasp, and the negotiations lasted for a long time.

unification

[jùːnəfikéiʃən]

□ 339

統一；統合；単一化

☞ unify 単一化する；1 つにする

☞ reunification 再統合；再統一

In addition, Morocco was approved to rejoin the African Union (AU) in January. Close attention is being paid to future trends such as the **unification** of Maghreb. (Diplomatic Bluebook 2017)

unilateral

[jùːnilǽtərəl]

□ 340

一方的な；片務的な；片側のみの

☞ unilaterally 一方的に

Furthermore, China continues **unilateral** development of resources in the maritime area pending delimitation between Japan and China, and has repeatedly carried out maritime surveys without Japan's consent. (Diplomatic Bluebook 2018)

また、10月の首脳会談でも、安倍総理大臣より、カンボジアの民主化を求めつつ、若手政治関係者の招へいなどガバナンス支援を拡充する考えを伝えた。（外交青書 2019）

和文中には undergo に相当する日本語表現は直接見られない。解釈としては「民主化を経ること（経験すること）」が "to undergo democratization" に相当すると考えられ、さらに省略されて「民主化」となっている。

その外交官の言葉の背後にある意図を汲み取ることは容易ではなく、交渉は長時間に及んだ。

grasp：握る；把握する；把握；理解
last：続く；持続する；最後の；最もしそうにない

また1月には、モロッコのアフリカ連合（AU）への再加盟が承認された。マグレブ地域統合を始めとする今後の動向が注目される。（外交青書 2017）

rejoin：再び加わる；再結合
close attention：細心の注意
trend：傾向；動向；トレンド

さらに、日中間の境界未画定海域での中国による一方的な資源開発も継続しているほか、日本の同意を得ない海洋調査も繰り返されている。（外交青書 2018）

development of resources：資源開発
maritime area：海域
pending：未解決の；係争中の

unipolarity

[jùːnipəulǽriti]

□ 341

単極性；一極性

☞ polar 極の；極地の

The post-Cold War composition of the American **unipolarity** is coming to an end. The world now is entering a new era of competition for hegemony.

unpredictable

[ʌ̀npridíktəbl]

□ 342

予測できない；予断を許さない；気まぐれな

☞ predictable 予測できる；予言できる

In addition, a cease-fire agreement brokered by Russia and Turkey came into effect on December 30, but it is **unpredictable** if this cease-fire will be honored by the disputing parties or lead to a subsequent political process. (Diplomatic Bluebook 2017)

upheaval

[ʌphíːvəl]

□ 343

動乱；激変；隆起

☞ political upheaval 政変

While domestic political **upheaval**, stagnant resource prices, and other factors led to negative economic growth for two consecutive years in 2015 and 2016, Japanese companies continue to have a strong faith in the Brazilian market. Evidence of this is clear from the participation of nearly 130 people in a joint meeting of the Japan-Brazil Economic Cooperation Committees in August, and the holding of a Japan Brazil Meeting for Cooperation on Infrastructure Improvements that same month. (Diplomatic Bluebook 2018)

冷戦後のアメリカの一極性の構図は終焉を迎え、世界は新たな覇権競争の時代を迎えつつある。

post-Cold War：冷戦後；ポスト冷戦
come to an end：終わる；終わりを迎える；途切れる

また、12月30日にロシア及びトルコが仲介した停戦合意が発効したが、この停戦が紛争当事者に遵守されるか、その後の政治プロセスにつなげていくことができるかについては予断を許さない。（外交青書 2017）

come into effect：発効する；効力を生じる
honor：尊重する；重んじる；栄誉となる；名誉
political process：政治過程（プロセス）

国内の政治混乱や、資源価格の低迷などにより、2015年から2016年にかけては2年連続のマイナス成長を記録したが、8月に開催された日本ブラジル経済合同委員会には日本から約130名が参加し、同月には日本ブラジルインフラ協力会合が開催されるなど、日本企業はブラジル市場に引き続き高い期待を寄せている。（外交青書 2018）

two consecutive years：2年連続（consecutive：連続した）
faith：信頼；信用；信念
participation：参加

100

urge

[ə́ːrdʒ]

□ 344

促す；駆り立てる；衝動

☞ urgency 緊急；切迫

☞ urgent 緊急の；切迫した

The international community has continued to **urge** both Israel and Palestine to resume the negotiations at an early date to improve such situation. (Diplomatic Bluebook 2017)

verify

[vérəfài]

□ 345

実証する；検証する；立証する

☞ verification 検証；実証；立証

☞ verifiable 検証可能な

The political statement was approved at the opening ceremony, clearly setting out efforts to strengthen measures to end tuberculosis, secure funds for these measures, strengthen research and development, and strengthen frameworks to **verify** progress. (Diplomatic Bluebook 2019)

vessel

[vésəl]

□ 346

大型船；血管；容器

☞ drilling vessel 掘削船

When the Government of Japan strongly suspects that ship-to-ship transfers with North Korean **vessels** banned by the UN Security Council resolutions are conducted, Japan has been taking measures such as notification to the Security Council Committee established pursuant to Resolution 1718, sharing of information with related countries, and releasing of information to the public. (Diplomatic Bluebook 2019)

この状況を改善しようと、国際社会は、イスラエル・パレスチナ双方に対して、早期交渉再開の呼びかけを続けた。（外交青書 2017）

Palestine：パレスチナ
at an early date：近い将来；近々（date：期日；日取り）
continue：続ける；継続する

開会式において、政治宣言が了承され、結核対策の強化、対策資金の確保、研究開発の強化、進捗を確認する仕組みの強化に取り組むことが明記された。（外交青書 2019）

opening ceremony：開会式
set out：着手する；出発する
tuberculosis：結核
fund：資金；基金

安保理決議で禁止されている北朝鮮船舶との「瀬取り」（洋上での物資の積替え）を実施していること等違反が強く疑われることが確認された場合には、国連安保理北朝鮮制裁委員会への通報、関係国への関心表明、対外公表等の措置を採ってきている。（外交青書 2019）

ship-to-ship transfer：瀬取り
conduct：実施する；行為
notification：通知（notify：通知する；知らせる）
pursuant to X：X に準じて；応じて

101

veto

[víːtou]

□ 347

拒否権（の行使）；拒否（する）；厳禁（する）

☞ power of veto 拒否権

The Japanese Ministry of Foreign Affairs issued the following statement in response to Russia and China's **veto** of the Security Council resolution.

vigorously

[vígərəsli]

□ 348

活気あふれて；精力的に；力強く

☞ vigor 活力；活発さ

The two countries affirmed that, based on the results of February's summit meeting, concrete cooperation between Japan and the U.S. would be pursued yet more **vigorously**. (Diplomatic Bluebook 2018)

warfare

[wɔ́ːrfèər]

□ 349

戦争（状態）；交戦；戦い

☞ psychological warfare 心理戦；神経戦

Cautious debate continues in the Diet on whether it is appropriate for Japan to send the Self-Defense Forces to Country A, which is in a state of a de facto **warfare**.

withdraw

[wiðdrɔ́ː, wiθ-0]

□ 350

撤退する；退く；引き出す

☞ withdrawn
withdraw の過去分詞形

On the issue of the ongoing standoff between the forces of Country A and Country B in Area C, government and military officials of both countries have agreed to **withdraw** their respective forces in a phased manner.

日本国外務省は、今回の安保理決議でロシアと中国が拒否権を行使したことを受け、次のように声明を発表した。

"(power of) veto over X" で「X に対する（関する）拒否権（の行使）」を意味し、veto は名詞・動詞どちらで用いることも可能。

両者は、2月の日米首脳会談の結果を踏まえ、日米間の具体的協力をより一層進めていくことを確認した。（外交青書 2018）

affirm：確認する；賛同する；肯定する
concrete：具体的な；明確な
yet：さらに；まだ；しかし

事実上の戦争状態にある A 国に、日本が自衛隊を派遣することは適切なのか、今国会で慎重な議論が続いている。

cautious：慎重な；用心深い
debate：論争；ディベート；論争する
Self-Defense Forces：自衛隊

A 国と B 国の両軍が C 地域でにらみ合いを続けている問題について、両国の政府・軍関係者は段階的にそれぞれの軍を撤退させることで同意した。

ongoing：進行中の
standoff：睨み合い；膠着状態
phased manner：段階的に（phase：段階）

PART III

英語学習コラム

私達は皆「ノイラートの船」の乗組員

「ノイラートの船」をご存知でしょうか。これはオーストリアの科学哲学者であるノイラート (Otto Neurath, 1882-1945) が用いた船の喩えのことで、後に言語哲学者のクワイン (Willard Van Orman Quine, 1908-2000) が好んで用いたことで知られるようになりました。

話のポイントは、皆さんが大海原で航海を続ける船の乗組員だということです。例として、皆さんが木造のそれほど大きくない船に 3、4 人で乗って航海をしていると考えて下さい。すると急にその船が壊れてしまい、改修の必要が生じました。さあ大変です。

ここで重要なことは、「理想を言えば」、船を一旦港に戻し、全て解体の上、一から組み直すことがベストな改修方法です。しかしそれは不可能です。なぜなら皆さんは今、海の真っ只中にいるからです。修理をしながら、しかし船自体沈まないようにしながらの作業が否応なしに求められます。使えるものは流れてくる流木でも何でも使わざるを得ませんし、船は一気には修理されず、徐々にしか改修できません。

全く同じことが英語学習についても言えます。私達は海の上にいるということを忘れないで下さい。つまり事態は決して理想的ではないのです。これまでの己の境遇を嘆いてみたところで、はたまた周囲の環境を非難してみたところで、皆さんの英語力の向上には何の役にも立ちません。

現実的にできることをやるしかありません。しかしそうすることによって、皆さんの英語力は確実に伸びます。これこそ、プラグマティズムが取るスタンスです。言語社会学者の鈴木孝夫 (1926-) は、日本人が陥りがちな「完璧な英語」を目指す態度を「蜃気楼」だと喝破しました。英語の出来不出来は単に程度の問題でしかありません。身の回りのありとあらゆる機会を使い、さらにはそうした機会を新たに創出して、自らの英語力を高め続けることが大切です。

一番良くないのは、単なる批評家に成り下がり、できない理由を並べ立てて、結局何もしない人です。船の上にそんな人がいたらどう思うか、考えてみれば明らかなことです。

外国語習得はコスト、戦略的に分野を特化して！

意外と私達が認識していないことの１つに、外国語学習はコストだという考えがあります。１つの外国語をモノにするために私達は多大なお金と時間をかけます。中には趣味で何カ国語も好んで学ぶ人もいますが、そうした人を除いて、外国語習得はできれば避けて通りたいですし、避けて通るべきです。言うまでもなく、その分の「コスト」が他のことに使えるからです。本来は母語である日本語が世界に広く普及していれば良かったのですが、残念ながら現状そうはなっていません。今更日本語をそこまでの地位に押し上げることは不可能ですから、私達は「仕方なく」まず英語を習得しています。一方、英語やフランス語の母語話者からしたら、自分達の言語が世界中で使われている（使わせている）わけですから圧倒的に有利です。どう考えてもフェアではありませんが、それが現状ですから私達は「仕方なく」英語を、加えてさらに他の言語を習得するのです。

外国語習得がコストであるならば、なるべく効率的かつ効果的に、そして戦略的に習得するべきです。特に明確目標も定めず、ただ外国人と仲良くしたいという程度のものなら、AI（人工知能）の自動翻訳で十分です。国際的な舞台で交渉に臨む、発表する、取り引きするなど、本書を手に取った皆さんであれば、自分が英語を用いて何をしたいのか、その具体的な姿を目に浮かべることができるはずです。まずはその場面で英語が使えれば良いのです。逆に言えば、それ以外の場面での優先度は低くて構いません。母語でない以上、母語話者と同じだけの語彙力を身に付けることは至難の技ですし、そもそもそういったことを誰も期待していません。国際交渉で英語を使うことが主目的であるならば、例えば花の名前や魚の名前を知っておく必要はほとんどないのです。つまり「全部できる」必要はないのです。英語において「完璧主義」に陥る日本人は少なくありません。謙虚で素晴らしい態度ですが、しかし「割り切って考える」ことも、時にそれ以上に必要なことです。

国際会議などで行われるコーヒーブレークで、なかなか話の輪に入っていけず、自分の英語力の無さを責める日本人から相談を受けることがよくあります。しかしどうでしょう、コーヒーブレークで話の中心にいることがあなたが英語を学ぶ主目的なのでしょうか？ そうでないならば、そうした英語力は後回しでよいのです。割り切りましょう。そして完璧主義を捨てましょう。これが英語上達のコツです。10 年後、20 年後、思うように英語が使えるようになっていればそれでよいのです。

<英語＋多言語習得> マルチリンガルのススメ

筆者は日本で英語教育を受けた典型的な人間だ。ネイティブ・スピーカーと会話をすると「L と R の発音」の間違いを指摘され、リスニングは大の苦手である。書店に行くと「冠詞の使い方」といった類のテキストをついつい手に取ってしまう。そんな筆者は、大学時代に英語力がなかなか上がらないまま、2003 年に韓国での交換留学の機会に恵まれた。

留学先の大学で到着早々待ち受けていたのは図らずも英語のシャワーだった。校内にある外国人寄宿舎には、世界中から来た留学生が生活していて共通言語は英語だった。そこで多数を占めていたのが、韓国企業のサムソンが新興国で選抜した「サムソン・プログラム」の学生であった。当時の韓国ではすべて英語で講義を行う国際大学院・国際学部の新設が盛んで、こうした留学生が韓国人に混ざって大学院の講義を受け、修士課程終了後にサムソンへそのまま入社し、自らの出身国とのビジネスを担当するという仕組みだ。

当初韓国語を一から学ぼうとした筆者であったが、留学生活最初の 3 ヶ月は英語漬けの生活に。この間思い知らされたのは、留学生も韓国人学生も英語力の高さだけでなく、母国語＋ 2 言語を駆使するトライリンガルが当たり前のようにいたことである。留学生であれば、母国語に加えて英語＋母国語に近い言語、韓国人であれば、英語に加えて、日本語か中国語。そういえば、この頃から韓国では日本語に代わって中国語学習者が激増していた。

当時から大卒の就職競争が激しかった韓国では、如何に他の学生との能力差を身につけるか、履歴書に書ける資格試験に合格できるかが問われていた。TOEIC 900 点以上がないと大企業に就職できないという話を頻繁に聞いたものである。さらに、TOEIC の点数勝負で差が出ないと考えた学生は、自らの英語力に磨きをかけるため、英語プレゼンテーション能力を磨く勉強会に参加したり、海外の大学に留学する学生がたくさんいた。欧米の大学はもちろん、フィリピンの語学学校に行くという友人の話を聞いて、当時はフィリピンで学ぶメリットを理解できない、理解しようともしない自分がいたのである。

勉強熱心な留学生や韓国人学生とは対照的に、筆者は最初の交換留学で納得のいく韓国語能力を身につけることができず、もう一度韓国へ留学することになる。2 回目の留学で驚いたことは、現地で出会った中国朝鮮族留学生の言語能力である。

母国語である中国語に加え、民族語である朝鮮語がネイティブ、さらに高校での第２外国語として日本語を学んだという学生に多く出会った。その中の何人かは高校の授業だけで相当高いレベルの日本語能力を身につけていて本当に驚いたものである。

この２回の留学で出会ったトライリンガルの学生に共通していることは、自分の競争力を高め、母国だけに止まらず、近隣国、あるいは欧米などグローバルな人材市場で勝負しようとする気概（きがい）を持っていたことである。そのために必要な複数の言語を習得した上で、英語はペーパーテストの点数よりも実践的に高いレベルを目指して切磋琢磨（せっさたくま）していたのだ。

押し付けがましく聞こえるかもしれないが、英語に加えてもう一言語習得するメリットは計（はか）り知れない。例えば、初めて出会った人が無愛想に流暢（りゅうちょう）な英語で話しかけてきたとする。話の内容から相手が韓国語を話せると分かり、韓国語で話しかけると一転して柔和（にゅうわ）な表情になり会話が弾（はず）む。こちらが同じ言語をできると分かるとお互いの距離感がグッと近づく。相手の違った「人となり」を見ることもできるのである。

この教材を手にした皆さんは本コラムを読んで、「英語だけでなく複数の言語を勉強するべきだ」という筆者の主張を負担に感じるかもしれない。そこは気持ちを楽にして、英語学習の合間に、気分転換で他言語の基礎的な教科書を眺（なが）めるだけでも相乗効果が期待できると思う。「まずは英語だけに専念して極めるべきだ」という考える人もいるだろう。人によってやり方は様々だ。学習量の大小はさておき、その言語の背景にある文化や世界観を知るだけでも勉強になる。国際社会で活躍することを夢見る人はぜひ複数言語の習得に挑戦して欲しい。

発信の大切さ

20 世紀を代表する言語学者の筆頭であるチョムスキー (Noam Chomsky, 1928-) は、言語能力を、言語知識 (linguistic competence) と言語運用 (linguistic performance) に区分しました。この分類が象徴するように、言語はたとえそれを知識としてどれだけ持っていようとも、それが使えるかどうかとは別問題です。皆さんは多くの英語の動詞を耳で聞いて理解できるでしょうが、しかし自分が即座(そくざ)に発信で使える動詞は、その中のごく一部であることに気づくはずです。どれだけ受信能力に長(た)けていようとも、発信のための持ち駒は自然には増えません。発信には発信のための取り組みが不可欠となります。

使えるようにするためには、使うしかありません。そしてここが重要なのですが、練習ではダメなのです。本番、もしくはそれに近い状況でどれだけの場数が踏(ふ)めるか、運用能力の向上はそれにかかっています。運用能力は「鍛(きた)える」ものだからです。

sink or swim という言葉があります。直訳すれば「泳ぐかそれとも溺(おぼ)れるか」ということになりますが、これはまさに、水の中に突き落とされることで、必死になって「できるようになる」ことを意味します。差し迫(せま)った必然性 (urgent needs) のもと、しどろもどろになって失敗を繰り返しながら、徐々に運用能力は身につきます。皆さんがあこがれるロールモデルがいるとしたら、その人は初めから英語がうまかったわけではありません。単に、それだけ失敗した経験を積み重ねているだけです。挑戦を恐れてはいけません。

以前のコラムで指摘した「完璧主義」はここでも完全な弊害(へいがい)です。もっと文法をやってから、もっと語彙を増やしてから、もっと練習してから…というのは単にやらないための口実です。今の自分の英語力で挑戦しましょう。はじめからうまくいくことを考えずに、鍛え、磨き続けるのです。

もう 1 つ強調しておきたい点があります。それは日本人がよく口にする「ペラペラ信仰」です。断言しますが、英語をペラペラ話すことをゴールにすることは間違っています。日本語ですらペラペラ話す人は一部ですし、ペラペラ話せることは単に発話の流暢(りゅうちょう)性を評価しているだけです。逆に重要な交渉の場面でペラペラとマシンガントークで話せば、一言一言に重みがなくなり、相手にとって嫌気が差すことさえあるくらいです。ゆっくりと、はっきりと、そして大きな声で話すこと、これは発話において大変重要なことです。子ども染(じ)みて聞こえるかもしれませんが、どの道の専門家であっても、このことを否定する人はいないでしょう。

2 ランク上の英語力を目指して

ここまで英語学習コラムでは、皆さんが今持つ英語力に自信と誇(ほこ)りを持ち、堂々と、そして果敢(かかん)に英語を使うべきことを述べてきました。すると当然、次のような意見が出てくると思います。「じゃあどんな英語であれ、通じれば、もっというと通じさせればそれで OK なのか ?」、「文法的な間違いや、単語の言い間違えなど気にせず、とにかく話せれば大丈夫なのか ?」・・・こういった問いです。

答えは、大部分の日本人に取っては「Yes」でしょう。しかし、本書を手に取る皆さんの多くにとっては「No」です。

国益を代表して交渉に臨む外交官はもちろんのこと、企業や教育機関、その他の諸団体など、組織の利益を代表して英語で交渉する場合、「通じれば良い」では話になりません。初歩的な文法ミスは相手の信頼すら損ねるかもしれませんし、話すだけでなく、高度な英文を「書く」能力がなければ相手にしてもらえません。

ただしこうした高いレベルの英語能力は、全員には決して求められていません。どれだけ多く見積もっても、こうした能力が期待されるのは、全人口の数パーセント程度でしょう。皆さんが既にそこに入っているのか、入ることを目指して一生懸命努力しているのかについては、皆さん自身が一番よく分かっていることだと思います。

トップ数パーセントに期待される英語力は、単なる日常会話程度では困ります。試験で満点が取れても意味がありません。そして本書は国際関係、外交に特化した英対話、単語、表現を取り上げていますが、分野ごとに異なることは言うまでもありません。

そこで、「2 ランク上の英語力」と比喩(ひゆ)してみたいと思います。皆さんが現在目標としている次のレベルの英語力の、さらにもう 1 つ先の英語力が求められていると思って下さい。当然一朝一夕(いっちょういっせき)では身につきません。日々努力を重ね、磨き続けて、やっと数年後、数十年後に大成するような英語力です。容易(たやす)いことではありません。

繰り返しますが、ほぼ全ての日本人にとって、このレベルの英語力は必要ありません。冷たい言い方をしているのではなく、本当に必要ないからです。自分がどうなりたいのか、どうしたいのか、改めて皆さんの決意と覚悟が求められていると言ってよいでしょう。

英語力が必要とされる国家公務員は「外交官」だけではない

本書を手に取った読者の中で、将来国家公務員、特に外務省で外交官として働くことを夢見ている人も多いだろう。また、国連などの国際公務員を目指す人もいるかもしれない。いずれも国際社会を舞台に高度な英語を駆使する語学力が求められる職業である。一般的に、国家公務員の中で語学力が入省時に求められるのは外務省、あるいは防衛省専門職員（英語など）が挙げられる。それでは日本の他省庁では高度な英語力を必要とされないのだろうか。

筆者が 2015 年 1 月から 2 年半勤務した内閣官房国家安全保障局（以下「NSS」:National Security Secretariat）は、これまで縦割りだった外交安全保障政策の立案過程を一本化し、関係省庁から必要な情報を要求・分析し、内閣総理大臣のリーダーシップの下に迅速かつ効率的な政策決定することを目的に、2013 年 12 月に創設された組織である。NSS には外務・防衛・警察・そして陸海空の各自衛隊からの出向者に加え、公安調査庁や海上保安庁などの関係省庁の職員も集められ、日本の外交安全保障政策の司令塔に相応しい布陣となった。

NSS が独自に果たす役割の中で特に重要なことは、「カウンターパート」である外国政府の NSS、あるいは類似組織との普段の情報交換による関係構築を通じて、必要に応じて直接外交交渉を行うことを可能にした点である。NSS が最も緊密に連絡を取り合うのは、同盟国アメリカの大統領直属スタッフ組織である NSC（National Security Council）だ。最近の各国が展開する外交スタイルは、首脳個々人のリーダーシップによるトップダウン型が目立つ。こうした首脳外交を直接補佐する各国の NSC との関係構築は、今日の外交活動の成否を左右すると言っても過言ではない。そこで、NSS での業務遂行に必要とされるのが個々人の英語力である。具体的に必要とされる場面を挙げると、①カウンターパートとなる組織や在京各国大使館との情報交換や交渉、②外国出張、③外国からの来客（政府高官など）対応などである。省庁横断的で重要な政策決定を迅速にできるようになった背景には、裏方のスタッフである行政官の語学能力が貢献しているのである。

最近では外務省以外でも、高度な英語力が求められる場面が増えている。従来の伝統的な安全保障概念に加えて、経済安全保障の強化が叫ばれている昨今、日本独自の技術流出を防ぎ、国外からのサイバー攻撃への対処能力向上などが求められている。どれも従来型の「外交官」では太刀打ちできない分野ばかりで、経済産業省や総務省などの行政官が他国との折衝(せっしょう)の前面に立つことが増えた。これに加えて、情報技術の発達によって、世界の動きは速まるばかりである。政策決定にスピードが求められる中で、通訳を必要としない行政官の個々の能力が求められている。今後はどの省庁に入省しても国際社会の最前線に送り込まれることを想定すべきだろう。そのために、大学で一定程度の英語力を磨き、入省後はその英語力をより実践的なものに切磋琢磨して、成長させることができる人材が求められている。

PART IV

チェックリスト
（総索引）

<総索引の使い方>

PART III には、本書で使用した合計 2,194 の英対話定型表現、英単語・英熟語（注釈を含む）などがアルファベット順に並べられています。各項目には本書の使用箇所についての情報も付記されていますので、これら全ての語彙・表現が確実に身に付いているか、本パートを何度も活用して記憶の定着をはかって下さい。

本書全体を通して、どなたにとっても新出の語彙があったはずです。語根は同じでも品詞を違えることで意味も少しずつ変化します。例文等で使用した語彙の中には相当ハイレベルなものも含まれます。PART I に記載されている全ての表現を含め、自分のものにできるよう取り組んで下さい。

まずは意味が分かることが大切ですが、それだけではなく、自分の語彙としてモノにして下さい。言えるだけでなく、書けることも同時に重要です。妥協することなく取り組んで下さい。

No.		使用箇所	English	日本語
1	□	33	a-	(否定を意味する接頭辞)
2	□	210	a number of	多数の;多くの
3	□	28	a series of X	一連のX
4	□	241	(a) verbal pledge	口約束
5	□	**2-9b**	abandon	廃棄する;諦める;捨て去る
6	□	1	abbreviated	省略された;簡略化された
7	□	1	abbreviation	短縮;省略(形);略語
8	□	300	abductee	拉致被害者;誘拐された被害者
9	□	300	abduction	誘拐;拉致
10	□	300	abduction issue	拉致問題
11	□	243	abroad	海外で(に);広く
12	□	**3-1**	abrupt	急な;突然の
13	□	**3-1**	abruptly	突然;不意に
14	□	**1-20c**	Absolutely!	もちろんです。;その通りですとも。
15	□	34	abuse	乱用;悪用;乱用する;悪用する
16	□	99	accede	即位する;就く;継承する;加盟する
17	□	183	accelerate	加速する;前倒しする
18	□	82	accept	受け入れる;承服する;受諾する
19	□	165	acceptable	容認できる;受け入れられる
20	□	2	accession	接近;加盟;即位
21	□	2	accession negotiation	加盟交渉
22	□	182	accompany	伴う;同行する
23	□	48	accomplish	成し遂げる;達成する
24	□	166	accord	一致する;調和する
25	□	12	according to X	Xによると;と一致して
26	□	195	accuracy	正確さ
27	□	3	accusation	非難;告発
28	□	3	accuse	非難する;告発する;責める
29	□	3	accuse X of Y	(Xに対してYのことで)非難する
30	□	4	acknowledge	認識する;認める;承認する;感謝する
31	□	4	acknowledgement	承認;感謝;謝辞
32	□	156	acquisition	取得;買収
33	□	**3-22a**	activist	活動家;運動家

No.		使用箇所	English	日本語
34	□	5	actor	行為主体；当事者；俳優
35	□	6	actual	実際の，現実の
36	□	6	actuality	現実（味）；アクチュアリティ；実在
37	□	174	add insult to injury	泣きっ面に蜂の状態にさせる；踏んだり蹴ったりにさせる
38	□	197	additional	追加の；付加的な
39	□	7	adhere	固執する；粘着する；支持する
40	□	7	adherence	固守；執着；支持
41	□	85	adherent	支持者；信奉者
42	□	14	administration	政権
43	□	221	adolescent	思春期の
44	□	38	adopt	採択する；可決する；承認する；養子にする
45	□	175	advance	前進させる；進展させる
46	□	73	advantage	優位；利益；好都合
47	□	73	advantageous	有利な；好都合な
48	□	8	adversarial	敵対的な；対立する
49	□	8	adversary	敵（の）；敵国（の）；敵対者
50	□	9	adviser/advisor	相談役；顧問；助言者
51	□	10	advocacy	擁護；支援運動；提唱
52	□	10	advocate	主張する；擁護者
53	□	107	affect	影響を与える；作用する
54	□	11	affiliation	所属；提携；加入
55	□	348	affirm	確認する；賛同する；肯定する
56	□	24	aftermath	直後の時期；余波；後(あと)の状態
57	□	55	against X	X に対して；反対して
58	□	12	agency	機関；局；取り次ぎ
59	□	**1-22c**	agenda	議題；予定
60	□	12	agent	工作員；調査官；代理人
61	□	153	aggravate	悪化させる；より重くする；悩ます
62	□	234	aggression	侵略；攻撃
63	□	189	aggressive	攻撃的な
64	□	5	aggrieved	被害を受けた；権利を侵害された
65	□	13	agreeable	賛同できる；好ましい

No.		使用箇所	English	日本語
66	□	13	agreement	合意；協定；一致
67	□	**3-28a**	agricultural product	農産物
68	□	54	agriculture	農業
69	□	108	aid	援助；支援；援助する；支援する
70	□	148	aim	意図する；向ける；狙う
71	□	55	aircraft	航空機
72	□	165	airspace	空域
73	□	59	airstrike	空爆；空からの攻撃
74	□	81	all-out	全面的な
75	□	20	allegation	疑惑
76	□	14	allege	言い張る；断言する；言い訳をする
77	□	14	alleged	申し立てられた；言われている
78	□	15	allegiance	忠誠；義務；献身
79	□	16	alleviate	緩和する；軽減する；緩める
80	□	16	alleviation	緩和；軽減
81	□	17	alliance	同盟（関係）；提携（国）；類似性
82	□	280	allocate	割り当てる；配分する
83	□	49	allow	許す；許可する
84	□	49	allow me to express X	Xを言わせて下さい
85	□	17	ally	同盟（する）；同盟を結ぶ；結び付ける
86	□	173	alone	単独で；孤立して
87	□	287	alongside	並行して；同時に；横に
88	□	**3-5a**	alter	変える；変更する
89	□	18	alternate	交互に行う；互い違いにする
90	□	18	alternative	代替手段；選択肢；二者択一の
91	□	18	alternatively	その代わりに；代案として
92	□	**3-23b**	altogether	全体で；総計で；完全に
93	□	19	ambassador	大使；代表；使者
94	□	19	ambassador extraordinary and plenipotentiary	特命全権大使
95	□	305	amended	修正された；補正された
96	□	20	amid	囲まれて；真っ只中に；取り巻かれて
97	□	20	amid great applause	拍手喝采の中

No.		使用箇所	English	日本語
98	□	57	amount	量；額
99	□	21	anarchist	無政府主義者；アナーキスト
100	□	21	anarchy	無政府状態；混乱；無秩序
101	□	152	ancestor	先祖；祖先
102	□	152	ancestral	先祖の；先祖から伝わる
103	□	331	angry	怒って；憤慨して
104	□	22	annex	併合する；付け足す；付属書類；別館
105	□	22	annexation	併合；合併；付属
106	□	29	anniversary	記念日（祭）；周忌
107	□	40	announce	公表する；発表する
108	□	331	antagonistic	敵対（対立）関係にある
109	□	222	anti-whaling	反捕鯨の；捕鯨に反対の
110	□	220	any country that meets its obligations	その義務を満たすいかなる国にとっても
111	□	**1-33b**	anyhow	とにかく；いずれにせよ
112	□	**1-31b**	anyway	とにかく；いずれにせよ
113	□	90	apart from X	X とは別に；離れて
114	□	238	apology	謝罪
115	□	157	apparent	明らかな；明白な；見かけの
116	□	291	application	応募；申請；出願
117	□	32	apply for	申請する；申し込む；志願する
118	□	19	appoint	任命する；指名する
119	□	19	appointed	任命された
120	□	23	apprehend	懸念する；心配する；理解する；逮捕する
121	□	23	apprehension	懸念；理解；逮捕
122	□	24	appropriate	適切な；ふさわしく；充当する
123	□	24	appropriately	適切に；ふさわしく
124	□	25	approval	承認；同意；認可
125	□	25	approve	承認する；同意する；認可する
126	□	54	approximately	およそ；約
127	□	26	arbitrate	仲裁する；解決する
128	□	26	arbitration	仲裁（裁定）；調停
129	□	27	archive	保存記録；公文書；保管する

No.		使用箇所	English	日本語
130	□	219	arisen	arise（起こる；生じる）の過去分詞形
131	□	28	arm	武装する；腕
132	□	28	armed	武装した；武器を持った（伴った）
133	□	29	armistice	休戦；停戦
134	□	29	armistice agreement	休戦（停戦）協定
135	□	193	arms embargo	武器禁輸；武器輸出禁止
136	□	257	arms export	武器輸出
137	□	30	arrange	準備する；配置する；協定を結ぶ
138	□	30	arrangement	手配；配置；協定
139	□	79	arrest	逮捕する；拘束する
140	□	**3-7a**	arson	放火
141	□	5	Article 51	（第）51 条（"article" は条文における「条」を指す）
142	□	1	as a (direct) result of A	A の（直接的な）結果として
143	□	18	as a means to X	X するための手段として
144	□	138	as a whole	全体として；総じて
145	□	**2-24a**	as far as we understand it	私達が理解する限りでは； 私達の理解が及ぶ範囲では
146	□	**3-29b**	as for X	X に関しては
147	□	186	as many as X	X もの数の；X と同じ数だけ多くの
148	□	93	as soon as possible (ASAP)	できるだけ早く；すぐに；速やかに
149	□	**2-23b**	as soon as we can	できるだけ早く；すぐに；速やかに
150	□	247	as such	その結果；そうすることで； それ自体（は）；そのようなものとして
151	□	30	as well as	同様に；もちろん
152	□	333	Asia-Pacific region	アジア太平洋地域
153	□	179	aspect	側面；向き；相
154	□	264	assess	評価する；査定する
155	□	104	asset	資産；財産；資源
156	□	104	asset freezing	資産凍結
157	□	278	asset recovery	資産（財産）回復
158	□	87	assign	任命する；配属する；割り当てる
159	□	170	assist	援助；援助する

No.		使用箇所	English	日本語
160	□	76	assistance	援助；支援
161	□	31	assume	想定する；思い込む
162	□	31	assumption	想定；仮定；掌握
163	□	32	asylum	亡命；保護；避難所
164	□	33	asymmetric	非対称の；不均衡な
165	□	33	asymmetry	非対称；不均衡；不釣り合い
166	□	253	(肯定文での) at all	仮にも；いやしくも (条件節で用いる)
167	□	344	at an early date	近い将来；近々
168	□	324	at least	少なくとも
169	□	**2-28a**	at stake	危機に瀕して；問題となって
170	□	202	at the mercy of X	X のなすがままに；翻弄されて
171	□	294	at the request of X	X の依頼を受けて；要求により
172	□	204	atomic	原子力の；原子の
173	□	204	atomic bombing	原爆投下
174	□	223	attack	攻撃
175	□	216	attain	達成する；獲得する
176	□	51	attempt	試み
177	□	311	attend	出席する；参列する；随行する
178	□	126	austerity	緊縮；緊縮経済
179	□	34	authoritative	当局の；権限のある；きっぱりと
180	□	34	authority	権限；権威；当局
181	□	35	autonomous	自治の；自律的な
182	□	35	autonomy	自治 (権)；自律 (性)；自治国家
183	□	7	avoid	避ける
184	□	316	back	支援する；後押しする
185	□	264	back-and-forth	堂々巡りの；行ったり来たりの
186	□	316	backed	支援を受けた；後援された
187	□	56	baggage claim	(空港の) 手荷物受取所
188	□	36	balance of power	勢力均衡；力の均衡
189	□	36	balance	均衡；平衡；残高；釣り合う；拮抗する
190	□	37	ballistic	弾道 (の)；弾道学の
191	□	37	ballistic missile	弾道ミサイル
192	□	38	ban	禁止する；差し止める；禁 (止) 令

No.		使用箇所	English	日本語
193	□	39	bargain	交渉する；駆け引きをする
194	□	39	bargaining	交渉；取り引き；駆け引き
195	□	255	bargaining chip	交渉の切り札；交渉を有利にする材料
196	□	40	barter	物々交換；交換する；交易する
197	□	40	barter transaction	バーター取引
198	□	86	base	基地；ベース；土台
199	□	272	based on X	X に基づいて；を踏まえて
200	□	**3-21b**	basic human rights	基本的人権
201	□	112	battlefield	戦場
202	□	**3-17b**	(be) about to X	X しそうである； まさに X しようとしている
203	□	51	(be) capable of X	X の能力がある；できる
204	□	**1-23b**	(be) interested in X	X に関心がある；気になっている
205	□	**3-20a**	(be) kindly requested to X	どうか X して下さい； X するようお願いします
206	□	44	(be) known as X	X として知られる
207	□	60	(be) likely to X	X しそうである
208	□	313	(be) located	位置する
209	□	**1-16a**	(be) not supposed to X	X しないことになっている
210	□	**2-9b**	(be) ready to X	X する用意がある；厭わない； 覚悟がある；するつもりだ
211	□	80	(be) subject to X	X にさらされる；支配下にある； 左右される
212	□	**1-16a**	(be) supposed to X	X することになっている
213	□	**2-13a**	(be) up to you	あなた次第；あなたが決める
214	□	56	bear	生み出す；(責任を) 負う
215	□	**2-21b**	bear X in mind	X を覚えておく；心に留めておく
216	□	180	because of X	X のために；せいで
217	□	167	behalf	利益；支持
218	□	**1-35b**	behave	ふるまう；行儀よくする
219	□	85	believer	信者；信じる人
220	□	338	beneath	下に；下方に；真下に
221	□	41	bestow	与える；授ける；贈る
222	□	41	bestowment	授与

No.		使用箇所	English	日本語
223	□	42	betray	裏切る；漏らす；騙す
224	□	42	betrayal	裏切り；背信；密告
225	□	**1-10a**	between ourselves	ここだけの話ですが； 大きな声では言えませんが
226	□	36	between X and Y	X と Y の（2 つの）間に（で）
227	□	**1-10a**	between you and me	ここだけの話ですが； 大きな声では言えませんが
228	□	45	bi-/di-	2
229	□	50	bias	偏見；先入観
230	□	50	biased	偏った；偏見を抱いた
231	□	43	bilateral	二国間の；双務的な；両側の
232	□	43	bilaterally	二国間で；相互に
233	□	336	bill	法案；請求書；紙幣
234	□	44	biological and chemical weapons	生物化学兵器
235	□	44	biology	生物学
236	□	45	bipolar	二極の；両極端の；相反する
237	□	46	bolster	強化する；支援する；支持物
238	□	46	bolster morale	士気を高める（上げる）
239	□	3	border	国境；境
240	□	130	border control	国境管理；出入国管理；国境検問所
241	□	137	born	bear（生む）の過去分詞形
242	□	137	borne	bear（生む・産む）の過去分詞形（born は生命が生まれる時にのみ用い、それ以外は borne を用いる）
243	□	47	branch	部門；府；支店
244	□	331	break	断絶；中止；破損；壊す；破る
245	□	61	break down	失敗に終わる；決裂する
246	□	297	break out	勃発する；突発する；起こる
247	□	32	breaking news	ニュース速報；臨時ニュース
248	□	25	breakthrough	突破口；飛躍的進歩
249	□	34	bribe	賄賂
250	□	34	bribery	賄賂の授受；収賄；贈賄
251	□	235	briefing	説明（会）；概況；ブリーフィング
252	□	76	bring about	引き起こす

No.		使用箇所	English	日本語
253	□	324	bring to light	暴露する；明るみに出す；表沙汰にする
254	□	296	British	イギリスの；英国の
255	□	51	broad	広汎な；幅の広い
256	□	297	broke	break の過去形
257	□	79	broker	仲介業者；ブローカー；仲立ちする；調停する
258	□	76	brought	bring の過去形・過去分詞形
259	□	184	brush off	はねつける；無視する；一蹴する
260	□	67	budgetary	予算の；予算上の
261	□	196	build up	築き上げる；確立する
262	□	231	built	build（築く；建設する）の過去形・過去分詞形
263	□	48	bureau	事務局；局；支局
264	□	48	bureaucracy	官僚（主義）；官僚制；官僚組織
265	□	48	bureaucrat	官僚；役人
266	□	4	but one X	ただ 1 つの X；唯一の X
267	□	292	by itself	それ自体で；単独で；自然に
268	□	**2-20c**	by the way	ところで；それはそうと；ついでながら
269	□	23	cabinet	内閣
270	□	3	call on	要求する；訪問する
271	□	49	calumniate	中傷する；誹謗する；謗る
272	□	49	calumniation	中傷；誹謗；謗り
273	□	50	campaign	（組織的）運動；選挙運動
274	□	50	campaigner	運動員；活動家；従軍者
275	□	191	candid	率直な；偏見のない
276	□	51	capability	能力；可能性；性能
277	□	52	capitalism	資本主義；資本制；キャピタリズム
278	□	52	capitalist	資本主義者；資本家
279	□	252	captive	捕虜；人質
280	□	59	carry out	実行する；遂行する；執行する
281	□	155	case	事例；場合；問題
282	□	240	catch the plague	疫病にかかる
283	□	130	cause	原因
284	□	349	cautious	慎重な；用心深い

No.		使用箇所	English	日本語
285	□	53	cease	終わる；中止する；終止
286	□	53	cease fire	停戦，休戦
287	□	317	cease-fire agreement	停戦（休戦）合意（協定）
288	□	152	cessation	停止；中止；中断
289	□	284	chair	議長を務める；議長
290	□	102	Chairman (Chairperson) of State Affairs Commission	国務委員長
291	□	143	challenge	挑む；挑戦する；異議を唱える
292	□	330	change X into Y	X を Y に変える
293	□	90	channel	チャンネル；ルート；手段
294	□	283	chaos	混乱；混沌；カオス
295	□	150	characteristic	特徴；特性；特徴のある
296	□	159	charge	起訴する；請求する；責める
297	□	95	charter	憲章
298	□	13	chemical	化学（の）
299	□	44	chemistry	化学
300	□	92	chief	長官；長；上司
301	□	23	Chief Cabinet Secretary	内閣官房長官
302	□	315	chilly	冷淡な；冷ややかな
303	□	54	circumstance (s)	状況；環境；境遇
304	□	55	citizen	民間人；市民；国民
305	□	55	citizenship	市民権；公民権
306	□	266	civil servant	公務員
307	□	14	civil war	内戦
308	□	59	civilian	一般人；文民；非戦闘員
309	□	56	claim	主張する；要求する；苦情
310	□	**2-13a**	clarifications	説明；明確化
311	□	**2-13a**	clarify	明確にする；解明する
312	□	117	clear	はっきりとした；疑う余地のない
313	□	242	clear	明らかな；確実な；はっきりした；疑う余地のない
314	□	89	close	近い；親密な；閉じる；閉鎖する
315	□	339	close attention	最新の注意
316	□	66	closely	緊密に；接近して

No.		使用箇所	English	日本語
317	□	**2-26a**	closure	閉鎖；撤退
318	□	38	coal	石炭；炭
319	□	216	coalition	連立；連合
320	□	57	coerce	強要する；抑圧する
321	□	182	coercion	強制（力）；抑圧
322	□	57	coercive	強制的な；威圧的な；強引な
323	□	**2-8c**	coincidence	一致；同時発生
324	□	52	Cold War	冷戦
325	□	58	collapse	崩壊（する）；倒壊させる；倒れる
326	□	59	collateral	二次的な；付帯的な；巻き添え
327	□	59	collateral damage	付帯的損害；巻き添え被害
328	□	60	collect	集める；収集する
329	□	60	collective	集合的な；集団の；共同の
330	□	48	collision	衝突；対立
331	□	**3-4a**	collusion	共謀；談合
332	□	58	colonial	植民地の；植民の
333	□	259	com-	(「共に」を意味する接頭辞)
334	□	16	combine	結合する
335	□	342	come into effect	発効する；効力を生じる
336	□	341	come to an end	終わる；終わりを迎える；途切れる
337	□	225	commence	開始する；始める
338	□	148	commend	褒める；称賛する
339	□	292	commensurate	釣り合った；等しい；同等の
340	□	61	commerce	商業；貿易；商科
341	□	72	commercial	商業の；商売の
342	□	102	commission	委員会；職務；委託；委託する
343	□	34	commit	犯す；委ねる；全力を傾ける
344	□	111	commodity	一次産品；鉱物；農作物；商品；日用品
345	□	51	common	共通の
346	□	296	commonwealth	連邦；共和国；団体
347	□	68	communicate	伝達する
348	□	82	community	共同体；団体；地域社会
349	□	119	comparably	比較できるほどに；同程度に

No.		使用箇所	English	日本語
350	□	54	compared to X	X と比較して
351	□	62	compassion	思いやり；同情；憐れみ
352	□	62	compassionate	思いやりのある；情け深い
353	□	168	compatible	互換性のある；両立可能な；相性がよい
354	□	63	compel	強要する；強制する；強いる
355	□	64	compete	競争する；競い合う；匹敵する
356	□	64	competition	競技；試合；競争
357	□	64	competitive	競争の激しい；競合する
358	□	113	complete	完全な
359	□	113	complete, verifiable and irreversible dismantlement (CVID)	完全な；検証可能な；かつ；不可逆的な廃棄
360	□	48	complex	複雑な
361	□	66	compliance	遵守；コンプライアンス
362	□	65	complicate	複雑にする；分かりにくくする
363	□	65	complicated	複雑な；交錯した；難解な
364	□	66	comply	遵守する；従う；応じる
365	□	259	component	構成要素；成分
366	□	65	composition	構図；構成
367	□	84	comprehensive	包括的な；理解のある
368	□	67	compromise	妥協（する）；和解（する）；折衷案
369	□	63	compulsion	無理強い
370	□	68	conceal	隠蔽する；隠す
371	□	68	concealment	隠蔽；潜伏；隠匿
372	□	235	concentration	集中；濃度
373	□	81	concern	懸念；心配事；心配する；憂慮する
374	□	67	concerning X	X に関して；について
375	□	69	concession	譲歩；容認；利権
376	□	69	concession speech	敗北宣言
377	□	309	conclude	締結する；結論を下す
378	□	348	concrete	具体的な；明確な
379	□	70	condemn	非難する；糾弾する
380	□	70	condemnation	非難；有罪判決；没収

No.		使用箇所	English	日本語
381	□	346	conduct	実施する；行為
382	□	132	confidence-building	信頼醸成（の）
383	□	151	confine	監禁する；制限する
384	□	151	confinement	監禁；幽閉
385	□	75	confirm	確認する；承認する；確かにする
386	□	278	confiscate	没収する；差し押さえる
387	□	71	conflict	紛争；論争；対立（する）
388	□	72	conformity	符合；一致；服従
389	□	73	confront	直面する；対決させる；対立させる
390	□	73	confrontation	対決；対立；衝突
391	□	16	congestion	渋滞；密集
392	□	324	congratulate	祝う；祝いの言葉を述べる
393	□	**2-18c**	Congratulations!	おめでとう。
394	□	74	congress	国会；議会；大会
395	□	74	Congress	アメリカ連邦議会
396	□	262	conjunction	接続；結合
397	□	343	consecutive	連続した
398	□	75	consensus	意見の一致
399	□	75	consent	同意（する）；承諾（する）；許可（する）
400	□	76	consequence	結果；帰結；重大性
401	□	76	consequently	（≒ as a consequence）その結果；それ故に
402	□	64	consist	成る；構成する
403	□	77	conspiracy	陰謀；謀議；共謀
404	□	77	conspiracy theory	陰謀論
405	□	77	conspire	共謀する；たくらむ
406	□	83	constant	絶えず続く；継続的な
407	□	78	constitute	構成する；制定する；任命する
408	□	206	constitutional	憲法（上）の；合憲の；構成上の
409	□	277	constitutional amendment	憲法（の）修正；改憲
410	□	206	constitutional monarchy	立憲君主制；立憲君主国
411	□	24	construction	建設
412	□	134	constructive	建設的な

No.		使用箇所	English	日本語
413	□	151	consular mission	領事公館
414	□	79	consulate	領事館；領事の職権；領事の任期
415	□	79	consulate(-)general	総領事館
416	□	29	consultation	協議；話し合い； （専門家から）助言を求めること
417	□	272	consume	消費する；浪費する
418	□	272	consuming	消費する；消費しつくす
419	□	235	contaminate	汚染する；汚す
420	□	235	contaminated	汚染された
421	□	80	contemptuous	軽蔑した；さげすんだ；見下した
422	□	80	contemptuously	軽蔑して；見下して； 小馬鹿にしたように
423	□	125	contentious	議論を引き起こす；議論のある
424	□	7	continent	大陸
425	□	81	contingency	偶発性；偶有性；不測の事態
426	□	81	contingent	偶発的な；不測の；左右されて
427	□	81	contingent on X	X 次第で；を条件として
428	□	344	continue	続ける；継続する
429	□	263	continuously	継続的に
430	□	122	contract	契約；協定
431	□	82	contrary to X	X に反して；とは逆に；裏腹に
432	□	213	contribute	貢献する；寄与する
433	□	58	control	支配；制限；管理
434	□	83	controversial	物議を醸している；論争を引き起こす
435	□	83	controversy	論争；（対立点のある）議論；物議
436	□	84	convene	開催する；召集する
437	□	84	convention	協定；条約；慣習
438	□	254	conventional	従来（型）の；慣習的な
439	□	85	conversion	変更；転換；改宗
440	□	85	convert	変更する；改心させる；改宗させる
441	□	86	convoy	護衛（する）；護送（する）；護衛隊
442	□	17	cooperation	協力
443	□	329	corporation	民間企業；法人
444	□	**3-19b**	corps	団；団体；隊

No.		使用箇所	English	日本語
445	□	33	correct	是正する；修正する；矯正する
446	□	47	correspondent	担当記者；特派員
447	□	79	corrupt	買収された；腐敗した；堕落する
448	□	79	corruptly	不正に
449	□	262	council	地方議会；評議会；審議会
450	□	176	counter intelligence	防諜；対敵諜報活動
451	□	61	counter-	敵対して；逆の
452	□	87	counterfeit	偽造の；偽の
453	□	61	countermeasure	対抗策；対抗手段
454	□	87	counterpart	相当するもの（人）；対の片方；片われ
455	□	87	counterparty	相手方；契約相手
456	□	97	counterterrorism	テロ対策；テロへの対抗措置
457	□	266	coup	政変；クーデター
458	□	88	courier	特使；密使；急使
459	□	159	court	裁判所
460	□	159	court ruling	判決
461	□	89	courtesy	丁寧な行為；厚意；礼儀
462	□	89	courtesy shuttle service	（無料の）シャトルサービス
463	□	95	covenant	規約
464	□	90	covert	隠れた；覆われた；暗に示した
465	□	57	crackdown	取り締まり；弾圧
466	□	91	credential	信任状；資格；信任の
467	□	92	credibility	信憑性；信用（性）；確からしさ
468	□	92	credible	信頼できる；信用できる
469	□	156	crime	罪；犯罪
470	□	**3-18a**	criminal	犯罪者；犯人；犯罪の
471	□	**2-3**	crises	crisis（危機）の複数形
472	□	68	crisis management	危機管理
473	□	173	critical	重要な；批判的な；危機的な
474	□	177	criticism	批判；非難
475	□	10	criticize	批判する
476	□	**2-1**	cross the border	越境する；国境を越える
477	□	113	crucial	決定的な；極めて重要な

No.		使用箇所	English	日本語
478	□	111	crude	加工されていない；粗雑な
479	□	111	crude oil	原油
480	□	98	cruel	残酷な；残忍な；無慈悲の
481	□	57	currently	現在は；目下
482	□	93	custom	関税；税関；慣習
483	□	93	customary	慣習法の；慣習となっている
484	□	268	cyberattack	サイバー攻撃；サイバーアタック
485	□	164	cyberspace	サイバー空間；サイバースペース
486	□	**2-33b**	Damn.	ちくしょう。；しまった。
487	□	**3-7a**	dangerous	危険な；危害を加える
488	□	313	dare	あえてする；大胆にもする； 思い切ってする（助動詞として同様の 意味で用いることも可能）
489	□	344	date	期日；日取り
490	□	94	de facto	事実上；事実上の（は）；実際にある
491	□	94	de facto standard	デファクトスタンダード；業界標準
492	□	24	deal	取引；契約
493	□	24	deal (with)	扱う；処理する
494	□	99	death	死（婉曲表現が demise）
495	□	349	debate	論争；ディベート；論争する
496	□	54	decade	10 年
497	□	227	decide	決定する
498	□	95	declaration	宣言；布告；申告
499	□	255	declaration of war	宣戦布告
500	□	95	declare	宣言する；布告する
501	□	27	declassify	機密指定から解く； 機密扱いから解除する
502	□	187	decline	減少する；辞退する；拒否する
503	□	235	decommission	廃止する；閉鎖する
504	□	161	dedicated to X	X のために尽くす；捧げる
505	□	96	deed	行為；行動；偉業
506	□	201	deepen	深める
507	□	144	deeply	深く；深刻に
508	□	227	defeat	打ち負かす；勝つ；破る

No.		使用箇所	English	日本語
509	□	333	defense strategy	防衛戦略
510	□	223	defensive	防御の；守勢の
511	□	33	deficit	不足額；赤字
512	□	98	define	定義する
513	□	181	definitely	確かに；厳密に；はっきりと
514	□	98	degrade	品位を落とす
515	□	98	degrading	品位を下げるような；下劣な
516	□	35	degree	程度；段階
517	□	68	delay	遅れ；遅滞
518	□	97	delegate	代表として派遣する；委任する；使節；代表
519	□	97	delegation	代表団；使節派遣；権限移譲
520	□	98	deliberate	意図的な；計画的な
521	□	98	deliberately	故意に；慎重に；計画的に
522	□	94	demand	要求する；求める
523	□	203	demilitarize	非武装化する；武装解除された
524	□	99	demise	死去；逝去：活動停止
525	□	110	demobilization	動員解除；復員
526	□	177	democratic	民主的な；民主制の；民主主義の
527	□	177	Democratic Party	(米国) 民主党
528	□	100	demographic	人口統計 (学) の；人口動態；デモグラフィック
529	□	100	demography	人口統計学；デモグラフィー
530	□	271	demonstrate	はっきり示す；実演する；デモをする
531	□	**3-12b**	demonstrator	デモ参加者；実演者
532	□	63	denied	deny (否定する；拒否する) の過去・過去分詞形
533	□	101	denounce	非難する；糾弾する；告発する
534	□	101	denounce the elections as invalid	選挙が無効であるとして非難する
535	□	102	denuclearization	非核化；核武装をやめること；核兵器撤去
536	□	101	denunciation	非難；糾弾；告発
537	□	291	departure	出発；出国

No.		使用箇所	English	日本語
538	□	103	deploy	（軍などを）展開する；配置する
539	□	103	deployment	配置；展開；配備
540	□	94	deport	追放する
541	□	94	deportation	国外追放；国外退去
542	□	260	deprive	奪う；取り上げる
543	□	276	Deputy Assistant Minister	官房審議官
544	□	276	Deputy Minister	官房長
545	□	299	describe	述べる；記述する；描写する
546	□	104	designate	指定する；任命する；指名を受けた
547	□	104	designation	指定；任命
548	□	142	despite X	X にもかかわらず
549	□	44	destroy	破壊する
550	□	**3-5a**	detail	詳細；細目
551	□	**3-23b**	detain	拘束する；留置する；拘留する
552	□	**3-24c**	detention	拘留；抑留；引き留め
553	□	81	deteriorate	悪化する
554	□	105	determinate	決定的な；限定的な；明確な
555	□	105	determine	決定する；決心する；終結させる
556	□	106	deterrence	抑止（力）；戦争抑止；阻止
557	□	106	deterrent	抑止する；引き止める；制止する
558	□	107	devastated area	荒廃地；被災地
559	□	107	devastating	壊滅的な；圧倒的な；悲惨な
560	□	127	develop	発展する；開発する；発達する
561	□	7	development	開発
562	□	108	development cooperation	開発協力
563	□	340	development of resources	資源開発
564	□	108	dialog box	ダイアログボックス
565	□	108	dialogue	対話（する）；会話；協議
566	□	295	Diet	国会
567	□	**3-12b**	dignitary	高官；要人
568	□	302	dignity	威厳；高位；品格
569	□	**3-13a**	dilemma	板挟み；難問；ジレンマ
570	□	179	diminish	少なくする；減少させる

No.		使用箇所	English	日本語
571	☐	109	diplomacy	外交；外交関係；外交手腕
572	☐	109	diplomat	外交官；外交家
573	☐	109	diplomatic	外交（上）の；外交的手段による
574	☐	39	diplomatic bargaining	外交交渉
575	☐	251	diplomatic document	外交文書
576	☐	323	diplomatic efforts	外交（的）努力
577	☐	279	diplomatic missions abroad	在外公館
578	☐	279	diplomatic missions overseas	在外公館
579	☐	325	diplomatic negotiation	外交交渉
580	☐	218	diplomatic privilege	外交特権；外交官特権
581	☐	300	diplomatic solution	外交的解決
582	☐	188	diplomatically	外交的に
583	☐	195	diplomatist	diplomat（外交官）と同義
584	☐	188	direct dialog	直接対話
585	☐	**3-17b**	director-general	長官；総裁；事務総長；会長
586	☐	110	dis-	（否定の意味）
587	☐	48	disappointing	失望させる；期待外れの
588	☐	110	disarm	武装（を）解除する；武器を取り上げる
589	☐	110	disarmament	武装解除；軍備縮小（撤廃）
590	☐	16	disaster	災害；大惨事
591	☐	111	disaster drill	避難（災害）訓練
592	☐	111	disastrous	破滅的な；災害の；悲惨な
593	☐	112	discern	識別する；見分ける；分かる
594	☐	112	discernible	識別できる；認識できる
595	☐	113	dismantle	廃棄する；取り壊す
596	☐	113	dismantlement	廃棄；解体撤去；撤収
597	☐	160	dismiss	解雇する；免職する
598	☐	241	dispatch	派遣する；急送する
599	☐	245	dispel	払いのける；晴らす
600	☐	243	dispensable	なくても済む；必ずしも必要でない
601	☐	153	displaced	住むところを失った；立ち退かされた
602	☐	114	disputatious	論争的な；論争好きの

No.		使用箇所	English	日本語
603	□	114	dispute	論争（する）；異議を唱える；抵抗する
604	□	115	disregard	無視（する）；軽視（する）；度外視（する）
605	□	**3-6a**	disrupt	混乱させる；破壊する
606	□	24	disseminate	広める；ばらまく
607	□	**3-7a**	dissemination	散布；流布
608	□	116	dissidence	不一致；相違；不同意；異議
609	□	116	dissident	意見を異にする；反体制派；反体制の
610	□	116	dissident elements	反体制の要素（派閥；分子）
611	□	11	dissolution	解体
612	□	11	dissolve	解消する；解散する
613	□	131	distribute	分配する；配布する
614	□	131	distributed	分散型（の）
615	□	223	district	地区；地域；地方
616	□	280	divide	分ける；分割する
617	□	35	division	分割
618	□	**1-8a**	do me a favor	頼む；お願いがある
619	□	**2-25c**	do our best	最善（全力）を尽くす； できる限り努力する
620	□	**1-17b**	Do you have a minute?	ちょっといいですか？； 少々お時間いいですか？
621	□	**2-7b**	Do you mind if X?	Xして構いませんか?;よろしいですか?
622	□	117	doctrine	方針；教義；主義
623	□	118	domestic	国内の；自国の；家庭内の
624	□	60	domestic and external affairs	内外政の
625	□	230	domestic law	国内法
626	□	243	domestically	国内で；国内的に
627	□	247	dominance	優位；優越；支配
628	□	119	dominant	支配的な；主要な；最も有力な
629	□	119	dominate	支配する；最も重要である
630	□	**3-27a**	Don' t you remember X?	X を覚えていないのですか？； をお忘れですか？
631	□	235	dose rate	線量率
632	□	154	double standard	ダブルスタンダード；二重基準

No.		使用箇所	English	日本語
633	□	120	draft	起草する；下書きをする；草案
634	□	284	draft resolution	決議草案
635	□	114	draft statement	声明案；声明の原案（下書き）
636	□	16	drainage	排水；排水路；排水設備
637	□	346	drilling vessel	掘削船
638	□	109	dub	称する
639	□	111	due to X	X が原因で；のせいで
640	□	72	duly	正当に；期日通りに
641	□	297	during X	X の間中；間ずっと
642	□	321	dynasty	王朝；王家
643	□	121	dysfunctional	機能不全の；逆機能の； 機能が損なわれた
644	□	61	e-commerce	電子商取引；e コマース
645	□	65	each	それぞれの；各々の
646	□	77	easily	容易に；たやすく；気軽に
647	□	58	economic collapse	経済崩壊；経済破綻
648	□	119	economic diplomacy	経済外交
649	□	179	economic front	経済面；経済前線
650	□	169	economic growth	経済成長
651	□	111	economic policies	経済政策
652	□	194	economies in transition	経済移行国
653	□	6	editorial	論説
654	□	123	effective	効果的に
655	□	123	efficient	効率的に
656	□	166	effort	努力；尽力；骨折り
657	□	21	elect	選出する；選ぶ
658	□	21	election	選挙
659	□	285	electricity	電気；電力
660	□	308	elevate	高める；上げる；昇進させる
661	□	122	embargo	禁輸；通商禁止；出入港禁止を命じる
662	□	123	embark	着手する；乗り込む；積み込む
663	□	123	embarkation/ embarkment	積み込み；乗船；搭乗
664	□	124	embassy	大使館；使節団

No.		使用箇所	English	日本語
665	□	124	embassy official	大使館員
666	□	167	emerge	出現する；現れる
667	□	203	emergency	緊急；非常；突発
668	□	203	emergency situation	緊急事態；有事
669	□	167	emerging country	新興国
670	□	125	emigrant	移民；移住者；移民の
671	□	125	emigration	移住；移民
672	□	126	empathic no	強調された "ノー"；断固とした "否"
673	□	126	emphatic	強調された；際立った；語気の強い
674	□	124	employee	被雇用者；従業員；職員
675	□	303	employment rate	就職率；就業率
676	□	129	en-	(名詞を動詞化させる働き)
677	□	305	enact	制定する；上演する
678	□	67	enactment	(法律の) 制定
679	□	51	encourage	促す；励ます
680	□	**3-4a**	endanger	危険にさらす；危うくする
681	□	127	endorse	承認する；支援する
682	□	127	endorsement	支持；承認；保証
683	□	128	enforce	施行する；強制する；強化する
684	□	128	enforcement	施行；執行；強制
685	□	109	engage (in)	従事する；携わる
686	□	106	enhance	高める；強化する；向上させる
687	□	129	enlarge	大きくする；拡大する；拡張する
688	□	129	enlargement	拡大；拡張；増大
689	□	59	enormous	非常に大きな；巨大な；莫大な
690	□	129	enrich	豊かにする
691	□	225	enrichment	濃縮；豊かにすること；強化すること
692	□	49	ensure	確かにする；確実にする
693	□	130	entangle	もつれさせる；巻き込む；からませる
694	□	130	entanglement	紛糾；もつれ；鉄条網
695	□	237	enter	入る；出場する
696	□	147	entire	全体の；全くの
697	□	131	entity	存在；実体；実在物

No.		使用箇所	English	日本語
698	☐	183	environment	環境；周囲（の状況）；情勢
699	☐	132	envoy	特命使節（特使）；（特命全権）公使；使者
700	☐	132	envoy extraordinary and minister plenipotentiary	特命全権大使
701	☐	128	equipment	装備；備品
702	☐	11	era	時代
703	☐	**3-19b**	escalate	悪化する；増大する；上昇させる
704	☐	325	especially	特に；とりわけ
705	☐	244	essential	必須の；本質的な
706	☐	133	establish	設立する；確立する；制定する
707	☐	133	establishment	設立；確立；樹立；制定
708	☐	134	eternal	永遠の；不滅の；不変の
709	☐	157	ethnic	民族の；民族的な
710	☐	**3-1**	eve	直前；前夜
711	☐	17	event	（重要な）出来事；事件
712	☐	222	evidence	証拠；形跡
713	☐	137	example	例；例示
714	☐	281	excellent	極めて良い；優秀な
715	☐	237	except	除いて；以外は
716	☐	89	exception	例外
717	☐	89	exceptional	例外的な；異例の
718	☐	254	excessively	過度に；過剰に
719	☐	135	exclusive	排他的な；閉鎖的な；スクープ
720	☐	135	exclusive economic zone (EEZ)	排他的経済水域
721	☐	229	excusable	許される；申し訳の立つ
722	☐	**2-31b**	excuse myself	失礼する；辞退する；ご免被る
723	☐	136	execution	遂行；履行；処刑；死刑執行
724	☐	136	executive	行政府；重役；執行する
725	☐	47	executive branch	行政機関；行政府
726	☐	137	exemplify	例証する；実例を挙げて説明する；典型例となる
727	☐	212	exercise	行使する；用いる；鍛える
728	☐	138	exert	行使する；働かせる；努力する

No.		使用箇所	English	日本語
729	□	138	exertion	行使；発揮；骨折り
730	□	185	expand	拡大する；拡張する；膨張させる
731	□	51	expansion	拡大；拡張
732	□	178	expect	期待する
733	□	281	expert	専門家；熟達者
734	□	92	explain	説明する；明らかにする
735	□	139	explicit	明確な；明示的な；系統立った
736	□	139	explicitly	はっきりと；明白に
737	□	140	exploit	搾取する；食い物にする
738	□	140	exploitative	搾取的な；収奪的な；資源開発の
739	□	121	explore	探求する；探る
740	□	**3-7a**	explosion	爆発
741	□	40	export	輸出する
742	□	40	exported	輸出された
743	□	268	expose	さらす；暴く；露呈する
744	□	96	express	述べる；示す；表現する
745	□	228	expressed their opposition	反対の意思を表明した；異を唱えた
746	□	221	extend	延ばす；拡張する；延長する
747	□	60	external	外の；外部の
748	□	255	extract	引き出す；抜粋する
749	□	**3-25a**	extradite	引き渡す；送還する
750	□	**3-18a**	extradition	（本国）送還；引き渡し
751	□	19	extraordinary	特命の；特別の
752	□	53	extremely	極めて；極端に
753	□	143	extremism	過激主義；過激思想
754	□	183	extricate	解放する；自由にする；脱出させる
755	□	85	face	直面する
756	□	141	facilitate	促進する；円滑に進める；手助けする
757	□	141	facility	施設；設備；容易さ
758	□	67	factional	党派の；党派的な
759	□	142	fail to	し損なう；できない；しないで終わる
760	□	142	failure	失敗；失敗したもの；落第点
761	□	**1-31b**	Fair enough.	結構。；分かった。；取引成立。

No.		使用箇所	English	日本語
762	□	343	faith	信頼；信用；信念
763	□	249	faithfully	忠実に；誠実に
764	□	77	fake	偽の；でたらめな
765	□	184	false	間違った；誤った；偽りの
766	□	131	falsification	偽造；改竄
767	□	26	far from X	X から遠く離れて；少しも X ではない
768	□	322	fear	恐れ；恐怖；懸念
769	□	35	federal	連邦政府の；連邦の
770	□	35	federalism	連邦制
771	□	212	fictional	架空の；フィクションの
772	□	64	fiercely	激しく；猛烈に
773	□	99	figure	象徴；姿；形；図
774	□	320	file	申し立てる；提訴する
775	□	320	file a lawsuit	訴訟を起こす；告訴する；提訴する
776	□	241	finance	財政；財務
777	□	108	financial	財務の；財政的な；財政上の
778	□	150	fine	細かい；立派な
779	□	145	fire	発砲する；燃やす
780	□	256	firing	発射；発砲；点火
781	□	243	fiscal policy	財政政策
782	□	267	fisheries	fishery（漁業；水産業）の複数形
783	□	15	flag	旗
784	□	**1-4**	flare up	突発する；燃え上がる
785	□	37	flew	fly（飛行する）の過去形
786	□	288	flight	飛行；飛行機；飛行距離
787	□	112	foe	敵
788	□	9	follow	続く
789	□	**3-3a’**	follow-up	補足（質問）（follow-up question〔補足質問〕の question が省略された形）
790	□	328	followed by X	続いて X がある；後に X が続いて
791	□	11	following	続いて；受けて；次の
792	□	**1-3**	following year	翌年；次の年
793	□	**2-3**	food crises	食糧危機

No.		使用箇所	English	日本語
794	□	87	for the purpose of X	X のために；の目的で
795	□	**2-11b**	for the time being	当分の間；差し当たり
796	□	159	for-life	終身（の）
797	□	210	fora	forum（フォーラム；公開討論会）の複数形
798	□	143	force	力；軍隊；強引に押し進める
799	□	278	forced repatriation	強制送還
800	□	143	forcible	力づくの；強制的な
801	□	72	foreground	前景
802	□	118	foreign	外国の；対外の（domestic の反意語）
803	□	35	foreign affairs	外交
804	□	9	foreign affairs/ diplomatic adviser	外交顧問
805	□	305	Foreign Exchange and Foreign Trade Act	外為法（外国為替及び外国貿易法）
806	□	31	foreign policy	外交政策
807	□	228	forejudge	予断する
808	□	144	foresight	先見性；展望；洞察力
809	□	**3-27a**	Forget it.	忘れた方がいいですよ。； 今のはなかったことにして下さい。； そんなことはどうでもいい。
810	□	282	forgivable	許せる；容赦できる
811	□	260	formal	形式上の；公式の；儀礼的な
812	□	**3-24b**	formally	正式に；公式に
813	□	8	former	かつての；以前の；元の；前者（の）
814	□	123	foster	育成する；養育する
815	□	1	found	設立する
816	□	43	foundation	基盤
817	□	30	framework	枠組み；体制
818	□	209	free trade	自由貿易；自由貿易の
819	□	**3-26b**	free-market economy	自由主義経済
820	□	288	freedom	自由；解放
821	□	**3-29b**	freedom of speech	言論の自由
822	□	112	frequently	頻繁に；しばしば
823	□	142	fresh	新しい

No.		使用箇所	English	日本語
824	□	72	friction	摩擦
825	□	145	friendly fire	友軍射撃（味方からの誤射）；誤爆；同士討ち
826	□	272	friendly relation	友好関係
827	□	92	friendship	友好関係；友情
828	□	36	from balance of power to collective security	勢力均衡から集団安全保障へ
829	□	279	frontline	最前線；第一線
830	□	196	fully	十分に
831	□	121	functional	機能的な；実用的な
832	□	345	fund	資金；基金
833	□	117	fundamental	基本的な；根本的な
834	□	146	fundamentalism	原理主義；根本主義
835	□	146	fundamentalist	原理主義者；原理主義者の
836	□	282	further	さらに深く；さらに遠く
837	□	24	furthermore	さらに；その上；なお
838	□	122	FY2016	2016 年度
839	□	192	G7	Group of Seven (Countries)
840	□	127	gain	得る；増加する
841	□	29	general	大将；将軍
842	□	126	general election	総選挙
843	□	246	general law	一般法；一般法則
844	□	234	genocide	集団虐殺
845	□	147	geopolitical	地政学の；地政学的な；地政学に関する
846	□	147	geopolitics	地政学
847	□	224	germ	細菌
848	□	224	germ weapon	細菌兵器
849	□	252	German	ドイツ人の；ドイツ（語）の
850	□	40	get around	回避する；うまく避ける
851	□	**2-21b**	get back to you	折り返し連絡する；改めて連絡する
852	□	**3-3a'**	get to X	X に達する；着手する
853	□	121	given X	X を前提とすると；仮定すると；考えると
854	□	142	global market	世界市場

No.		使用箇所	English	日本語
855	□	329	globalization	グローバル化；グローバリゼーション
856	□	**1-30c**	go ahead	勝手にどうぞ；どうぞ；先へ進む
857	□	199	go out	外出する；公にされる；消える
858	□	**3-13a**	goal	目標；目的（地）
859	□	139	GOJ	日本政府（=government of Japan）
860	□	96	good deed	善行；善い行い
861	□	316	government forces	政府軍；官軍
862	□	173	government-led initiative	政府主導の（による）イニシアチブ
863	□	141	grant aid	無償資金協力；無償援助
864	□	32	grant asylum	亡命を認める
865	□	338	grasp	握る；把握する；把握；理解
866	□	37	grave	重大な；重要な
867	□	37	gravity	重力
868	□	301	grayzone	グレーゾーン（=gray zone）
869	□	139	ground	根拠；理由；立脚点
870	□	37	grow	増える；成長する；高まる
871	□	246	guarantee	保証する；請け合う
872	□	232	guerrilla	ゲリラ；ゲリラ兵
873	□	**2-8c**	Guess what X?	X について当ててごらん？； 何だか分かりますか？
874	□	**3-5a**	guilty	有罪の；罪を犯した
875	□	124	halt	停止させる；中断させる
876	□	91	hand over	手渡す；引き渡す
877	□	**2-11b**	handle	対処する；操縦する
878	□	150	hard-working	勤勉な；よく働く
879	□	118	harsh	厳しい；辛辣な
880	□	240	harsh economic conditions plague the former socialist countries	厳しい経済状況が旧社会主義国を苦しめる
881	□	**3-11a**	hate	ひどく嫌う；憎む
882	□	197	have a marginal effect	ほとんど効果がない
883	□	**1-17b**	have something to X	X するべきこと（もの）がある
884	□	148	having said that	そうはいっても；そうかといって； それでもやはり

No.		使用箇所	English	日本語
885	□	311	headquarters	本部；司令部；本社
886	□	107	health service	（公共）医療サービス
887	□	149	hegemonism	覇権主義
888	□	149	hegemony	覇権；主導権；ヘゲモニー
889	□	71	hence	それ故に；したがって
890	□	**1-15b**	Here comes X.	（さあ；ほら）Xがやって来た。
891	□	**3-24b**	hereby	ここに；これによって
892	□	150	heterogeneous	異種の； 異質の（homogeneousの反意語）
893	□	97	high-level meeting	ハイレベル（局長級）会合
894	□	226	high-technology	ハイテク（high-tech）の；先端技術の
895	□	130	highly	高く；大いに；非常に
896	□	232	hinder	妨げる；妨害する
897	□	144	hindsight	後知恵
898	□	91	His Majesty the Emperor	天皇陛下
899	□	92	historical	歴史的な
900	□	158	hold	開催する；保留する
901	□	330	hold a dialog	対話をする； やり取りする（dialogue = dialog）
902	□	150	homogeneous	同種の；均質の；同質的な
903	□	334	honest	誠実な；率直な
904	□	342	honor	尊重する；重んじる；栄誉となる；名誉
905	□	151	hostage	人質；抵当
906	□	151	hostage release	人質解放
907	□	152	hostile	敵意のある；敵の；反対して
908	□	152	hostilities	戦闘（行為）； 戦争（通常複数形で用いる）
909	□	152	hostility	敵意；敵対心；反抗
910	□	12	House and Senate	（米国）上下両院；上院と下院
911	□	280	House of Representatives	（米国）下院
912	□	**3-17b**	How have you been?	ご機嫌いかがですか？； 調子はどうですか？
913	□	221	human resources (HR)	人的資源；人材
914	□	10	human rights	人権
915	□	**3-27a**	Human Rights Council	人権理事会

No.		使用箇所	English	日本語
916	□	153	humanitarian	人道的な；人道主義の；博愛の
917	□	153	humanitarian aid	人道援助；人道支援
918	□	76	humanitarian consequences	（人道上の）帰結；結果
919	□	154	hypocrisy	偽善；偽善的行為；見せかけ
920	□	154	hypocritical	偽善の；偽善者の
921	□	155	hypothesis	仮説；仮定（複数形は hypotheses）
922	□	155	hypothetical	仮定（上）の；仮説（上）の；仮言の
923	□	**3-16a**	I (really) appreciate it.	感謝します。；ありがとうございます。
924	□	**2-31b**	I am afraid that	残念ながら；せっかくですが；あいにく
925	□	**2-21b**	I am not sure yet.	まだはっきりしたことは言えない。；まだ分からない。；まだ決めていない。
926	□	**2-7b**	I beg your pardon?	もう一度言って下さい。；失礼ですが。；すみません。
927	□	**1-6a**	I haven't seen you (for a while).	久しぶりですね。ご無沙汰していました。
928	□	**1-16a**	I must go now.	もう行かなければなりません。；もう失礼します。
929	□	**1-34a**	I owe you one.	恩に着る。；借りができたね。；ありがとう。
930	□	**1-8a**	I wondered	どうかと思って
931	□	**1-18c**	I'm in a hurry.	急いでいます。；急いでいるのですが。
932	□	**2-29b**	I'm on my way.	向かっているところだ。；今すぐ行く。
933	□	174	ideal	理想；極致
934	□	156	identification	身元確認；身分証明証；同一化
935	□	156	identify	身元を明らかにする；同定する；同一化する
936	□	156	identity	同一性；アイデンティティー；身元
937	□	157	ideological	イデオロギーに基づく；イデオロギー（上）の；非現実的な
938	□	157	ideology	イデオロギー；価値（信念）体系
939	□	**2-7b**	if that is the case	もしそうだとしたら；仮にそれが本当なら
940	□	**2-28c**	if you so wish	お望みであれば；もしそうしたいなら
941	□	155	ignite	点火する；燃え立たせる
942	□	155	ignition	発火；点火；着火

No.		使用箇所	English	日本語
943	□	**3-23b**	illegally	不法に；違法に
944	□	192	illegitimate	違法の；非合法の
945	□	156	illicit	違法な；不法な
946	□	236	Immanuel Kant	イマヌエル・カント（1724-1804）
947	□	158	immediate	即時の；差し迫った；直接の
948	□	158	immediately	即座に；直接に；すぐ近くに
949	□	218	immigration	移住；入国管理
950	□	218	immigration authorities	出入国管理局；入国審査官
951	□	37	imminent	差し迫った；切迫した
952	□	159	immune	免疫がある；免除された；免れる
953	□	159	immunity	特権；免除；免疫
954	□	160	impeach	弾劾する；告発する；問題にする
955	□	160	impeachment	弾劾；告発
956	□	161	Imperial Japanese Army	旧日本軍；帝国陸軍
957	□	161	imperial	帝国の；皇帝の；荘厳な
958	□	162	implement	実施する；実装する；用具
959	□	162	implementation	遂行；執行；実施
960	□	306	implementation structure	実施（体制）
961	□	163	implication	ほのめかし；含意；連座
962	□	164	implicit	暗に示された；暗黙の；潜在的な
963	□	164	implicitly	暗に；それとなく（explicitly の反意語）
964	□	163	imply	ほのめかす；暗示する
965	□	38	import	輸入；輸入する
966	□	154	importation	輸入；輸入品
967	□	294	importing country	輸入国
968	□	165	impose	課す；負わす；押し付ける
969	□	165	imposition	押し付け；強制；義務
970	□	225	impression	印象
971	□	69	in a hurry	急いで；焦って
972	□	166	in accordance with X	X にしたがって；一致して；則って
973	□	6	in actuality	実際は（に）
974	□	30	in addition (to X)	（X に）加えて

No.		使用箇所	English	日本語
975	□	170	in any way	決して；いかなる形であっても
976	□	167	in behalf of X/ on behalf of X	X を代表して；代理として；のために
977	□	262	in conjunction with X	X とあわせて；同時に
978	□	77	in conspiracy	共謀して；徒党を組んで
979	□	86	in convoy	(護衛のために) 船団を組んで
980	□	248	in earnest	本気で；本格的に
981	□	112	in fact	実際 (は)
982	□	322	in favor of X	X に賛成して；利益になるように
983	□	334	in general	一般の；概して
984	□	24	in order to X	X のために
985	□	225	in other words	つまり；言い換えれば
986	□	**1-23b**	in particular	特に；とりわけ
987	□	94	in question	問題の；問題になっている；当の
988	□	223	in response to X	X に応えて；応じて
989	□	43	in return	見返りとして；代償として；引き換えに
990	□	193	in terms of X	X に関して
991	□	294	in the past	従来は；かつて (昔) は
992	□	**2-19b**	in the world	一体 (全体)
993	□	232	in turn	今度は；順番に
994	□	**2-9b**	in what context	どういう事情で；どのような文脈で
995	□	**2-27b**	in writing	書面で；文書で
996	□	**1-32c**	in your capacity as X	X の立場で；の資格において
997	□	229	in-	(否定の接頭辞)
998	□	139	inappropriate	不適切な；ふさわしくない
999	□	158	inauguration	就任；開始；落成
1000	□	312	incarcerate	投獄する；監禁する；幽閉する
1001	□	312	incite	扇動する；駆り立てる；奮い立たせる
1002	□	12	include	含む
1003	□	37	including X	X を含む
1004	□	135	inclusive	包括的な；包摂的な
1005	□	119	incomparably	比較にならないほど
1006	□	168	incompatibility	不適合；不一致

No.		使用箇所	English	日本語
1007	□	168	incompatible	相いれない；両立しない；互換性のない
1008	□	169	incorporate	取り入れる；取り込む；合併する
1009	□	169	incorporate X into Y	X を Y に取り入れる；組み込む
1010	□	169	incorporation	組み込み；合併；法人設立
1011	□	325	increasingly	ますます；次第に
1012	□	207	incumbent	行う義務のある；現職の
1013	□	131	incur	招く；負担する；被る
1014	□	320	indicate	示す；指し示す；示唆する
1015	□	229	indignant	怒った；憤慨した
1016	□	254	indiscriminate	無差別の；見境のない
1017	□	243	indispensable	不可欠な；なくてはならない
1018	□	114	indisputable	議論の余地のない；疑う余地のない
1019	□	104	individual	個人；個人の
1020	□	15	indivisible	分割できない
1021	□	170	induce	誘導する；説得する；帰納する
1022	□	170	induction	誘導；導入；帰納
1023	□	142	industry	産業；工業；勤勉
1024	□	286	ineffective	効果がない；役に立たない
1025	□	48	inevitably	必然的に；否応なく
1026	□	229	inexcusable	許せない；弁解の余地のない
1027	□	**3-7a**	infectious	感染性の
1028	□	171	inflict	押し付ける；負わせる；与える
1029	□	171	infliction	苦しみ；刑罰
1030	□	105	influence on X	X への影響
1031	□	115	infrastructure	基盤；インフラ
1032	□	172	infringe	侵害する；破る；違反する
1033	□	172	infringement	違反（行為）；侵害；抵触
1034	□	275	initially	当初は；最初に
1035	□	173	initiative	主導権；進取の気性；取り組み
1036	□	254	injurious	傷つける；有害な
1037	□	**3-15a**	innate	生来の；生得的な
1038	□	202	innocent	純真な；無罪の；無害の
1039	□	87	inquiries	inquire（問い合わせ；照会）の複数形

No.		使用箇所	English	日本語
1040	□	302	instability	(stability の反意語) 不安定 (性)
1041	□	174	instead	その代わりに
1042	□	129	institution	制度；組織；機構
1043	□	129	institutional	制度の；組織の；機構の
1044	□	301	institutionalization	制度化；組織化；慣行化；収容
1045	□	301	insufficient	不十分な；不足して
1046	□	174	insult	侮辱 (する)；辱める；無礼
1047	□	175	integrate	統合する；調和させる
1048	□	175	integrated	統合した；一体の；人種差別をしない
1049	□	175	integration	統合；融合
1050	□	172	intellectual property right	知的所有権；知的財産権
1051	□	176	intelligence	諜報 (機関)；機密情報；インテリジェンス
1052	□	51	intend	するつもりである；意図がある
1053	□	177	intensify	強める；強化する；激しくする
1054	□	177	intensive	集中的な；激しい；強い
1055	□	16	intent	熱意
1056	□	286	intention	意図；意向
1057	□	16	intently	熱心に
1058	□	7	inter-	間の
1059	□	178	intercede	仲裁する；とりなす
1060	□	178	intercession	仲裁；斡旋；調停
1061	□	7	intercontinental	大陸間 (の)
1062	□	179	interdependence	相互依存；持ちつ持たれつの関係
1063	□	179	interdependent	相互依存の；相互依存的な；互いに頼り合う
1064	□	213	interest	利益；関心；興味を持たせる
1065	□	180	interfere	妨げる；干渉する；邪魔をする
1066	□	180	interference	干渉；妨害；邪魔
1067	□	290	intermediate	中間の；中間的な；中級の
1068	□	35	internal	内部の；内側の；国内の
1069	□	35	internal affairs	内政問題；国内事情
1070	□	219	internally displaced	国内避難した (国内で住む場所を追われた)

No.		使用箇所	English	日本語
1071	□	82	international community	国際社会
1072	□	88	international courier service	国際宅配便
1073	□	55	international law	国際法
1074	□	142	international standard	国際標準；国際規格；国際水準
1075	□	238	internment	抑留；収容
1076	□	5	interpretation	解釈；説明
1077	□	178	intersession	学期と学期の間；学期間休暇
1078	□	181	intervene	干渉する；介在する；調停する
1079	□	181	intervention	干渉；介入；仲裁
1080	□	96	interview	インタビュー；取材訪問；記者会見；面接する
1081	□	182	intimidate	脅す；威嚇する；怖がらせる
1082	□	182	intimidation	威嚇；脅し；脅迫（行為）
1083	□	183	intricate	複雑な；入り組んだ；込み入った
1084	□	184	intrigue	陰謀（を企てる）；術策をめぐらす；好奇心をそそる
1085	□	184	intriguer	陰謀者；策士
1086	□	185	intrude	侵入する；押し入る；立ち入る
1087	□	185	intruder	侵入者；乱入者；邪魔者
1088	□	22	invade	侵略する；侵攻する
1089	□	186	invest	投資する；出資する
1090	□	177	investigation	調査；捜査
1091	□	186	investor	投資家；出資者；資本主
1092	□	5	invoke	発動する；引き起こす
1093	□	181	involve	関与する；巻き込む；関わる
1094	□	88	involvement	関与；関係
1095	□	187	ironically	皮肉なことに；皮肉にも；反語的に
1096	□	187	irony	皮肉；アイロニー
1097	□	140	irresponsible	無責任な；責任のない；責任を負わない
1098	□	113	irreversible	不可逆的な
1099	□	146	-ism	主義；学説；イズム
1100	□	188	isolate	孤立させる；分離する；隔離する
1101	□	188	isolated	孤立した；隔絶された

No.		使用箇所	English	日本語
1102	□	188	isolation	孤立；分離；隔離
1103	□	88	Israeli	イスラエルの；イスラエル人
1104	□	124	issuance	発行；支給
1105	□	10	issue	問題；論点；発行する
1106	□	**3-28a**	It doesn't make sense.	それはおかしい。；意味をなさない。；筋が通っていない。
1107	□	**2-11b**	It is (very) nice of you to X.	X に対し感謝する；どうもありがとう。
1108	□	**3-29b**	It is high time X.	もう当然 X してよい時だ。；既に X し終わっている時間だ。
1109	□	**3-29b**	It is highly likely that X.	X の可能性が高い。;が十分考えられる。
1110	□	**2-8c**	It is my pleasure.	喜んで。；こちらこそ。
1111	□	121	it is no wonder X	X は驚くに値しない；明らかだ
1112	□	**2-22c**	It is none of my business.	それは私には関係のないことだ。
1113	□	**2-22c**	It is none of your business.	余計な口出しをするな。；あなたには関係のないことだ。
1114	□	**2-10c**	It is time for you to X.	X する時が来た。；もう X する時間だ。
1115	□	**1-35b**	It will be a piece of cake.	簡単なことさ。;たいしたことじゃない。
1116	□	**1-34a**	It's very kind of you to X.	X してもらい親切にありがとうございます。；恐縮しています。
1117	□	106	Japan-U.S. Security Arrangements	日米安全保障体制；日米安保
1118	□	86	Japanese national	日本人；邦人
1119	□	**3-7a**	jeopardize	危険にさらす；危うくする
1120	□	120	joint	共同の；共有の；結合；つなぐ
1121	□	66	joint statement	共同声明
1122	□	94	journalist	ジャーナリスト；記者
1123	□	47	judicial branch	司法機関；司法府
1124	□	**1-25a**	jump in	割り込む；飛び込む
1125	□	334	justice	正義；司法
1126	□	334	justice system	司法制度
1127	□	249	Justice will prevail.	正義は勝つ
1128	□	189	justification	正当化；弁明
1129	□	189	justify	正当化する；弁明する；正当だと理由づける
1130	□	299	juvenile	若い；未熟な；年少者の

No.		使用箇所	English	日本語
1131	☐	**2-23b**	keep your fingers crossed	祈る
1132	☐	239	key pillar	重要な柱
1133	☐	28	kidnapping	誘拐
1134	☐	184	killing	殺害；致死の
1135	☐	261	Kyoto Protocol	（気候変動に関する国際連合枠組条約の）京都議定書
1136	☐	57	labor	労働（力）；仕事
1137	☐	150	lack	不足；欠乏；欠いている
1138	☐	299	laid	lay の過去形・過去分詞形
1139	☐	190	lame	正常に歩けない；歩行が困難な
1140	☐	190	lame duck	死に体；レームダック；役立たずな人
1141	☐	135	land	着弾する；着地する；上陸する；陸地
1142	☐	242	large-scale	スケールの大きい；大規模な
1143	☐	338	last	続く；持続する；最後の；最もしそうにない
1144	☐	308	late 1980s	1980年代後半
1145	☐	191	launch	着手する；発射する；進水させる
1146	☐	191	launch a missile	ミサイルを発射する
1147	☐	212	law of the sea	海洋法
1148	☐	299	lay down	制定する；横たえる
1149	☐	14	layer	層
1150	☐	69	lead	先導する；リードする
1151	☐	60	leadership	指導；統率力；リーダーシップ
1152	☐	115	leading newspaper	主要紙；有力紙
1153	☐	236	League of Nations	国際連盟
1154	☐	90	leak	リーク；漏洩
1155	☐	130	leave	去る；離れる
1156	☐	11	led	lead（導く）の過去形
1157	☐	84	legal	法的な
1158	☐	131	legal entity	法人（合法的な実体）
1159	☐	**3-5a**	legal status	法的地位
1160	☐	334	legal system	法制度；法体系；法律制度
1161	☐	67	legislation	法律；立法；立法行為
1162	☐	295	legislative session	立法府の（今次の）会期

No.		使用箇所	English	日本語
1163	□	192	legitimacy	正統（性）；合法性；嫡出
1164	□	192	legitimate	合法の；合法的な
1165	□	192	legitimately	合法的に
1166	□	**2-23b**	Let's see.	えっと。；どれ。；そうだなあ。
1167	□	52	liberal	寛大な；自由な；自由主義の；リベラルな
1168	□	**3-29b**	liberal democracy	自由民主主義
1169	□	52	liberalism	自由主義
1170	□	**3-4a**	life imprisonment	終身刑；無期懲役
1171	□	193	lift	解禁する（禁止を解く）；持ち上げる；向上させる
1172	□	193	lift off	離昇する；打ち上がる
1173	□	122	lift the embargo	輸出禁止を解く
1174	□	335	likewise	同様に；同じように
1175	□	194	limit	制限する；限る
1176	□	194	limitation	限界；制限；制約
1177	□	146	link	つながる；結びつく；関係づける
1178	□	12	lobbying	ロビー（陳情）活動
1179	□	314	local	その地域の；現地の
1180	□	35	local autonomous body	地方自治体
1181	□	246	local government	地方自治体；地方政府
1182	□	**1-7b**	Long time no see.	久しぶりですね。ご無沙汰していました。
1183	□	317	long-term	長期の；長期間にわたる
1184	□	93	lower	下げる；減じる
1185	□	195	loyal	忠実な；誠実な
1186	□	195	loyalty	忠実；忠誠（心）；誠実
1187	□	169	mainly	主として；大部分は
1188	□	134	maintain	維持する；主張する
1189	□	91	majesty	陛下；尊厳；威厳
1190	□	298	major	大きい；主要な；専攻
1191	□	129	majority voting	多数決；多数決投票
1192	□	132	make an effort to	努力する
1193	□	316	make it clear	はっきりさせる；明らかにする

No.		使用箇所	English	日本語
1194	□	118	make the most of X	X を最大限活用する； できるだけ利用する
1195	□	196	manifest	明白な；はっきり表れた；表明する
1196	□	196	manifestation	示威運動；示威行動
1197	□	77	manipulate	操作する；操縦する；操る
1198	□	**3-12b**	march	デモ行進；行軍；マーチ
1199	□	39	margin	余白；余地；縁；周辺
1200	□	197	marginal	周辺的な；取るに足りない； ぎりぎりの
1201	□	128	marine law	海洋法；海法
1202	□	198	maritime	海の；海事の；船員特有の
1203	□	340	maritime area	海域
1204	□	198	maritime delimitation	海の限界の決定；（EEZ や大陸棚の） 海洋境界の画定
1205	□	198	maritime insurance	海上保険
1206	□	231	market	市場；需要
1207	□	199	martial	軍の；戦争の
1208	□	199	martial law	戒厳令
1209	□	266	massive	大規模な；大量の；巨大な
1210	□	251	matter	問題；問題である
1211	□	183	maximize	最大化する；極大化する
1212	□	**3-4a**	maximum	最大の；最大限度の；最大値
1213	□	**1-17b**	May I?	よろしいですか？；いいですか？
1214	□	18	means	手段；方法
1215	□	288	measure(s)	法案；対策；措置
1216	□	200	mediate	仲裁する；調停する
1217	□	200	mediation	調停；仲裁；媒介
1218	□	120	meeting	会合；会議
1219	□	285	Meiji Restoration	明治維新
1220	□	201	memorandum	覚書；備忘録；メモ
1221	□	161	memorial	記念碑；記念館
1222	□	110	-ment	（名詞化する接尾辞）
1223	□	23	mention	言及する；述べる
1224	□	202	mercy	慈悲；容赦；情け

No.		使用箇所	English	日本語
1225	□	315	mere	単なる；ほんの
1226	□	190	mid-term election	中間選挙
1227	□	88	Middle East	中東
1228	□	203	military	軍事的な；軍（人）の；軍隊
1229	□	35	military affairs	軍事
1230	□	286	military force	軍事力
1231	□	203	military government	軍事政権；軍政
1232	□	251	military presence	軍の駐留；軍事的存在
1233	□	313	military superpower	軍事大国
1234	□	314	military support for X	X への軍事支援
1235	□	205	military tension	軍事的緊張
1236	□	**1-32c**	mind you	いいかい；よく聞いて
1237	□	62	minded	心がある；志向がある
1238	□	111	mineral	鉱物；採掘物
1239	□	326	minimize	最小限に抑える；最小化する
1240	□	**3-1**	minimum level	最低水準
1241	□	70	minister	大臣
1242	□	257	ministerial	閣僚級の；閣僚レベルの
1243	□	70	ministerial-level	閣僚級（の）
1244	□	34	misconduct	不正行為；違法行為
1245	□	204	mission	任務；派遣団；布教
1246	□	204	missionary	布教の；伝道の
1247	□	**3-20a**	misunderstanding	誤解；意見の相違
1248	□	205	mitigate	軽減する；緩和する；鎮静する
1249	□	205	mitigation	緩和；軽減
1250	□	332	mobilize	動員する；結集する
1251	□	195	modesty	謙虚；慎み深さ
1252	□	27	MOFA (Ministry of Foreign Affairs of Japan)	外務省
1253	□	58	momentum	勢い；機運
1254	□	206	monarchy	君主制；君主国；王政
1255	□	23	monitor	注視する；観察する；監視する
1256	□	250	Monroeism	モンロー主義

No.		使用箇所	English	日本語
1257	□	207	moral	道徳上の；良心の
1258	□	207	morality	道徳（性）；倫理；教訓
1259	□	289	more and more	ますます
1260	□	273	more than ever before	かつてないほどに；これまで以上に
1261	□	**3-10b**	mostly	大部分は；たいていは
1262	□	25	motion	動議；提案；動き
1263	□	201	MOU (=memorandum of understanding)	覚書；基本合意書
1264	□	208	mount	登る；据えつける；開始する
1265	□	208	mounting	高まる；台；据えつけ
1266	□	144	move	感動させる；動く
1267	□	45	multi-	多
1268	□	209	multilateral	多国間（参加）の；多面的な；多角的な
1269	□	209	multilaterally	多国間で；多面的に
1270	□	210	multinational	多国籍の；多国間の；多国籍企業
1271	□	210	multinational force	多国籍軍
1272	□	45	multipolarization	多極化
1273	□	76	munition	武器弾薬
1274	□	28	murder	殺人；殺害
1275	□	**2-9b**	must	違いない；しなければならない
1276	□	211	mutual	相互の；共通の；相互的な
1277	□	250	mutual non-interference	相互不干渉
1278	□	211	mutuality	相互関係；相互依存
1279	□	211	mutually	お互いに；相互に
1280	□	167	nanosatellite	（超）小型衛星
1281	□	**3-1**	narrow	狭い；限られた；やっとの
1282	□	**3-1**	narrowly	辛うじて；狭く
1283	□	73	nation	国家；国民
1284	□	212	nation-state	国民国家；民族国家
1285	□	214	national	国の
1286	□	27	National Archives and Records Administration (NARA)	米国国立公文書館
1287	□	292	national capability	国力；国の能力

No.		使用箇所	English	日本語
1288	☐	147	national credit	国家信用
1289	☐	213	national interests	国益；国の利益
1290	☐	214	national security	国家安全保障；国家の安全
1291	☐	214	National Security Council (NSC)	国家安全保障会議
1292	☐	301	national sovereignty	国家主権
1293	☐	212	national state	国民国家
1294	☐	**3-5a**	national unification	国家統一
1295	☐	**1-5**	nationalist	国家主義者；国粋主義者
1296	☐	26	nationalities	nationality（国籍）の複数形
1297	☐	26	nationality	国籍
1298	☐	53	natural resource	天然資源
1299	☐	188	nature	本質；特質；性質；自然
1300	☐	75	nature that are different from X	X とは異なった種類（性質）の
1301	☐	215	naval	海軍の；海軍に属する；軍艦の
1302	☐	215	naval vessel(s)	艦艇
1303	☐	215	navy	海軍；艦隊
1304	☐	24	necessary	必要な
1305	☐	216	negotiate	交渉する；協議する
1306	☐	216	negotiation	交渉；折衝；克服
1307	☐	8	neighboring	近隣の；隣接した
1308	☐	81	neither X	（双方とも）X でない
1309	☐	**1-22c**	Never mind.	まあいいです。；気にしないで。
1310	☐	136	next to impossible	ほとんど不可能な；無理な
1311	☐	136	next to X	X の次に
1312	☐	**3-22a**	no problem	問題ない；大丈夫だ
1313	☐	**1-13b**	No way.	冗談でしょう。；駄目です。；そんなこと絶対にあり得ない。
1314	☐	312	Nobel Laureate	ノーベル賞受賞者
1315	☐	217	non-governmental organization (NGO)	非政府組織
1316	☐	250	non-interference	不干渉
1317	☐	204	non-proliferation	不拡散；拡散防止の

No.		使用箇所	English	日本語
1318	□	5	non-state actor	非国家主体
1319	□	217	non(-)governmental	非政府（の）；民間の；政府と無関係の
1320	□	**3-12b**	non(-)violent	非暴力の
1321	□	148	nonetheless	それでもなお；といっても
1322	□	55	nonmilitary	非軍事（の）；非軍事的な
1323	□	39	nonnegotiable	譲れない；交渉の余地がない
1324	□	**3-12b**	nonpartisan	無党派の
1325	□	234	norm	規範；標準
1326	□	171	normalization	正常化
1327	□	**2-8c**	Not at all.	全くそんなことはありません（構いません）。；どういたしまして。
1328	□	**1-21b**	not have the slightest idea	考えもしない；思いもよらない；皆目見当もつかない
1329	□	**2-5**	not only X but (also) Y	X だけでなく Y も；X 同様 Y も
1330	□	**2-19b**	not say a word	一言も言わない；発しない
1331	□	253	not X at all	全く X ではない；全然 X ではない
1332	□	346	notification	通知
1333	□	346	notify	通知する；知らせる
1334	□	244	now that X	今や X なので（X には that 節の文章が来る）
1335	□	287	nuclear activities	原子力活動
1336	□	**2-5**	nuclear power	核の力；核保有国；原子力
1337	□	37	nuclear test	核実験
1338	□	44	nuclear weapon	核兵器
1339	□	102	nuke	核兵器；原子力
1340	□	218	nullification	無効化；取り消し
1341	□	218	nullify	無効にする；無価値にする；取り消す
1342	□	156	nurture	助長する；養育する；育む
1343	□	219	obedience	服従；従順；忠実
1344	□	219	obey	従う；服従する
1345	□	220	obligation	義務（感）；義理；債務
1346	□	220	oblige	強いる；余儀なくさせる
1347	□	249	observe	遵守する；観察する
1348	□	249	observer	（議決権を持たない）会議参加者

No.		使用箇所	English	日本語
1349	□	**3-9a**	obtain	得る；手に入れる
1350	□	221	occasion	機会；場合；行事
1351	□	221	occasionally	時々；時折
1352	□	222	occupation	占領；占有；職業
1353	□	222	occupy	占領する；占有する；占める
1354	□	112	occur	起こる；生じる；発生する
1355	□	**1-32c**	of course	もちろん；当然（ながら）
1356	□	**3-5a**	offense	違反；犯罪；攻撃
1357	□	223	offensive	攻撃態勢；攻撃的な；攻撃側の
1358	□	41	Office of the United States Trade Representative (USTR)	米通商代表部
1359	□	224	official	当局者；公式の；公務員
1360	□	238	official apology	公式謝罪；正式な謝罪
1361	□	224	officially	公式に；正式に；当局の発表では
1362	□	122	omnibus	包括する；オムニバス形式の
1363	□	**2-17a**	on a step-by-step basis	段階を経て；段階的方法で
1364	□	**2-19b**	on earth	一体（全体）
1365	□	314	on the back of X	X を背景に；という経緯があって
1366	□	82	on the contrary	それどころか；むしろ
1367	□	25	on the other hand	他方で；一方で
1368	□	225	on the verge of X	今にも X しようとして；X の間際に
1369	□	293	once	かつて；ひとたび；一旦
1370	□	**3-26b**	one country(,) two systems	一国二制度
1371	□	**1-1**	one second	2 分の 1
1372	□	**1-1**	one tenth of X	X の 10 分の 1
1373	□	350	ongoing	進行中の
1374	□	289	online	オンラインで；オンラインの；オンライン
1375	□	259	op-	（「反対側に」を意味する接頭辞）
1376	□	345	opening ceremony	開会式
1377	□	226	operation	軍事行動（作戦）；運転；作業
1378	□	226	operational	軍事行動の；操作の
1379	□	141	operational capability	運用能力

No.		使用箇所	English	日本語
1380	□	31	opinion	意見
1381	□	227	opponent	敵対者；競争相手；敵対する；対立する候補者
1382	□	49	opportunity	機会；好機
1383	□	227	oppose	反対する；敵対する
1384	□	228	opposed	反対した；対立した
1385	□	228	opposition	反対；対立；野党
1386	□	74	opposition party	野党；反対派
1387	□	42	optimism	楽観；楽観（楽天）主義
1388	□	212	oral proceeding	口頭弁論；口頭審理
1389	□	143	order	秩序；命令；静粛にする
1390	□	**3-10b**	ordinary	普通の；平凡な；一般の
1391	□	28	organization	組織；機構
1392	□	155	organize	組織する；計画する
1393	□	155	organizer	組織者；事務局；主催者
1394	□	291	orientation	方向づけ；オリエンテーション
1395	□	49	origin	生まれ；起源；先祖
1396	□	85	ostracism	追放；排斥
1397	□	**2-19b**	otherwise	反対の；別の；さもなければ
1398	□	229	-ous	（形容詞を作る接尾辞）
1399	□	**3-16a**	out of X	X の中から
1400	□	229	out-	（「外に」を意味する接頭辞）
1401	□	219	outflow	流出
1402	□	229	outra-/ultra-	（「超えて / 越えて」を意味する接頭辞）
1403	□	229	outrage	激怒；激しい怒り
1404	□	229	outrageous	とんでもない；法外な；奇抜な；常軌を逸して；一線を越えて
1405	□	196	outstanding	極めて優れた；目立った
1406	□	**3-13a**	over there	あちらに；あちらでは
1407	□	105	over X	X を通して；にわたって
1408	□	145	over-defense	過剰防衛
1409	□	72	overconformity	過度の服従
1410	□	125	overnight	夜通しの；徹夜の
1411	□	230	overridden	override の過去分詞形

No.		使用箇所	English	日本語
1412	□	230	override	優先する；無効にする；くつがえす
1413	□	231	overseas	海外の（で）；海外へ；外国へ
1414	□	231	overseas affiliated firm	現地法人；現地関連会社
1415	□	333	overseas dispatch of troops	海外派兵
1416	□	305	oversight	監視；監督；見落とし；過失
1417	□	90	overt	明白な；公然の
1418	□	171	overthrow	転覆させる；ひっくり返す；屈服させる
1419	□	80	overtly	公然と；明らかに
1420	□	**3-2a'**	overview	要旨；概説
1421	□	226	overwhelming	圧倒する；圧倒的な
1422	□	185	-owned	所有されている
1423	□	344	Palestine	パレスチナ
1424	□	332	Palestinian	パレスチナの；パレスチナ人（の）
1425	□	**2-4**	Panmunjom	板門店
1426	□	216	parliament	議会；国会
1427	□	216	parliamentary	議会の
1428	□	210	participate	参加する
1429	□	343	participation	参加
1430	□	72	particularly	特に；とりわけ
1431	□	232	partisan	ゲリラ（の）；パルチザン（の）；党派心の強い
1432	□	170	party	（行動を共にする）団体；関係者；政党
1433	□	11	party affiliation	政党所属；支持政党
1434	□	336	pass	通過する；可決する；合格する
1435	□	312	pass away	死亡する；逝去する
1436	□	74	passage	（法案などの）通過；可決；成立
1437	□	2	path	道筋；小道
1438	□	195	patience	我慢強さ
1439	□	238	payment	支払い；納入
1440	□	308	peace process	和平プロセス
1441	□	330	peace treaty	講和条約；平和条約（協定）
1442	□	206	peaceful	平和な；平和的な
1443	□	323	peaceful resolution	平和的解決

No.		使用箇所	English	日本語
1444	□	206	peacefully	平和（的）に；平和裏に
1445	□	18	peacekeeping	平和維持
1446	□	**3-4a**	penalty	罰則；刑罰；罰金
1447	□	340	pending	未解決の；係争中の
1448	□	233	peninsula	半島
1449	□	233	peninsular	半島（状）の
1450	□	128	People's Liberation Army	（中国）人民解放軍
1451	□	286	perceive	気づく；見抜く；知覚する
1452	□	234	peremptory	絶対の；横柄な；有無を言わせない
1453	□	234	peremptory norm	強行規範
1454	□	234	peremptory rule	確定的決定；確定命令
1455	□	235	period	期間；時代；時期
1456	□	235	periodically	定期（的）に；周期的に
1457	□	197	peripheral	周囲の；周辺的な；末梢の
1458	□	236	permanent	恒久的な；永続する；常置の
1459	□	237	permission	許可；認可；承諾
1460	□	237	permit	許可する；認める；許可証
1461	□	265	perpetrator	加害者；犯罪者；犯人
1462	□	236	perpetual	永遠の；永久の
1463	□	238	perseverance	忍耐（力）；根気；辛抱強さ
1464	□	238	perseverant	忍耐強い；我慢強い
1465	□	222	persistent	粘り強い；持続的な
1466	□	**3-21b**	personal	個人の；本人が直接行う
1467	□	**1-17b**	personally	個人的に；自分自身で
1468	□	266	personnel	人々；隊員；人事の
1469	□	235	perspective	見方；考え方；眺望
1470	□	239	persuade	説得する；説得してさせる；確信させる
1471	□	239	persuasion	説得（力）；信条；宗派
1472	□	350	phase	段階
1473	□	**2-24a**	phased approach	段階的実施（方策）
1474	□	350	phased manner	段階的に
1475	□	**2-26a**	phased process	段階的な過程（プロセス）
1476	□	182	physical	物理的な

No.		使用箇所	English	日本語
1477	□	239	pillar	柱
1478	□	234	piracy	海賊行為；著作権侵害
1479	□	317	PKO	平和維持活動 （peacekeeping operations の略）
1480	□	240	plague	悩ます；伝染病；ペスト
1481	□	327	plan	計画する；するつもりである；計画；企画
1482	□	292	play a role	役割を果たす
1483	□	241	pledge	誓う；誓約（する）；公約
1484	□	15	pledge of allegiance	忠誠の誓い
1485	□	19	plenipotentiary	全権を有する（委任された）
1486	□	242	plot	たくらむ；陰謀；構想
1487	□	242	plot an assassination	暗殺を謀る
1488	□	307	plunge	下落；急落；急落する
1489	□	177	point out	指摘する；注目させる
1490	□	**3-7a**	poisonous	有毒な；有害な
1491	□	341	polar	極の；極地の
1492	□	243	policy	政策；方針；手段
1493	□	295	policy speech	施政方針演説
1494	□	310	politburo	政治局
1495	□	310	politburo member	政治局員
1496	□	20	political decision	政治判断；政治決断
1497	□	302	political instability	政治的（な）不安定（さ）
1498	□	207	political morality	政治道徳
1499	□	342	political process	政治過程（プロセス）
1500	□	325	political trade-off	政治的取引
1501	□	343	political upheaval	政変
1502	□	72	politicize	政治化する；政治問題化する
1503	□	191	politics	政治
1504	□	259	-pon	（「置く」を意味する語根）
1505	□	187	populism	ポピュリズム；大衆迎合主義
1506	□	65	position	立場；位置；配置；置く；配置する
1507	□	319	possession	保有；所有；所持
1508	□	184	possibility	可能性

No.		使用箇所	English	日本語
1509	□	341	post-Cold War	冷戦後；ポスト冷戦
1510	□	71	post-conflict	紛争後
1511	□	2	postpone	延期する
1512	□	257	postponement	延期；先送り
1513	□	244	power	力；大国；強国
1514	□	244	power of attorney	委任状；委任権
1515	□	347	power of veto	拒否権
1516	□	347	(power of) veto over X	X に対する（関する）拒否権（の行使）
1517	□	245	pragmatic	実用的な；現実的な；実際的な；（理想や強がりではなく）現実的な状況を踏まえ、考えられうる最善の
1518	□	245	pragmatism	プラグマティズム；実用主義
1519	□	71	pre-conflict	紛争前の；紛争発生前の
1520	□	335	pre-emptive	先制の；先取りの
1521	□	335	pre-emptive strike	先制攻撃
1522	□	246	precede	先行する；先んじる
1523	□	246	precedence	優先（権）；先行；先立つこと
1524	□	236	predecessor	先行したもの；前任者
1525	□	342	predictable	予測できる；予言できる
1526	□	247	predominance	優勢；卓越：支配
1527	□	247	predominate	優位に立つ；支配する
1528	□	79	prefectural police	県警
1529	□	64	preliminary	予選の；準備の
1530	□	191	premium	高品質の；プレミア付きの；主要な
1531	□	61	prepare	準備する；構える
1532	□	248	prerequisite	前提条件；あらかじめ必要な；不可欠の
1533	□	248	prerequisite course	前提（必修）科目
1534	□	251	presence	存在；駐留
1535	□	279	present	存在する；出席している；現在の；提示する
1536	□	21	president	大統領
1537	□	69	presidential	大統領の
1538	□	47	press	記者団；マスコミ；出版物
1539	□	**3-2a’**	press briefing	記者会見

No.		使用箇所	English	日本語
1540	□	47	press conference	記者会見
1541	□	290	pressure	圧力；(圧力をかけて) 無理強いさせる
1542	□	**3-18a**	pretty	大いに；かなり；かわいい
1543	□	249	prevail	普及する；優勢である；(打ち) 勝つ
1544	□	64	previous	前の；以前の
1545	□	271	previously	以前に；前に
1546	□	217	primary	最上位の；初等の；一次の
1547	□	20	prime minister	総理大臣；首相
1548	□	230	principal	主な；主要な；校長
1549	□	230	principally	主に；主として；第一に
1550	□	250	principle	原理；主義；原則
1551	□	250	principle of Archimedes	アルキメデスの原理
1552	□	251	prior to X	X に先立って；より前に
1553	□	10	prioritize	優先する；優先順位をつける
1554	□	251	priority	優先すること；重要度が高いこと；優先順位
1555	□	252	prisoner-of-war	(戦争) 捕虜；俘虜
1556	□	252	prisoner-of-war camp	(戦争) 捕虜収容所
1557	□	217	private sector	民間部門
1558	□	253	privilege	特権；名誉；光栄
1559	□	253	privileged	特権の (ある)；光栄で；免責された
1560	□	259	pro-	(「賛成側に」を意味する接頭辞)
1561	□	259	pro/con (pros and cons)	賛成と反対
1562	□	109	proactive	積極的な；率先した
1563	□	109	proactively	積極的に；先を見越して
1564	□	117	problem solving	問題解決の
1565	□	254	procedure	手続き；方法；手順
1566	□	254	proceed	続行する；進む
1567	□	278	proceeds	収益；売上高
1568	□	255	proclaim	宣言する；公布する；示す
1569	□	255	proclaim an amnesty	恩赦を布告する
1570	□	256	profound	深い；深刻な；深遠な
1571	□	256	profoundly	深く；大いに

No.		使用箇所	English	日本語
1572	□	134	progress	進歩；進捗；進展
1573	□	257	prohibit	禁止する；差し止める；妨げる
1574	□	257	prohibition	禁止；禁（止）令；差し止め
1575	□	153	prolong	長くする；引き延ばす
1576	□	258	prominence	卓越；傑出；名声
1577	□	258	prominent	卓越した；目立った；著名な
1578	□	258	prominent diplomatic achievement	突出した外交（的）成果； 卓越した外交成果
1579	□	233	promise	約束（する）；誓う；誓約
1580	□	175	promotion	推進；促進；昇進
1581	□	83	promulgation	発布；普及
1582	□	208	pronounced	目立った；顕著な
1583	□	**3-20a**	properly	適切に；正しく
1584	□	259	proponent	提唱者；支持者；擁護者
1585	□	200	propose	提案する
1586	□	259	proposition	提案；計画；案
1587	□	78	prosperity	繁栄
1588	□	138	prosperous	繁栄している；豊かである
1589	□	260	protect	保護する；庇護する
1590	□	208	protection	保護
1591	□	208	protectionist	保護主義論者
1592	□	260	protectorate	保護国；保護関係；保護領
1593	□	133	protest	抗議；抗議行動；異議を申し立てる
1594	□	**3-10b**	protester	異議を申し立てる人；デモ参加者
1595	□	261	protocol	（外交）儀礼；（国家間）協定；手続き
1596	□	84	provide	与える；供給する
1597	□	262	province	地方；州（省・県）；田舎
1598	□	262	provincial	地方の；偏屈な；州（省・県）の
1599	□	13	provision	条項；提供
1600	□	238	provision	提供；準備
1601	□	22	provisional	暫定的な；仮の
1602	□	263	provocation	挑発；憤激
1603	□	263	provocative	挑発的な；怒らせる；刺激的な
1604	□	264	prudence	慎重さ；慎ましさ；用心深さ

No.		使用箇所	English	日本語
1605	☐	264	prudent	慎重な；分別のある；倹約する
1606	☐	264	prudently	慎重に；手堅く；用心深く
1607	☐	349	psychological warfare	心理戦；神経戦
1608	☐	**3-7a**	public health	公衆衛生
1609	☐	165	public notice	公告；公示
1610	☐	31	public opinion	世論
1611	☐	**3-22a**	public order	社会秩序
1612	☐	146	public security	治安；公安
1613	☐	176	Public Security Intelligence Agency	公安調査庁
1614	☐	166	public use	公用；公共用途
1615	☐	265	punish	罰する；罰則を科す
1616	☐	265	punishment	処罰；刑罰；懲罰
1617	☐	22	puppet	傀儡；操り人形
1618	☐	**3-28a**	purchase	購入する；買う
1619	☐	266	purge	粛清（する）；一掃（する）；追放する
1620	☐	87	purpose	目的
1621	☐	**34b**	pursuant to X	X に準じて；応じて
1622	☐	127	pursue	追求する；追いかける
1623	☐	140	push	推し進める；強要する；押す
1624	☐	265	put an end to	終わらせる；終止符を打つ；決着をつける
1625	☐	116	put down	鎮圧する；鎮める
1626	☐	129	qualified	条件付きの；限定された；資格のある
1627	☐	62	qualities	quality（質）の複数形
1628	☐	185	quality and quantity	質と量
1629	☐	267	quarantine	検疫（する）；隔離（する）；隔離期間
1630	☐	267	quarantine certificate	検疫証明書
1631	☐	192	question	問題として取り上げる；疑問を持つ；質問
1632	☐	148	questionable	疑問の余地がある；疑わしい
1633	☐	**3-18a**	quite	かなり；非常に；完全に
1634	☐	146	radical	過激派の；急進的な；根本的な
1635	☐	**3-7a**	radioactive	放射能の

No.		使用箇所	English	日本語
1636	☐	229	rage	怒り
1637	☐	161	raid	空襲；襲撃；奇襲
1638	☐	**2-8c**	raise	上げる；取り上げる
1639	☐	113	range	距離；範囲
1640	☐	268	ransom	身代金；受け戻し；取り戻す
1641	☐	268	ransom demand	身代金（の）要求
1642	☐	81	rapidly	急速に；迅速に
1643	☐	269	ratification	批准；承認；裁可
1644	☐	269	ratify	批准する；承認する；追認する
1645	☐	293	re-	（「再び」を意味する接頭辞）
1646	☐	144	re-read	再び読む；読み返す
1647	☐	13	reach	到達する；達する
1648	☐	31	reaction	反応；応答；反発
1649	☐	303	real wage	実質賃金
1650	☐	309	realization	実現；成就；認識
1651	☐	270	rebel	反逆者；反抗者；反抗する；反政府の
1652	☐	270	rebellion	反乱；暴動；謀反
1653	☐	162	recent	最近の；近頃の；先般の
1654	☐	162	recently	最近
1655	☐	213	recipient	受益者；受容者
1656	☐	271	reciprocal	相互の；互恵的な；相互的な
1657	☐	271	reciprocity	相互依存；互恵主義
1658	☐	15	recite	復唱する；朗唱する；暗唱する
1659	☐	272	recognition	認識；認知；見覚え
1660	☐	272	recognize	識別する；認める；承認する
1661	☐	14	reconcile	和解する
1662	☐	14	reconciliation	和解
1663	☐	273	reconnaissance	偵察（隊）；（予備）調査；踏査
1664	☐	273	reconnoiter	偵察する
1665	☐	24	reconstruction	再建；復興
1666	☐	166	record	記録；登録；記録する
1667	☐	232	recur	再発する
1668	☐	232	recurrence	再発；再帰

No.		使用箇所	English	日本語
1669	□	152	Red Cross	赤十字社；赤十字章
1670	□	266	Red Purge	レッドパージ；赤狩り
1671	□	129	redistribution	再配分；再分配
1672	□	194	reduction	減らすこと
1673	□	192	reelect	再選する
1674	□	227	reelection	再選
1675	□	95	refer	言及する；参照する
1676	□	298	referendum	国民投票；住民投票
1677	□	42	reflect	反映する；反射する
1678	□	274	refuge	避難；保護；避難所
1679	□	274	refugee	難民；亡命者；避難者
1680	□	**2-2**	regain	取り戻す；回復する
1681	□	115	regard	注視する；注意する；見なす；敬意
1682	□	275	regime	（政治）体制；政権；制度
1683	□	275	regime change	政権交代；体制変革
1684	□	205	region	地域；地方；領域
1685	□	71	regional	地域の；地方の
1686	□	149	regional hegemony	地域覇権
1687	□	53	regret	後悔する；遺憾に思う；気の毒に思う
1688	□	53	regrettable	遺憾な；残念な；気の毒な
1689	□	**3-22a**	regulation	規則；規制；法規
1690	□	110	reintegration	復帰
1691	□	92	reiterate	反復して言う；繰り返す
1692	□	25	reject	否決する；拒否する
1693	□	339	rejoin	再び加わる；再結合
1694	□	299	rejuvenation	復活；若返り；活性化
1695	□	71	rekindle	再燃する；よみがえらせる
1696	□	201	related	関連する；関係する
1697	□	193	relation	関係
1698	□	43	relationship	関係
1699	□	88	release	公開する；発出する；解放する；公開；解放
1700	□	276	relegate	左遷する；格下げする；追いやる
1701	□	276	relegation	左遷；追放；格下げ

No.		使用箇所	English	日本語
1702	□	66	relevant	関係する；関係のある
1703	□	85	religion	宗教
1704	□	58	relinquish	放棄する；断念する
1705	□	29	remain	遺骨；遺跡；残りもの； そのまま（の状態）である
1706	□	**3-2a'**	remark	言葉；批評；意見；述べる
1707	□	**3-25a**	remind	リマインドする；思い出させる； 注意する
1708	□	160	removal	解任；除去；廃止
1709	□	160	remove	取り除く；取り去る；廃絶する
1710	□	277	renounce	放棄する；破棄する；断念する
1711	□	248	renowned	有名な；高名な
1712	□	277	renunciation	放棄；棄権；拒否
1713	□	277	renunciation of war	戦争放棄
1714	□	278	repatriate	（本国へ）送還する；送り返す；帰還者
1715	□	115	repay	返金する；報いる
1716	□	321	repeated	度重なる；繰り返した
1717	□	68	repeatedly	繰り返し；再三にわたり
1718	□	157	replace	取りかえる；取ってかわる
1719	□	50	report	報告書；報道；報告する；伝える
1720	□	85	reportedly	報道によると；伝えられるところでは
1721	□	333	reposition	再配置；再配置する
1722	□	279	represent	代表する；象徴する；表現する
1723	□	280	representation	代表を務めること；代議制度；表現
1724	□	280	representative	代表の；（下院）議員；代議士
1725	□	15	republic	共和国；共和制
1726	□	190	Republican Party	共和党
1727	□	281	reputation	評判；名声；好評
1728	□	281	repute	評する；評判
1729	□	133	request	依頼する；要請する；依頼；要請
1730	□	17	require	要求する；求める
1731	□	282	resent	憤慨する；腹を立てる
1732	□	282	resentful	憤って；憤慨して；腹を立てて
1733	□	282	resentment	憤り；腹立たしさ

No.		使用箇所	English	日本語
1734	□	274	resettlement	再定住；再植民
1735	□	11	resident	住民
1736	□	283	resign	辞職する；断念する；身を任せる
1737	□	283	resignation	辞職；退陣；辞表
1738	□	284	resolution	決議；解決；解像度
1739	□	286	respect	点；尊敬（する）
1740	□	70	respective	各々の；個別の
1741	□	28	response	反応；対応；応答
1742	□	285	restoration	回復；復元；返還
1743	□	286	restrain	制限する；抑制する；拘束する
1744	□	286	restraint	抑制；制止；拘束
1745	□	287	restrict	制限する；限定する
1746	□	287	restriction	制限；制約；限定
1747	□	247	result in X	X という結果になる；に終わる
1748	□	53	resume	再開する；取り戻す；回復する
1749	□	152	resumption	再開；回復
1750	□	**3-1**	retain	保持する；維持する
1751	□	293	retake	取り戻す；再び受ける
1752	□	276	retaliate	仕返しする；報復する；応酬する
1753	□	276	retaliatory	報復的な；仕返しの
1754	□	42	return	帰還；返還
1755	□	339	reunification	再統合；再統一
1756	□	152	reunion	再会；再統合；同窓会
1757	□	13	reveal	明かす；明らかにする
1758	□	319	review	再検討；見直し；評価；再調査する；見直す
1759	□	288	revocable	取消可能な
1760	□	288	revoke	無効にする；廃止する；取り消す
1761	□	129	rich	豊かな
1762	□	5	right to self-defense	自衛権
1763	□	147	ripple	さざ波；波紋
1764	□	147	ripple effect	波及効果
1765	□	17	ROK	Republic of Korea（大韓民国）
1766	□	120	rough draft	草稿（大まかな原稿）

No.		使用箇所	English	日本語
1767	□	34	row	騒動；騒ぎ
1768	□	209	rule of law	法の支配；法治
1769	□	74	ruling	権力の座にある；優勢な
1770	□	74	ruling party	与党
1771	□	208	run counter to X	X に逆行する；反対の行動を取る
1772	□	101	run-off	決選投票；決勝戦
1773	□	289	ruthless	情け容赦ない；無慈悲な；残忍な
1774	□	289	ruthlessly	情け容赦なく
1775	□	290	sanction	制裁（を加える）；認可（する）；拘束力
1776	□	273	satellite	（人工）衛星；衛星都市
1777	□	242	scale	規模
1778	□	311	schedule	予定する；予定に入れる
1779	□	83	scope	範囲
1780	□	291	screen	隠す；覆う；遮断する
1781	□	291	screening	選考；ふるい分け；遮蔽
1782	□	175	SDGs	"Sustainable Development Goals" の略で「持続可能な開発目標」
1783	□	**3-4a**	secession	分離；脱退
1784	□	18	Secretary of Defense	国防長官
1785	□	256	secretary-general	事務局長；事務総長
1786	□	172	section	条；部分
1787	□	100	secularist	世俗主義者
1788	□	292	secure	確保する；保証する；安全な
1789	□	292	secure network	安全な（セキュリティーで確保された）ネットワーク
1790	□	214	security	安全保障
1791	□	284	Security Council	安全保障理事会；安保理
1792	□	284	Security Council resolution	安保理決議
1793	□	91	security credential	セキュリティー証明書
1794	□	**3-13a**	security dilemma	安全保障のジレンマ
1795	□	105	security policy	安全保障政策
1796	□	**1-35b**	See you then.	それではまた。；じゃあね。
1797	□	293	seize	つかむ；差し押さえる；逮捕する
1798	□	293	seizure	掌握；拿捕；押収（物）

No.		使用箇所	English	日本語
1799	□	201	self-	（「自己の；自分を」を意味する接頭辞）
1800	□	189	self-defense	自衛（の）；自己防衛（の）
1801	□	349	Self-Defense Forces	自衛隊
1802	□	294	self-restraint	自制；自主規制；自粛
1803	□	318	self-sustained development	自立的な発展； 自ら維持（持続）させられる発展
1804	□	12	Senate	（二院制議会の）上院
1805	□	224	senior official	高官（地位の高い官職にある人）
1806	□	100	sentiment	心情；感情
1807	□	**3-5a**	separate	離す；分離する；独立させる
1808	□	121	serious	深刻な；重大な
1809	□	76	seriously	深刻に；重く；真剣に
1810	□	43	serve	役に立つ；（目的を）果たす
1811	□	326	servicemen	serviceman（軍人）の複数形
1812	□	295	session	会期；会議；学期
1813	□	295	Session（国会の会期に関して）	（第 XX）回
1814	□	287	set forth	表明する；明記する
1815	□	345	set out	着手する；出発する
1816	□	149	set store	尊重する；重視する；価値を置く
1817	□	296	settle	落ち着く；定住する；解決する
1818	□	296	settlement	植民地；解決；精算
1819	□	328	severe	厳しい；深刻な
1820	□	151	severely	厳しく；激しく
1821	□	15	shall	しなければならない；すべきだ
1822	□	**2-1**	shape	形作る；輪郭
1823	□	209	share	共有する；共同使用する
1824	□	70	sharply	鋭く；激しく
1825	□	304	shield	盾；防御物；盾となる
1826	□	100	shift	変化；転換
1827	□	346	ship-to-ship transfer	瀬取り
1828	□	86	shipment	輸送；発送
1829	□	145	shortage	不足；欠乏
1830	□	74	shut down	閉鎖する；停止する
1831	□	297	shuttle	定期往復便；折り返し運転；往復する

No.		使用箇所	English	日本語
1832	□	297	shuttle bus	近距離往復バス
1833	□	177	sight	視野；視力
1834	□	201	sign	署名する；記入する；サインする
1835	□	233	signature	署名；サイン
1836	□	60	significant	重大な；重要な
1837	□	298	significantly	かなり；意義深いことに；有意に
1838	□	298	signify	示す；意味する；表す
1839	□	181	simultaneous interpretation	同時通訳
1840	□	181	simultaneously	同時に
1841	□	65	since X	X のため；なので；以来
1842	□	**2-22c**	sincerely	心から；誠実に；真摯に
1843	□	290	single	1 つの；単独の
1844	□	328	situation	状況；状態；場面
1845	□	234	slave	奴隷；奴隷の
1846	□	67	slow	遅くする；遅くなる；遅い
1847	□	326	smooth	円滑な；順調な；速やかな
1848	□	**2-12b**	So do you, don't you?	あなたもそうですよね？
1849	□	**2-19b**	So far, so good.	今のところ順調だ。； これまでのところはうまくいっている。
1850	□	190	so-called	いわゆる
1851	□	100	social structure	社会構造
1852	□	299	socialism	社会主義
1853	□	299	socialist	社会主義者；社会主義（の）
1854	□	252	soldier	軍人；兵士
1855	□	18	solely	もっぱら；単に
1856	□	300	solution	解決（策）；解答；溶液
1857	□	173	solve	解決する；解く
1858	□	32	sought	seek（求める）の過去形・過去分詞形
1859	□	147	sovereign	主権者；統治者；国王
1860	□	147	sovereign risk	ソブリン（カントリー）リスク
1861	□	301	sovereignty	主権（国家）の；統治権；独立国
1862	□	273	space	宇宙（空間）；間隔；場所
1863	□	137	span	わたる；及ぶ

No.		使用箇所	English	日本語
1864	□	132	special envoy	特使
1865	□	93	special measure	特別措置；特措；特例措置
1866	□	20	speculation	憶測
1867	□	140	speech	演説；スピーチ；発話
1868	□	122	spending bill	歳出（支出）法案
1869	□	99	spiritual	精神的な；崇高な
1870	□	56	spokesman	報道官；広報担当者；代弁者
1871	□	96	spokesperson	報道官；スポークスパーソン；代弁者
1872	□	**3-9a**	spy	スパイをする；諜報活動をする
1873	□	302	stability	安定（性）；着実；確固
1874	□	302	stable	安定した；変動のない
1875	□	303	stagnancy	停滞；よどみ
1876	□	303	stagnant	よどんでいる；不景気な；停滞した
1877	□	134	stance	立場；姿勢
1878	□	142	standard	基準；標準
1879	□	350	standoff	睨み合い；膠着状態
1880	□	35	state	国；国家；州；状態
1881	□	237	state of emergency	非常事態；緊急事態
1882	□	170	state party	締約国
1883	□	326	stationing	駐留
1884	□	143	status quo	現状
1885	□	**3-20a**	stay away	離れている；近寄らない
1886	□	162	steadily	着実に；絶え間なく
1887	□	162	steady	安定した；揺るぎない
1888	□	**3-9a**	steal	盗む；盗用する
1889	□	57	step up	強化する；増す
1890	□	133	stern	強固な；容赦ない
1891	□	277	stipulate	規定する；明記する
1892	□	**2-5**	stockpile	貯蔵；備蓄；貯蔵する
1893	□	304	strategic	戦略的な；戦略（上）の；戦略上重要な
1894	□	213	strategically	戦略的に
1895	□	304	strategist	戦略家；ブレイン
1896	□	305	strength	力；強み；強さ

No.		使用箇所	English	日本語
1897	□	305	strengthen	強化する；丈夫にする；増強する
1898	□	62	stress	強調する；重視する
1899	□	156	stringent	厳しい；厳重な；緊縮の
1900	□	108	strive	努力する；励む
1901	□	63	strongly	断固として；強硬に；堅調に
1902	□	306	structural	構造（上）の；構築物の
1903	□	306	structure	構造；体制；構成
1904	□	307	struggle	もがく；争う；努力（する）
1905	□	307	struggle against X	X との（に対する）抗争
1906	□	307	struggle with the plunge of	急落に（もろに影響を受け）悪戦苦闘しながら（苦しみながら；もがきながら）；急落の影響を受けながら
1907	□	63	submit	提出する；屈服する
1908	□	308	subsequent	その次の；その後の；それに続く
1909	□	308	subsequently	その後；それ以降
1910	□	309	subsidiary	補助の；従属の；付属物
1911	□	309	subsidiary organization	下部組織；補助組織
1912	□	310	substance	物質；実質；重要性
1913	□	310	substantial	実質的な；相当な；しっかりした
1914	□	310	substantially	大幅に；実質的には
1915	□	311	substitute	代用する；代理をする；代替
1916	□	311	substitution	代理；代用；代理出席
1917	□	312	subversion	（国家）転覆；打倒；破壊
1918	□	312	subvert	倒す；転覆させる；滅亡させる
1919	□	125	successfully	成功裏に；うまく
1920	□	6	such	そのような；とても
1921	□	164	such as X	例えば X；X などの
1922	□	22	suddenly	突如；突然
1923	□	158	summit	首脳（会談）；首脳級；頂上
1924	□	142	superior	優れた；上質の；まさる
1925	□	313	superpower	超大国
1926	□	86	supplies	supply（物資；支給物）の複数形
1927	□	314	support	支援；援助；サポート
1928	□	314	suppress	抑圧する；鎮圧する；隠す

No.		使用箇所	English	日本語
1929	☐	314	suppression	抑圧；鎮圧；隠蔽
1930	☐	**3-21b**	sure	本気で；確かに
1931	☐	315	surreal	非現実的な；現実離れした； 超現実主義の
1932	☐	315	surrealism	超現実主義；シュールレアリズム
1933	☐	316	surrender	降伏（する）；放棄（する）；明け渡す
1934	☐	75	surrounding	周囲の；囲む
1935	☐	317	surveillance	偵察；監視；査察
1936	☐	317	survey	調査する；見渡す；調査；検査
1937	☐	57	suspect	疑う
1938	☐	49	suspend	一時的に止める；吊るす
1939	☐	180	suspicion	疑い；疑念
1940	☐	318	sustain	維持する；持続させる；耐える
1941	☐	318	sustainable	持続可能な；維持できる
1942	☐	101	sweeping victory	圧勝；完全な勝利
1943	☐	271	symbolize	象徴する；表す
1944	☐	33	symmetry	（左右）対称；調和
1945	☐	319	tactic	戦術（の）；作戦；戦略
1946	☐	319	tactical	戦術的な；戦術（上）の；巧妙な
1947	☐	293	take	受ける
1948	☐	**1-35b**	Take it easy.	気楽に行こう。；気をつけて。； じゃあまた。
1949	☐	**1-5**	take over	接収する；乗っ取る；引き継ぐ
1950	☐	**3-16a**	take time	時間を取る
1951	☐	264	tanker	タンカー；油槽船
1952	☐	320	tariff	関税（を課す）；関税率；税率表
1953	☐	320	tariff barrier	関税障壁
1954	☐	35	tax collection	徴税
1955	☐	141	technical cooperation	技術協力
1956	☐	172	technology	技術；科学技術
1957	☐	172	technology transfer	技術移転
1958	☐	309	technology transfer agreement	技術移転契約（協定）
1959	☐	327	temporarily	一時的に；当座のところ；当面は

No.		使用箇所	English	日本語
1960	□	327	temporary	一時的な；仮の
1961	□	205	tension	緊張；緊張状態
1962	□	**1-22c**	tentative	仮の；一時的な
1963	□	95	term	用語；期間；条件
1964	□	321	territorial	領土の；領土に関する
1965	□	133	territorial rights	領土権
1966	□	185	territorial waters	領海
1967	□	321	territory	領土；領域；縄張り
1968	□	5	terrorism	テロ行為；テロリズム
1969	□	28	terrorist	テロリスト
1970	□	156	tertiary	三次の；第三の
1971	□	256	test-firing	試射
1972	□	322	testify	証言する；証拠となる；立証する
1973	□	322	testimony	証言；証明
1974	□	**2-32a**	Thanks a million.	どうもありがとう。
1975	□	9	that followed	その後の
1976	□	**1-19b**	That's a shame.	それは残念です。
1977	□	176	the Cabinet Intelligence and Research Office	内閣官房内閣情報調査室
1978	□	296	the Commonwealth	英連邦；イギリス連邦
1979	□	78	the Constitution of Japan	日本国憲法
1980	□	**3-17b**	the day after tomorrow	明後日
1981	□	95	the Declaration of Independence	米国独立宣言
1982	□	52	the East	東欧諸国
1983	□	134	the Eternal	神
1984	□	165	(the) high sea(s)	公海；外洋
1985	□	176	the National Police Agency	警察庁
1986	□	26	the number of X	X の数（X の名刺は複数形になる）
1987	□	44	the poor	貧者（= poor people）
1988	□	57	the said	前述の；上記の
1989	□	52	the West	西側諸国；欧米諸国
1990	□	**2-23b**	There is no room for X.	X の余地はない。；出る幕はない。
1991	□	106	thereby	それによって；したがって

No.		使用箇所	English	日本語
1992	□	**3-29b**	think twice	考え直す；よく考える
1993	□	274	third-country	第三国
1994	□	322	those who	人々
1995	□	323	threat	脅し；脅迫；威嚇
1996	□	323	threaten	脅す；脅迫する；脅威を与える
1997	□	323	threatening	威嚇的な；脅迫的な；険悪な
1998	□	99	throne	王位；王座
1999	□	260	throughout X	X の間中ずっと；あらゆる場所に
2000	□	**3-11a**	thug	悪党；凶悪犯
2001	□	189	thus	それゆえに；だから；結果として
2002	□	117	tie	絆；連携；関係
2003	□	137	tireless	休むことのない；不断の
2004	□	**2-14b**	to be honest with you	率直に言うと；正直なところ
2005	□	**2-12b**	to cut a long story short	早い話が；端的に言えば
2006	□	**2-3**	to no avail	無駄に；その甲斐なく
2007	□	337	to undergo democratization	民主化を経ること；民主化
2008	□	96	tolerate	許容する；我慢する
2009	□	164	too X	X 過ぎる;あまりにX 過ぎて(できない)
2010	□	98	torture	拷問；激しい苦痛
2011	□	38	total ban	全面禁止；完全禁止
2012	□	298	tough	厳しい；難しい；屈強な
2013	□	248	tough negotiator	手強い交渉人；タフ・ネゴシエーター
2014	□	263	towards X	X に向かって；を目指して(=toward)
2015	□	324	trace	形跡；痕跡；追跡する
2016	□	324	traceability	追跡可能性；履歴管理
2017	□	41	trade	貿易；通商
2018	□	33	trade deficit	貿易赤字
2019	□	290	trade sanction	貿易制裁
2020	□	325	trade-off	両立しないこと；(相殺) 取引；交換
2021	□	217	traditionally	伝統的に
2022	□	326	tragedy	悲劇；惨事
2023	□	326	tragic	悲劇的な；悲惨な；痛ましい

No.		使用箇所	English	日本語
2024	□	326	tragically	悲劇的に；あえなく
2025	□	**3-8a**	training	訓練；練習
2026	□	327	transfer	移す；移動させる；伝達する
2027	□	327	transferee	転任者；被譲渡人
2028	□	328	transition	移行；変遷；過渡期
2029	□	21	transitional	暫定の；仮の；過渡的な；移り変わりの
2030	□	328	transitionally	過渡的に
2031	□	329	transnational	多国籍の；国を跨いで；多国籍企業
2032	□	329	transnationally	国境を越えて
2033	□	51	transparency	透明性
2034	□	29	transport	輸送；移送；運搬
2035	□	80	treat	扱う；とらえる
2036	□	98	treatment	待遇；扱い；手当て
2037	□	330	treaty	条約（文書）；協定（書）；契約
2038	□	339	trend	傾向；動向；トレンド
2039	□	45	tri-	3
2040	□	331	trigger	引き金（を引く）；きっかけ（となる）；起こす
2041	□	331	triggering device	起爆装置
2042	□	43	trilateral	三カ国の；三者の
2043	□	332	trinity	三つ組；三位一体
2044	□	332	tripartite	三者（間）の；三者加盟の；3つに分かれた
2045	□	332	tripartite cooperation	三角協力
2046	□	333	troop	軍隊；一団；群をなして動く
2047	□	117	Truman Doctrine	トルーマン・ドクトリン
2048	□	334	trustworthiness	信頼性；信用性；頼りがい
2049	□	334	trustworthy	信頼できる；信用できる
2050	□	195	truth	真実
2051	□	189	try to X	Xしようとする
2052	□	345	tuberculosis	結核
2053	□	275	turmoil	騒動；混乱；動揺
2054	□	**3-3a’**	turn (it) over X	Xに譲る；引き継ぐ
2055	□	275	turn around	好転する；回復する；方向転換する

No.		使用箇所	English	日本語
2056	☐	304	turning point	転換点；岐路；ターニングポイント
2057	☐	343	two consecutive years	2 年連続
2058	☐	**1-1**	two thirds	3 分の 2
2059	☐	122	U.S.-produced	米国産の
2060	☐	180	Ukrainian	ウクライナの；ウクライナ人（語）の
2061	☐	335	ultimata	ultimatum の複数形
2062	☐	335	ultimatum	最後通牒；最後通告；最終的申し入れ
2063	☐	7	un-	（否定の意味）
2064	☐	165	unacceptable	容認できない；受け入れられない
2065	☐	336	unanimous	全員一致の；全会一致の；同意見で
2066	☐	336	unanimously	満場一致で；全員異議なく；全会一致で
2067	☐	28	unarmed	非武装の；丸腰の
2068	☐	7	unavoidable	避けられない
2069	☐	316	unconditional surrender	無条件降伏
2070	☐	321	under the control of X	X の支配を受けて；X の制御下で
2071	☐	337	undergo	経験する；受ける；耐え忍ぶ
2072	☐	**3-5a**	undermine	弱体化させる；間接的に攻撃する
2073	☐	338	underneath	下（部）に；底面に；背後に
2074	☐	143	underpin	支える；支持する
2075	☐	40	undertaken	undertake（引き受ける；請け負う；着手する）の過去・過去分詞形
2076	☐	100	underway	進行中で；既に始まって
2077	☐	337	underwent	undergo の過去形
2078	☐	72	unduly	過度に；不当に
2079	☐	303	unemployment rate	失業率
2080	☐	320	unfair	不公平な；不当な
2081	☐	282	unforgivable	許されない；容赦できない
2082	☐	274	UNHCR	the Office of the United Nations High Commissioner for Refugees
2083	☐	45	uni-/mono-	1
2084	☐	339	unification	統一；統合；単一化
2085	☐	339	unify	単一化する；1 つにする
2086	☐	340	unilateral	一方的な；片務的な；片側のみの
2087	☐	340	unilaterally	一方的に

No.		使用箇所	English	日本語
2088	□	341	unipolarity	単極性；一極性
2089	□	1	United Nations General Assembly	国連総会
2090	□	134	unity	結束；一致；単一性
2091	□	207	universal	普遍的な
2092	□	76	universalization	普遍化；一般化
2093	□	56	unjustified	正当化できない；不当な；根拠のない
2094	□	**3-9a**	unlawful	非合法的な；違法の
2095	□	**3-9a**	unlawfully	非合法的に；不法に
2096	□	37	unprecedented	前例のない；異例の
2097	□	342	unpredictable	予測できない；予断を許さない；気まぐれな
2098	□	**3-10b**	unrest	混乱；動揺；不安
2099	□	318	unsustainable	持続不可能な；維持できない
2100	□	174	unwanted	求められない；不必要な
2101	□	**2-13a**	upcoming	次回の；近づきつつある
2102	□	**3-2a’**	update	最新情報；更新する
2103	□	343	upheaval	動乱；激変；隆起
2104	□	336	Upper House	上院
2105	□	225	uranium enrichment	ウラン濃縮
2106	□	344	urge	促す；駆り立てる；衝動
2107	□	344	urgency	緊急；切迫
2108	□	344	urgent	緊急の；切迫した
2109	□	289	useless	役に立たない；無益な
2110	□	177	utilize	利用する；活用する
2111	□	**3-17b**	vacation	休暇；休み
2112	□	100	various	様々な；多様な
2113	□	65	vary	変わる；変化する
2114	□	154	vehement	激しく；猛烈な
2115	□	154	vehemently	強く；猛烈に
2116	□	**2-23b**	venue	場所
2117	□	225	verge	瀬戸際；ふち
2118	□	345	verifiable	検証可能な
2119	□	345	verification	検証；実証；立証

No.		使用箇所	English	日本語
2120	□	345	verify	実証する；検証する；立証する
2121	□	346	vessel	大型船；血管；容器
2122	□	347	veto	拒否権（の行使）；拒否（する）；厳禁（する）
2123	□	326	vicinity	周辺；周辺地
2124	□	164	victim	被害者；犠牲者
2125	□	50	view	見方；見解
2126	□	348	vigor	活力；活発さ
2127	□	169	vigorous	活気のある；活発な
2128	□	348	vigorously	活気あふれて；精力的に；力強く
2129	□	171	violate	違反する；犯す；破る
2130	□	14	violation	違反；侵害；暴行
2131	□	199	violence	暴力；猛威；激しさ
2132	□	199	violent	激しい；暴力的な
2133	□	211	VIP	要人
2134	□	8	virtual	仮想の
2135	□	8	virtual adversary	仮想敵国
2136	□	89	visit	訪問；訪れる
2137	□	231	vitality	活力；持続力
2138	□	27	voluntarily	自発的に；任意に
2139	□	126	vote	票；投票；投票する
2140	□	126	voter	有権者；投票者
2141	□	303	wage	賃金
2142	□	303	wage war	（戦争を）仕掛ける；行う
2143	□	**1-15b**	Wait a minute.	ちょっと待って。；もう少し待って。
2144	□	**2-27b**	walk out	退席する；突然去る
2145	□	285	war-related	戦争関連の；戦争に関連する
2146	□	349	warfare	戦争（状態）；交戦；戦い
2147	□	56	warn	警告する
2148	□	149	wary	慎重な；警戒する
2149	□	174	waste	無駄；浪費する
2150	□	**3-22a**	wave	振る；うねらせる；波
2151	□	107	weaken	弱める；弱体化させる
2152	□	258	wealth of experience	豊富な経験

No.		使用箇所	English	日本語
2153	□	13	weapon	武器；兵器
2154	□	**2-8c**	What a coincidence!	何という偶然でしょう。；奇遇ですね。
2155	□	**1-9b**	What can I do for you?	何をしましょうか？；ご用件は何ですか？
2156	□	**3-27a**	What do you mean by X?	X とはどういう意味ですか？
2157	□	**2-10c**	what he/she said	彼 / 彼女が言ったこと
2158	□	**3-19b**	what you call	いわゆる
2159	□	**2-25c**	what we need now	今私達が必要なこと（もの）
2160	□	**1-7b**	What's up?	どうしたの？；調子はどう？
2161	□	**1-19b**	Where are you off to?	どちらへ向かうのですか？； どこへお出かけですか？
2162	□	203	whether X	X かどうか；いずれにせよ
2163	□	114	, which	（前部分に書かれた内容〔直前の語とは限らない〕に対し、追加的に説明を加える際に主として用いる。）
2164	□	**2-30a**	Why don't we X?	X しませんか？；しましょうよ。
2165	□	263	will	意思；決意；意向
2166	□	**3-28a**	wise	賢明な；思慮深い
2167	□	**1-30c**	wish	強く望む；願う
2168	□	315	wishful	望んでいる
2169	□	315	wishful thinking	希望的観測
2170	□	**3-5a**	with a view to X	X するために；を目的として； する目的で
2171	□	286	with respect to X	X に関しては；については
2172	□	350	withdraw	撤退する；退く；引き出す
2173	□	25	withdrawal	離脱；撤退；引き出し
2174	□	350	withdrawn	withdraw の過去分詞形
2175	□	278	within the context of X	X の脈略（文脈）の中で
2176	□	202	without any mercy	いかなる慈悲もなしに；無残にも
2177	□	67	without compromise	妥協なしに
2178	□	323	words and actions	言動；言行
2179	□	107	work together	協力する；共に働く
2180	□	120	working group	作業部会；作業グループ
2181	□	147	world economy	世界経済
2182	□	281	worldwide	世界的に見て；世界的な

No.		使用箇所	English	日本語
2183	□	54	worsen	悪化する；より悪くなる
2184	□	233	written document	文書
2185	□	83	X years have passed since Y	Y 以来（から）X 年が経つ
2186	□	285	yen loan project	円借款事業
2187	□	348	yet	さらに；まだ；しかし
2188	□	310	yield	生む；産出する；もたらす
2189	□	**2-10c**	You bet!	おっしゃる通り。；確かに。
2190	□	**1-32c**	You better not. (= You'd better not.)	やめておいた方がいい。；しない方がいいですよ。
2191	□	**1-8a**	you could do me a favor	頼みごとを聞いてくれる
2192	□	**1-13b**	you know	ご存知でしょうが；えっと；あのね；いいかい
2193	□	**2-9b**	You must be kidding me!	まさか冗談だろう。；からかわないでくれ。
2194	□	**1-33b**	You said it.	確かに。；よくぞ言った。；同意するよ。

参考・引用文献

A Comprehensive Grammar of the English Language. Randolph Quirk, Sidney Greenbaum, Geoffrey Leech, and Jan Svartvik. London: Longman. 1985

「英語の語源」THE ENGLISH CLUB.（http://www.etn.co.jp/etymology/）

「英辞郎 on the WEB Pro Lite」アルク . (https://eowf.alc.co.jp/)

『英単語ターゲット 1900：5 訂版』宮川幸久 (著) , ターゲット編集部 (編) . 旺文社 . 2011

『オックスフォード現代英英辞典 第 10 版』オックスフォード大学出版局 (編) . 2020

「『外交青書』一覧（1957-2020）」外務省 .（https://www.mofa.go.jp/mofaj/gaiko/bluebook/index.html）(*Diplomatic Bluebook*（1971-2020）. Ministry of Foreign Affairs of Japan.（https://www.mofa.go.jp/policy/other/bluebook/index.html））

「【外交文書公開】イスラエルのペレス首相が「密使」派遣も日本は肩入れ拒否 1985 年 1 月」産経新聞 (2017 年 12 月 20 日) .（https://www.sankei.com/politics/news/171220/plt1712200024-n1.html）

『外国人との交渉に成功するビジネス英語』Rochelle Kopp・小野智世子・増田真紀子 (著) . 語研 . 2011

『科学的英会話独習法（改訂新版）』吉野義人 (著) . 研究者 . 1986

『国際標準 CEFR の英単語 中・上級』日向清人・狩野みき・迫村純男 (著) . 秀和システム . 2018

「条約の国会承認に関する制度・運用と国会における議論：条約締結に対する民主的統制の在り方とは」中内康夫 (著) .『立法と調査』No.330. 参議院事務局企画調整室編集・発行 . 2012

「信任状捧呈式」宮内庁 .（https://www.kunaicho.go.jp/about/gokomu/kyuchu/shinninjo/shinninjo01.html）(“Ceremony of the Presentation of Credentials” The Imperial Household Agency.（https://www.kunaicho.go.jp/e-about/kyuchu/shinninjo01.html))

『ジーニアス英和辞典：第 4 版』小西友七・南出康世 (編) . 大修館書店 . 2006

“Joint Communique Between the People's Republic of China and the United States” , "The World and Japan" Database (Project Leader: TANAKA Akihiko), Database of Japanese Politics and International Relations, National Graduate Institute for Policy Studies (GRIPS); Institute for Advanced Studies on Asia (IASA), The University of Tokyo. (https://worldjpn.grips.ac.jp/documents/texts/docs/19720228.D1E.html)

「生物兵器禁止条約 (BWC) の概要」外務省 .（https://www.mofa.go.jp/mofaj/gaiko/bwc/bwc/gaiyo.html) (“Convention on Certain Conventional Weapons（CCW）” Delegation of Japan to the Conference on Disarmament.（https://www.disarm.emb-japan.go.jp/itpr_ja/CCW_info.html））

「第 43 回人権理事会ハイレベルセグメントにおける尾身外務大臣政務官ステートメント (仮訳)」外務省 .（https://www.mofa.go.jp/mofaj/fp/hr_ha/page3_002814.html)（“Statement Parliamentary Vice-Minister for Foreign Affairs Omi at the High-Level Segment of the 43th Session of the Human Rights Council” Ministry of Foreign

Affairs of Japan.（https://www.mofa.go.jp/fp/hr_ha/page3e_001052.html））

Diplomacy. Harold Nicolson. Oxford University Press. 1960（『外交』ハロルド・ニコルソン（著）. 斎藤眞・深谷満雄（訳）. 東京大学出版会．1968）

『DUO 3.0』鈴木陽一（著）. アイシーピー . 2000

『2013 年版 政府開発援助（ODA）白書：日本の国際協力』外務省 .（https://www.mofa.go.jp/mofaj/gaiko/oda/shiryo/hakusyo/13_hakusho/index.html）（*Japan's Official Development Assistance White Paper 2013: Japan's International Cooperation*. Ministry of Foreign Affairs of Japan.（https://www.mofa.go.jp/policy/oda/white/2013/html/index.html））

「人間の安全保障を求めて」緒方貞子. UN Chronicle, 国際連合広報センター .（https://www.unic.or.jp/activities/international_observances/un70/un_chronicle/ogata/）（"Striving for Human Security" Sadako Ogata. UN Chronicle, United Nations.（https://www.un.org/en/chronicle/article/striving-human-security））

「ブリーフィング・メモ：国際テロに対する自衛権の援用について」森田桂子（著）. 防衛研究所 .（http://www.nids.mod.go.jp/publication/briefing/pdf/2004/200404.pdf）

"Press Briefing with Secretary of State Mike Pompeo and Secretary of the Treasury Steve Mnuchin" The White House.（https://www.youtube.com/watch?v=lTCErLFbu4Q）

"UNIT 1 INTERNATIONAL RELATIONS: PRINCIPAL THEORIES" Faculty of International Relations, The Ivan Franko National University of Lviv.（https://intrel.lnu.edu.ua/wp-content/uploads/2016/09/03_Theories-of-IR.pdf）

『理系国際学会のためのビギナーズガイド』山中司・西澤幹雄・山下美朋（著）. 裳華房 . 2019

『ロイヤル英文法：徹底例解（改訂新版）』綿貫陽・須貝猛敏・宮川幸久・高松尚弘（著）. 旺文社 . 2000

Longman Advanced American Dictionary. Pearson Japan. 2002

「Weblio 辞書：英和辞典：和英辞典」ウェブリオ .（https://ejje.weblio.jp/）

執筆者一覧

宮家 邦彦

1953年、神奈川県生まれ。キヤノングローバル戦略研究所研究主幹。元外交官。東京大学法学部を卒業後、外務省に入省。外務大臣秘書官、中近東第一・第二課長、日米安全保障条約課長、在中国・在イラク大使館公使、中東アフリカ局参事官を歴任。2005年に退官。現在、内閣官房参与、立命館大学客員教授、外交政策研究所代表。著書に『「力の大真空」が世界史を変える』(PHP研究所)、『AI時代の新・地政学』(新潮社) など多数。

山中 司

1979年、岐阜県生まれ。立命館大学教授、博士(政策・メディア)。一般社団法人大学英語教育学会(JACET)本部運営委員(研究促進委員会)。IEEE Professional Communication Society, Japan Chapter, Secretary of PCSJ。慶應義塾大学卒業、慶應義塾大学大学院政策・メディア研究科博士課程修了。専門は大学英語教育、言語論、言語哲学。著書に『自分を肯定して生きる―プラグマティックな生き方入門―』(海竜社)、『プロジェクト発信型英語プログラム―自分軸を鍛える「教えない」教育』(共著・北大路書店)『理系 国際学会のためのビギナーズガイド』(共著・裳華房) などがある。

伊藤 弘太郎

1977年、愛知県生まれ。キヤノングローバル戦略研究所主任研究員。中央大学大学院法学研究科政治学専攻博士後期課程満期退学。衆議院議員事務所、公益財団法人日本国際交流センター、内閣官房国家安全保障局等での勤務を経て現職。立命館大学客員准教授、淑徳大学兼任講師を兼任。専門は韓国の外交安全保障政策。著作に「韓国の戦力増強政策の展開と軍事産業の発展 新技術獲得を目指す執念とその弊害」道下徳成編著『「技術」が変える戦争と平和』(芙蓉書房出版)、"Japan's Security Pledge in the Korean Peninsula", Jagannath P. Panda ed., The Korean Peninsula and Indo-Pacific Power Politics: Status Security at Stake (Routledge) などがある。

外交的英対話学習法
国際社会で活躍するための必須英対話・用語用例集 [IG-77]

1 刷 2021年5月13日

著 者 宮家 邦彦 Kunihiko Miyake
山中 司 Tsukasa Yamanaka
伊藤 弘太郎 Kohtaro Ito

発行者 南雲 一範 Kazunori Nagumo
発行所 株式会社 南雲堂
〒162-0801 東京都新宿区山吹町361
NAN'UN-DO Co., Ltd.
361 Yamabuki-cho, Shinjuku-ku, Tokyo 162-0801, Japan
振替口座：00160-0-46863
TEL: 03-3268-2311（営業部：学校関係）
03-3268-2384（営業部：書店関係）
03-3268-2387（編集部）
FAX: 03-3269-2486

編集者 加藤 敦

組 版 中西 史子

装 丁 銀 月 堂

検 印 省 略

コード ISBN978-4-523-30077-9 C0082

Printed in Japan

E-mail : nanundo@post.email.ne.jp
URL : https://www.nanun-do.co.jp/